Tolerant Allies

Tolerant Allies

Canada and the United States
1963–1968

GREG DONAGHY

McGill-Queen's University Press
Montreal & Kingston • London • Ithaca

© McGill-Queen's University Press 2002
ISBN 0-7735-2431-2

Legal deposit fourth quarter 2002
Bibliothèque nationale du Québec

Printed in Canada on acid-free paper that is 100%
ancient forest free (100% post-consumer recycled),
processed chlorine free.

This book has been published with the help of a grant
from the Humanities and Social Sciences Federation of
Canada, using funds provided by the Social Sciences and
Humanities Research Council of Canada.

McGill-Queen's University Press acknowledges the
support of the Canada Council for the Arts for our
publishing program. We also acknowledge the financial
support of the Government of Canada through the Book
Publishing Industry Development Program (BPIDP) for
our publishing activities.

National Library of Canada Cataloguing in Publication Data

Donaghy, Greg
    Tolerant allies : Canada and the United States, 1963–1968
/ Greg Donaghy.

Includes bibliographical references and index.
ISBN 0-7735-2431-2
    1. Canada – Foreign relations – 1945–   2. United States
– Foreign relations – 1963–1969.   3. Canada – Foreign
relations – United States.   4. United States – Foreign
relations – Canada.   I. Title.

FC249.D63 2002   327.71073   C2002-902479-X
E183.8.C2D64 2002

For Katherine, Michael, and Stephen

Contents

Acknowledgments

During its long period of gestation, this book has benefited immeasurably from the kind help of many friends, both Canadian and American. Laura and Tim Gaughan, Ian Sempowski, and Sean Meagher shared with me the results of their research in the John F. Kennedy and Lyndon B. Johnson libraries. John Wilson, an archivist at the Johnson Library, was especially helpful in locating material and speeding declassification. Ciuineas Boyle, Herb Barrett, and Michael Way of the Privy Council Office's Access to Information and Privacy Unit responded to my requests for access in a genuinely open and professional manner. Paulette Dozois and Maureen Hoogenraad of the National Archives of Canada also provided assistance and encouragement.

Over the years, many historians of Canadian foreign policy have generously shared their knowledge and wisdom with me. Geoffrey Pearson, Basil Robinson, Saul Grey, Bruce Muirhead, Denis Stairs, Michael Stevenson, Christopher Cook, Michael Hart, Stephen Azzi, and Boris Stipernitz read and commented helpfully on portions of the book. The anonymous readers for McGill-Queen's also provided constructive and useful criticisms that made their way into the text.

My colleagues in the Historical Section of the Department of Foreign Affairs and International Trade have demonstrated their friendship and support for this project. John Hilliker, my supervisor, graciously made the leave arrangements that allowed me to begin this project in 1990. Since then, he has provided plenty of good advice and encouragement. He also read and commented on the entire manuscript. Hector

Mackenzie, E.A. Kelly, and Mary Halloran have been supportive colleagues, always ready with help when needed.

John English, who supervised the dissertation from which this book eventually came, was the perfect advisor – always available and unreasonably optimistic. Norman Hillmer, who helped me through an earlier degree, read much of the book, and his comments forced me to develop my ideas and sharpen my prose.

Finally, my family was closely involved in this project. My parents, Michael and Maureen Donaghy, lent considerable emotional, intellectual, and financial support to the enterprise.

My wife, Mary, was a constant source of strength and inspiration. Just as important, she cheerfully ignored the mass of notes, papers, and books that cluttered up our small house during this project. My children, Katherine, Michael, and Stephen, provided perspective and delightful diversion. This book is dedicated to them.

Tolerant Allies

Introduction

Lyndon Johnson ignored Mike Pearson. Over lunch, the president talked on the phone and ordered his aides about while Canada's fourteenth prime minister, Lester B. Pearson, waited for the outburst he knew was coming. Since being summoned to Camp David that morning in April 1965 to answer for a speech that dared to question American bombing in Vietnam, Pearson had dreaded the encounter. After their meal, the towering Texan took Pearson by the arm and led him into the garden. From a distance, Canadian ambassador Charles Ritchie watched the pantomime as the two men talked in the sunshine. The president "strode the terrace, he sawed the air with his arms, with upraised fist he drove home the verbal hammer blows ... from time to time, Mike attempted a sentence – only to have it swept away on the tide."[1] For many Canadians, this compelling image of bilateral conflict neatly and indelibly captured the fundamental differences that seemed to divide Canada and the United States during the 1960s.

Pearson's confrontation with Johnson, however, was only a single episode in a much more complex story of economic integration and political differentiation. At a time when economic nationalists began to flex their muscles in Ottawa, Canada and the United States developed a framework for economic cooperation that drew the two countries more closely together than ever. In helping to create this framework, Washington showed itself a patient and tolerant ally. As Pearson's government tackled the structural weaknesses in Canada's economy by unilateral action that targeted its trading and financial

relationship with the United States, the Kennedy and Johnson administrations responded in imaginative and thoughtful ways. Though
determined not to sacrifice its legitimate interests for bilateral harmony, Washington was ready to seek equitable arrangements for sharing
the North American economy in ways that acknowledged the unique
conditions confronting Canada, the smaller neighbour of an economic giant. In doing so, it posed the fundamental question that Pearson's
government confronted in determining its approach to economic relations with the United States: should Canada agree to the further integration of the two North American economies in exchange for the
material benefits that greater access to the United States market would
make possible?

In accepting American proposals for closer economic partnership,
did Pearson's government sacrifice Canada's political independence?
This question, too, is a central theme in this study. The collapsing postwar political order of the 1960s offered Ottawa numerous opportunities to distinguish itself from its American neighbour on the world
stage. Carefully and with due regard for genuine American interests,
Pearson's government adopted new military and diplomatic roles for
Canada that were designed to reflect a unique perspective on international affairs. Here too, in responding to these Canadian initiatives,
Washington was a tolerant ally. It acknowledged these developments as
legitimate and inevitable, adjusting its attitudes and policies accordingly. As a result, Canada and the United States found ways to accommodate each other's diverging political interests without seriously
impairing bilateral cooperation.

Canada emerged as an important United States ally in its own right
in the years just after the Second World War. Canadians, anxious to
avoid the mistakes of the interwar years, looked to and encouraged
Washington to play a leading role in the search for an effective means
of collective security. While Western Europe struggled to recover from
the war, Washington came to count on Canada as a close and reliable
North Atlantic partner. When the nascent United Nations proved ineffectual in the face of Soviet aggression, Canada helped the United
States create the North Atlantic Treaty Organization (NATO). At the
peak of the Canadian military effort in 1953–54, Canada spent 8.8
percent of its gross national product (GNP) on defence, the fourth
largest defence budget in NATO.[2] Canada was there when it mattered.
In 1950, Canadian troops challenged communist aggression in Korea;
in 1954, Canadian diplomats took on the Western burden to help
France escape from Indochina; and in 1956, it was a Canadian, the
secretary of state for external affairs, Lester B. Pearson, who helped
prevent the Western alliance from tearing itself apart during the Suez

Crisis. Certainly, Ottawa and Washington sometimes differed – over NATO, over Asia, and over continental defence – but these differences were mostly tactical and easily reconciled.

During the immediate postwar period, the wartime changes in the economic relationship between the United States and Canada were cemented into place. Britain was exhausted, and the prewar North Atlantic triangle, within which Canada balanced its imports from the United States with its exports to Britain, was gone forever.[3] In the future, American imports would have to be paid for with dollars earned by exports to the United States and imports of American capital. Investors in the United States, which emerged from the war with the world's strongest economy, were happy to oblige, delighted at the prospect of investing in their safe, familiar, and profitable neighbour.

Unimpeded, American capital flowed northward, and the economy boomed. Canadians cheered C.D. Howe, the ubiquitous "minister of everything" who trumpeted the benefits of North American economic cooperation, and they elected majority Liberal governments in 1945, 1949, and 1953. The GNP grew steadily from just over $15.4 billion in 1945 to $21.5 billion in 1955.[4] By the mid-1950s, American investment in Canada totalled $10.2 billion, up from approximately $5 billion in 1945.[5] In 1955, American-owned companies accounted for 73 percent of Canada's oil and gas production, 55 percent of its mining and smelting operations, and 42 percent of its manufacturing.[6]

Cross-border trade grew as well. In 1945, Canada sent 38.7 percent of its exports, worth $878 million, to the United States. By the mid-1950s, this trade had increased to $2.54 billion and represented almost 60 percent of Canada's exports.[7] The buoyant economy fed the sense of national self-confidence that had developed during the war. United under the tranquil, if uninspired, leadership of Prime Minister Louis St Laurent, Canadians lapped up American magazines and movies and books without questioning who or what they were. As one of Canada's leading syndicated columnists pointed out, the answer was evident: Canada was "tomorrow's giant."[8]

Still, in many quarters there was an imprecise but disturbing sense that too cosy a relationship with the United States was somehow not good for Canada. In 1951 Vincent Massey's Royal Commission on National Development in the Arts, Letters and Sciences dismissed American movies, advertising, and television as "alien."[9] The anti-communist witch hunts of Senator Joseph McCarthy disturbed Canadians, who were outraged when one of their diplomats, Herbert Norman, leaped to his death in 1957 in the wake of allegations that he was a communist. Many Canadians, especially the roughly 45 percent who

were British in origin, waxed nostalgic for the receding imperial con-
nection, and they recoiled at St Laurent's refusal to support Britain
during the Suez Crisis.[10] John G. Diefenbaker, the Progressive Conservative leader, touched this anti-American nerve in the federal election
of June 1957 and drove the Liberals from power after twenty-two
years in office.

During his first three years as prime minister, Diefenbaker pursued a
policy towards the United States that hardly differed from the one followed by his Liberal predecessors. His anti-Americanism remained
more apparent than real, a matter of style rather than substance. The
deep admiration he felt for President Dwight Eisenhower, who had
served as supreme allied commander in Europe during the Second
World War (and who carefully cultivated the prime minister's friendship), tempered his hostility.[11] The Conservative leader's only attempt
to reverse the postwar pattern of economic relations was a whimsical
promise to divert 15 percent of Canada's trade from the United States
to Britain. Uttered spontaneously in the emotional aftermath of Diefenbaker's first Commonwealth prime ministers' meeting, it was a pledge
that he disavowed when he learned how disastrous it would be for the
Canadian economy.[12]

Under Diefenbaker several pieces of important, unfinished defence
business with the United States were quickly settled. In 1957 he signed
the agreement establishing the joint North American Air Defence Command (NORAD), which replaced the ad hoc bilateral measures for continental defence then in effect with a formal, integrated system for
defending the continent. Later that year he agreed that NATO forces
would accept tactical nuclear weapons. The Conservative government
accepted the implications of this arrangement in deciding to equip the
Canadian Air Division in Europe with nuclear-armed CF-104s and to
arm Canadian ground troops with a battery of Honest John missiles,
weapons that also relied on nuclear warheads. Similarly, in replacing
the ill-fated Avro Arrow (CF-105), a Canadian fighter that was cancelled in 1959 after huge cost overruns, the prime minister adopted the
Bomarc B missile, which was effective only when armed with nuclear
warheads.[13] The negotiations to determine the conditions under which
Canada's NATO and NORAD contingents would receive American
nuclear weapons initially went well.

Relations between Ottawa and Washington began to deteriorate in
1961, however. Howard Green, Diefenbaker's secretary of state for
external affairs, was an ardent champion of nuclear disarmament.
Convinced that Ottawa's capacity to advance this cause would be
reduced by accepting American nuclear weapons, Green pressed the
prime minister to repudiate his commitment to equip Canadian forces

in Europe and North America with atomic weapons. Caught between his secretary of state for external affairs and his minister of defence, who urged him to cooperate fully with Washington, Diefenbaker played for time.[14]

But John F. Kennedy, Eisenhower's successor, had little time to spare. He and his advisors were determined to increase the West's capacity to confront the Soviet Union, and they did not understand or sympathize with Diefenbaker's predicament.[15] Personal animosity soon exacerbated the differences over Canada's ambiguous nuclear weapons policy. Diefenbaker resented the American's popularity and felt slighted when Kennedy gossiped at length with Lester Pearson, then the opposition leader, during a presidential visit to Ottawa in 1961. Kennedy found the prime minister boring; later, when Diefenbaker refused to return a note from Kennedy's briefing book, the u.s. president dismissed him as contemptible. Relations reached their nadir during the Cuban missile crisis in October 1962. Diefenbaker's hesitant response to Washington's request for help in stopping the Soviet Union from basing nuclear weapons in Cuba was, from the American point of view, wholly inadequate.

Canadians thought so too. After the Cuban crisis, defence minister Douglas Harkness tried once more to convince Green and Diefenbaker to accept nuclear weapons, but he failed. When Diefenbaker insisted in Parliament that a Canadian nuclear role in NATO and NORAD was not in fact necessary, he provoked a public dispute with Harkness. The u.s. State Department issued a statement repudiating the prime minister's claim. On 3 February 1963 Harkness resigned, and the Diefenbaker government began to collapse in disarray.

At its deepest level, the confrontation between Kennedy and Diefenbaker reflected growing differences between Canada and the United States in their strategic outlook. As Europe settled into an uneasy but stable peace, Canadian policymakers were anxious to pursue détente with the Soviet Union and normalize relations with Communist China. Western Europe's economic and political recovery sparked a restiveness in NATO. France and West Germany sought new and larger roles for themselves, raising questions about Canada's place in the alliance. As the likelihood of war in Europe declined, Canadians diverted resources from defence to domestic social programs and development assistance.

By contrast, the United States was sceptical about détente. For Kennedy, in particular, the threat remained unchanged, though the front had shifted from Europe to the developing world. Communism mixed easily with nationalist movements throughout Africa, Asia, and the Caribbean as Britain and Europe abandoned their colonial empires.

By the early 1960s, it was no longer clear exactly how Canada would fit into this new international order.

Even more disturbing for future relations between Canada and the United States, the postwar economic order started to crumble between 1957 and 1963. Canada's resource boom, fuelled by the Korean War, NATO rearmament, and European reconstruction, ended in 1956 and revealed disturbing structural weaknesses in the Canadian economy. The dollar and its floating exchange rate were vulnerable to movements in American capital, which pushed the Canadian dollar to artificially high levels, encouraging imports, deterring exports, and driving unemployment to over 7.5 percent by 1960. In June 1962 the investors and their American dollars finally fled, sparking a Canadian financial crisis.[16]

The Conservative government responded belatedly by introducing several measures to reduce the current account deficit. In May 1962 the government pegged the dollar at U.S. 92.5 cents, a level that guaranteed an expansion in exports and a contraction in imports. More important, it tackled the largest single contributor to the current account deficit, the lacklustre Canadian automobile industry. Vincent Bladen, dean of arts at the University of Toronto, was appointed a one-man royal commission that proposed a series of measures to improve the industry's capacity to export its products.[17] In October 1962 the first of these proposals, a program providing for the remission of duties on imported transmissions incorporated by Canadian automotive manufacturers into their exports, went into effect despite American protests. The implication was clear: any move to address Canada's current account deficit would necessarily involve some adjustment in the terms of its economic relationship with the United States.

The international economy was changing as well, confronting the Kennedy administration with problems of its own. An overvalued dollar, large external financial obligations related to Washington's global security interests, and the expanding economy in Western Europe placed enormous demands on the United States balance of payments. By 1960 the current account, which had enjoyed a $6 billion surplus in 1945, was running a $3.1 billion deficit. The trend showed no sign of abating.[18] Moreover, the creation of the European Economic Community (EEC) in 1958 signalled a movement toward greater economic regionalism and threatened the multilateral liberal trading system to which the United States remained committed. Kennedy's response to both these problems would involve considerations that went to the heart of Canada's relations with the United States.

The Liberal Party that was returned to power in 1963 was not the party that had been defeated in 1957 and 1958. Diefenbaker's triumph in the 1958 general election had reduced the Liberal Party to forty-nine seats, ravaged the party's leadership, and forced it to rebuild both its organization and its platform. "Mike" Pearson, who had succeeded St Laurent as leader in January 1958, turned to Tom Kent and Walter Gordon for advice. Kent, an Englishman who had edited the liberal-minded *Winnipeg Free Press* from 1954 to 1956, warned Pearson that "[l]iberalism must 'mean' something if was to survive."[19] The new opposition leader, who had often supported progressive social causes in St Laurent's Cabinet, was easily convinced. He delighted in Kent's enthusiasm for government, and welcomed his proposals for new federal initiatives in health, education, and welfare. By 1960–61 the Liberal Party was armed with an expensive program for social spending, with obvious implications for Canada's defence budget.[20]

Gordon, who had helped ease Pearson's transition from bureaucrat to politician in 1948 and who had organized his leadership bid in 1958, also exerted a profound influence on the Liberal Party and its leader in opposition. His principal preoccupation, which had developed during the early 1950s and was confirmed by his work as chairman of the Royal Commission on Canada's Economic Prospects of 1957, was American investment in Canada. In his view the level of u.s. investment since 1945 had produced a host of ills. Gordon argued that American subsidiaries concentrated their research and decision making in the United States, favoured American suppliers, and refused to compete with their parent companies for exports to third countries. Most worrying of all, he contended, this close economic relationship must inevitably give way to political union.

In March 1960 he made it clear that his continued support depended on Pearson's willingness to address this issue: "I am unhappy about the gradual economic and financial take-over by the United States, or rather by the owners of United States capital that is taking place, and if I were in public life I would wish to urge some modest steps to counteract what is presently going on in this direction."[21] Gordon was also vaguely concerned with defence policy and the more general question of Canada's approach to the world: "I am becoming more of the opinion that Canada should begin to take an independent line ... I do not profess to know too much about this subject or all its implications, but I assume that this line of thinking might lead to the cancellation of the Norad deal and thus to a full dress argument, or showdown, with the Americans."[22]

Pearson needed Gordon's help. The Toronto businessman was a talented fund-raiser and organizer. The successful Study Conference on National Problems of 1960, an important meeting of liberal thinkers that he attended, made Gordon the acknowledged leader of the party's progressive wing. Pearson, according to Gordon, promised his support. "Mike called," he wrote. "He said he agreed *completely* with my ideas."[23]

But while Pearson did share Kent's interest in social policy, he did not in fact fully accept Gordon's views on American investment or Canadian foreign policy. The Liberal leader was never an economic nationalist. Pearson was concerned about too great a dependence on American markets and capital but was inclined to seek a solution in a broader North Atlantic context.[24] As secretary of state for external affairs from 1948 to 1957 (and under-secretary from 1946 to 1948), he was one of the main architects of Canada's postwar economic and political relationship with the United States. This partnership might need adjusting from time to time, but the structure was sound. Pearson recognized that Canada's central foreign policy objective was to secure sound and friendly relations with the United States. To achieve this goal, Pearson overcame his own opposition to equipping Canadian forces with nuclear weapons and declared in January 1963 that a Liberal government would honour Diefenbaker's unfulfilled pledge.

Pearson's decision angered many Liberals, including Gordon, who was not consulted. But it was supported by many in the party who had served under St Laurent. This group also wielded influence and power in Pearson's Liberal Party. For six years they had confronted and baited Diefenbaker in Parliament, pointing up the contradictions in his policies and driving him to distraction. While Kent and Gordon drafted policy papers, they had stumped the country, riding by riding. Like Gordon, Paul Martin and the "old guard" were a valuable source of advice, and they reinforced Pearson's views on the importance of good relations with Washington. Martin, who had often filled in for Pearson at the United Nations and at the Cabinet table under St Laurent, shared his leader's views on Canadian foreign policy almost completely.

An ambiguity, then, characterized the Liberal Party's approach to its relations with Washington in the spring of 1963. Uneasily, Pearson held together the two wings of the party. During the federal election that year, one of the few Canadian contests in which foreign policy played a major role, the party repeated its promise to accept Canada's nuclear commitments and assured voters that it would improve the country's relations with the United States. At the same time, Liberal candidates promised to take steps to reduce the level of American investment in Canada. Gordon grumbled that the Liberal leader was paying too much attention to foreign policy questions, and perhaps he was right. By election night, Diefenbaker's formidable campaigning abilities had sharply reduced Pearson's popular support. On 8 April the Liberals drew just 41 percent of the popular vote and won only 129 seats. The Tories retained 95 seats. The two smaller parties, Social Credit and the New Democratic Party, held the balance of power with 24 and 17 seats respectively. Though 4 seats short of a majority, Pearson's slim victory was enough to make him prime minister on 22 April 1963.[25]

Historians are ambivalent about bilateral relations in the 1960s and stress the differences dividing Canada and the United States. Robert Bothwell's study of Canada's postwar relations with the United States generally emphasizes "the convergence of Canadian and American attitudes and habits," arguing that the Johnson and Pearson governments "got on moderately well."[26] However, the University of Toronto historian argues that the growing divergence over foreign and defence policies, especially over the Vietnam War, was much more significant. "What was national security south of the border," he writes, "became social security to the north. In the long run, that was what would count most."[27]

John Herd Thompson and Stephen Randall share Bothwell's assumptions about the basic similarity of Canadian and American society. Their study of bilateral relations, *Canada and the United States: Ambivalent Allies*, is inspired by the view that American economic and cultural vitality drew a willing Canada into the United States orbit. They also hold the view that Pearson's government restored "the equilibrium" to official relations, but they stress the long-term importance of the differences over Cold War priorities, particularly the Vietnam conflict, that emerged during the 1960s.[28] They echo Bothwell: "America battled the Communist threat around the globe, and in the process, built a warfare state instead of a welfare state."[29]

Norman Hillmer and J.L. Granatstein begin their study of Canada's relations with the United States with very different premises, but their conclusions are much the same. These two historians argue that bilateral relations are defined by the "continued tension between conflict and cooperation."[30] Yet their treatment of relations under Johnson and Pearson, in a chapter succinctly and revealingly entitled "You Screwed Us," is long on conflict and short on cooperation. The differences over Vietnam epitomized the division between the two countries. "The Temple speech [on Vietnam] was symptomatic. A long list of clashes between U.S. and Canadian interests and values had replaced the relative calm and consensus of the ten years after the end of the Second World War."[31]

There are good reasons for this constrained view of the bilateral relationship under Pearson and Johnson. In narrative terms, the emphasis on conflict is dramatically satisfying. Early success gives way in 1965, the middle of the period and an election year in Canada, to a string of bilateral controversies and a sharp deterioration in relations, paving the way for Pierre Trudeau and a new generation. In addition, there are few detailed case studies of relations during this period, encouraging historians working on broad interpretations to focus on the most readily accessible and often the most controversial events. The problem is compounded, as Michael Hart observes, by the reluctance of Canadian historians to wrestle seriously with economic and trade policy, subjects where one might expect common values and interests to persist most strongly.[32]

Good relations between Ottawa and Washington, as the opening chapter of this book demonstrates, were not automatic under the new Liberal government. Though Pearson and Kennedy, who met at the president's retreat in Hyannisport in May 1963, respected and liked each other, this was not enough to ensure bilateral harmony, even in the short period before Kennedy's assassination. Finance Minister Walter Gordon's first budget, which included provisions to reduce foreign (American) ownership of the Canadian economy, angered the American administration. At the same time, Washington's efforts to reduce its own balance of payments problems threatened the Canadian dollar and worried Ottawa. Chapter 1 of this book thus explores the different lessons each country drew from these experiences. While Washington redoubled its efforts to seek a renewed basis for continental partnership, Ottawa was determined to seek greater economic independence. It expanded Diefenbaker's automotive duty remission scheme and unilaterally tried to alter the balance of trade with the United States. On the eve of Kennedy's death, two competing visions for the future of the North American economy seemed destined to collide.

Lyndon Johnson's accession to the presidency delayed this confrontation. The president and the prime minister initially got on well together, and Washington tried hard to persuade Ottawa to resolve their differences over automotive products in a cooperative manner that stressed their common economic interests. At the same time, Canada was offered the chance to improve its access to the United States market by negotiating extensive bilateral tariff reductions under the General Agreement on Tariffs and Trade (GATT). Finding a solution to the automotive dispute and developing a position on tariff negotiations forced the Pearson government to decide if it was prepared to accept further integration of the two North American economies in exchange for the improved standard of living that greater access to the United States market would make possible.

This question, which pitted economic nationalists against "continentalists," also lies at the centre of chapter 3, a study in Canadian-American financial relations during the Pearson era. American efforts to stem the flow of United States dollars abroad accelerated between 1963 and 1968. Ever more elaborate measures were erected to limit the circulation of American dollars overseas. While Pearson's government was able to protect Canada's access to American capital, Washington exacted its price. Canada was exempted from the American balance of payments measures on condition that it too regulated the flow of American dollars, a situation that effectively created a common North American capital market by 1968 and reinforced the view of many policymakers that Canada's economic security lay with still closer relations with the United States.

Nationalist fears that closer economic integration would eliminate Canada's capacity to pursue its own foreign and defence policy were unfounded. Under Pearson, Canada adopted a defence policy that emphasized new international roles in keeping with the altered foreign policy environment. Chapter 4 challenges the view that this change inevitably led to resentment in Washington. Instead, it draws on American sources to demonstrate that both the State Department and the Pentagon possessed an acute understanding of the influences on Canadian policy. Washington adjusted its expectations to meet Canadian realities. Consequently, by the time Pearson left office in the spring of 1968, the two countries had started to refashion the close political and military alliance that had developed during the height of the Cold War.

Not all differences could be reconciled, however. Johnson's decision in 1965 to take the United States to war in Southeast Asia reflected the perspective of a world power, a perspective that was alien to the Canadian experience. Squeezed between American demands for support and growing popular opposition to the conflict, Ottawa had little room to manoeuvre. Still, as chapter 5 demonstrates, Paul Martin, the secretary of state for external affairs, exploited every available opportunity to advance the prospects for a negotiated settlement in Indochina. This was a risky strategy, one that seemed likely to provoke a direct confrontation with the United States. As the war intensified and the scope for Canadian diplomatic initiative narrowed, Pearson assumed responsibility for Canada's Asian policy, overcoming his minister's temptation to pursue a course too independent of Washington.

The sixth and final chapter explores how policymakers in Ottawa and Washington worked hard to preserve cooperative relations in the face of rising nationalist sentiment in Canada. The two countries successfully contained and resolved their differences over legislation to protect Canadian magazines from American competition. This experience is implicitly contrasted with the crisis that resulted when Ottawa tried to stop a large American bank from taking over a smaller Canadian one. The virulent strain of Canadian nationalism that this confrontation released forced Pearson to adopt a more critical attitude to American policy in Southeast Asia. Nevertheless, Pearson made sure that the change in Canada's attitude was gradual and carefully managed. When Canada finally questioned United States policy in Vietnam – with a muted and ambiguous call for a bombing halt in September 1967 – it hardly registered in Washington, where the administration was by then almost impervious to criticism.

Over five years, Pearson's government virtually redefined the parameters of postwar Canadian-American relations. The economic relationship was increasingly grounded in a shared recognition of the value of formalized structures for continental cooperation. These in turn were slowly uncoupled from political considerations. Rather than compromising Canada's independence, Pearson's pursuit of closer economic relations with the United States rescued Canada from the parochial influence of Walter Gordon and his nationalist allies.

CHAPTER ONE

An Unsteady Start

Although discouraged by Pearson's failure to secure a parliamentary majority in 1963, many observers on both sides of the border were buoyed by the hope that the new prime minister would quickly recreate a basis for cooperation with Washington. They were not disappointed. Within weeks of the new ministry assuming office, Pearson and Kennedy retreated to the president's family compound in New England. For two days they chuckled at Diefenbaker's eccentricities as they sliced through the backlog of business that had been allowed to accumulate. Bilateral relations seemed about to settle into the easy familiarity that characterized the partnership before 1957.

Yet many of the most important questions that the two men addressed – Canada's acquisition of nuclear weapons, for example, and the ratification of the Columbia River Treaty – were firmly rooted in the preoccupations of an earlier era. The two men paid almost no attention to the new set of important issues that had already begun to clamour for serious attention. Indeed, to ensure the success of his meeting with Kennedy, the Canadian prime minister glossed over the importance his government attached to curbing the American stake in the Canadian economy. Yet within a month of the New England summit, Pearson's Cabinet had endorsed a budget that questioned the benefits of unfettered American investment in Canada and struck at the very basis of the postwar alliance.

Washington's hostile reaction to Finance Minister Walter Gordon's first budget gave his colleagues plenty of reason to question his

nationalist policies and his standing in Pearson's cabinet. The minister's difficulties were compounded in early July when the Kennedy
administration tried to solve its balance of payments problems by
reducing the flow of American capital to Canada and other foreign
markets. While the financial crisis that subsequently rocked the Canadian dollar further eroded Gordon's reputation, it also demonstrated
how much the Canadian economy depended on Washington's forbearance. As a result, by early September a new sense of urgency characterized the government's determination to create a stronger and
more independent Canadian economy.

The summer's economic difficulties resonated just as loudly in Washington. Disturbed by Gordon's nationalist budget, the u.s. under secretary of state, George Ball, ordered his department to examine the
nature of North American relations. Its conclusion, that the solution to
the current bilateral difficulties lay in redoubling efforts to integrate
the two economies, contrasted sharply with Ottawa's views. When the
minister of industry, Bud Drury, announced his proposals for developing Canada's domestic automotive industry in the fall of 1963, these
two irreconcilable visions for the future of the North American partnership seemed certain to collide.

For a few prescient observers in the Department of External
Affairs, Pearson's poor election results meant only trouble. Worried
that Washington expected more from the new prime minister than he
could possibly deliver and wary of the nationalist lobby on the government's left, one official wondered whether the two countries
would "be able to get through the immediate future without too
much antagonism being stirred up."[1] Most members of the department, however, were much more confident of Pearson's ability to
restore the relationship to its former robust condition. After all, as
Canada's ambassador to the United States, Charles Ritchie, noted in
his diary on election day, "the Liberals seem a sort of normalcy which
is called stable government and seem to mean a return to the old mid-
dle-class, middle-of-the-way, reasonable, responsible, familiar Canada."[2] While he waited for the new ministry to take final shape, Ed
Ritchie, an assistant under-secretary of state for external affairs,
began to develop a broad and coordinated strategy for normalizing
relations with the United States.

Ritchie contended that Canadian-American relations were shaped in
part by the atmosphere produced by the "nature and timing" of key
decisions. Pearson should meet Kennedy soon to orchestrate a
sequence of decisions that would "get the new period ... off to the right
kind of start." This might begin with a series of decisions favourable
to the United States on matters where the Americans believed that

Canada had been unreasonable in the past. These decisions would be balanced by unprovocative statements that reiterated the Canadian position on issues where Canada had legitimately differed with the United States. The bilateral relationship would subsequently be driven forward by announcing conspicuously and dramatically the intensification of joint efforts to address any outstanding problems that were of mutual interest.[3]

Ritchie's strategic approach to bilateral relations, a departure from the traditional ad hoc diplomacy that typified exchanges between Ottawa and Washington, failed to impress the prime minister. With one eye fixed on the country's nationalist movement, which already wielded substantial influence within his own party, and another locked on the Liberal party's precarious standing in the House of Commons, Pearson was reluctant to move too quickly. In requesting an interview with Kennedy, he made it clear to White House officials that he was not ready to use a heads-of-government meeting to announce any bilateral agreements. Instead, he insisted on limiting the agenda to an informal *tour d'horizon*, during which he and the president would simply identify problems in the relationship and set in motion the means for solving them.[4]

Aware of the pressures that faced the new prime minister, officials in the State Department and the White House were ready to give Pearson ample time to settle in and room to set the bilateral agenda. They cautioned the president against assuming that relations with Canada under Pearson would be relaxed and assured. "[E]ven though Diefenbaker was not there any more," the State Department warned, "the Canadians were still going to be difficult to deal with on a lot of subjects."[5] Pearson's minority government, added the president's national security advisor, McGeorge Bundy, heralded "a period of considerable uncertainty" and complicated the problem of manoeuvring around tender Canadian nationalist sensibilities.[6] The Central Intelligence Agency (CIA) echoed these concerns and warned the president that Pearson was "a moderately strong nationalist" who was inclined to question "the whole course of U.S.-Canadian defense relationships."[7]

In response to these concerns, the president reined in any agencies that might have been tempted to immediately resume negotiations that had been broken off during Diefenbaker's tenure. Kennedy himself seized control of American policy, resolved to regulate the timing and the direction of any new departures: "The advent of a new government in Canada has naturally stirred nearly all branches of the government to new hope that progress can be made in effective negotiations with this most important neighbor on all sorts of problems. It is the President's wish that these negotiations should be most carefully coordinated under his personal direction through the Department of State."[8]

Kennedy and his advisors maintained this restrained and cautious posture during preparations for the president's meeting with Pearson. Rather than trying to advance particular bilateral objectives, Kennedy was encouraged simply to use the meeting to "gauge Pearson's attitudes on world problems and provide him with a clear picture of [American] views." Though he might reasonably raise bilateral issues that concerned Washington, like nuclear weapons or the Columbia River Treaty, he was reminded that Pearson would not wish to appear as an American pawn and would avoid reaching any substantive decisions.[9]

In an off-the-record press briefing designed to counter growing public expectations of a breakthrough in bilateral relations, Bundy acknowledged that the United States expected the meeting to resolve none of the contentious issues facing the two countries. He hoped that the two leaders would avoid being drawn into any detailed discussions on bilateral issues and focus instead on larger international questions where agreement might provide the basis for a close relationship between the two men. The president, Bundy noted in regard to continental defense, "would desire only to follow the prime minister's timetable ... much would depend on what the prime minister judged politically feasible in Canada."[10]

Kennedy's restrained approach to his meeting with Pearson and his decision to host the talks at his family's New England retreat rather than in a formal Washington setting removed some but not all of the pressure associated with the occasion. On the eve of his departure for Hyannisport, Pearson nervously confessed to his cabinet colleagues that "he had never approached an international discussion with deeper concern."[11] His anxieties were unwarranted. The easy laughter and casual banter that slid back and forth as Kennedy's press secretary tested Pearson's knowledge of baseball was striking evidence of the warm and cosy environment that was immediately established when the two leaders met. Pearson reflected the patrician, East Coast establishment to which the president and his family had long aspired. Kennedy looked with admiration at Pearson's Nobel Prize and envied his friendships with influential journalists like James Reston, Walter Lippmann, and Marquis Childs. The American also respected Pearson's profound grasp of international affairs, which in turn helped the Canadian prime minister appreciate the pressures under which the American president laboured.[12] Struck by the president's "quick mind ... great capacity and ... forward-looking attitude," Pearson was favourably impressed by

Kennedy's determination "to bring [about] a reduction in world tensions and to promote disarmament."[13]

The two men made their way quickly through a lengthy agenda. Pearson retained the initiative during the two days of talks and determined most of the agenda. He astutely began by informing Kennedy of his government's determination to honour Diefenbaker's promise to arm Canada's NATO and NORAD forces with nuclear weapons. Kennedy was clearly relieved. He assured Pearson that he understood the political difficulties that his minority government faced in reaching this decision. Indeed, he informed the delighted prime minister that outstanding American requests for nuclear storage facilities for antisubmarine weapons and the Strategic Air Command were "well down" the list of American priorities. Until the two countries had concluded a general agreement that established the conditions under which Canada would accept nuclear weapons, these requests could be safely postponed.

After their lengthy discussion of nuclear questions, Kennedy and Pearson tackled the long list of irksome issues whose resolution had been hampered by Diefenbaker's shaky relationship with the American president. Few of these problems were immediately solved. Instead, the two men described to each other the issue as defined in their respective capitals, and together they decided on the mechanism to be used in seeking a solution. Pearson, for instance, complained of the Pentagon's plans to stem the flow of American defence dollars to Canadian contractors as part of Washington's efforts to resolve its balance of payments problems. Kennedy promptly responded by explaining the logic behind the American position, before eventually agreeing to ask the two responsible cabinet members to discuss Canadian concerns in greater detail.

The same fate awaited other troublesome problems. Pearson reiterated his desire to see the Columbia River Treaty ratified and work started on the massive hydroelectric project. When he proposed adding a brief protocol to the treaty in order to defuse nationalist critics in Canada by specifying the benefits accruing to Canada under the treaty, Kennedy responded constructively with a promise of "immediate consultations." The two men also promised "to get a high level meeting going as soon as possible" to deal with the intractable problems plaguing Canadian shipping on the Great Lakes, where the American Seafarer's International Union (SIU) continued to boycott Canadian ships in retaliation against Ottawa's effort to clean up its corrupt Canadian affiliate. Pearson and Kennedy similarly agreed that senior officials would begin discussing Canada's plans to extend unilaterally its sovereignty over Canadian territorial waters to a distance of twelve miles. Finally, Ottawa's efforts to renegotiate the outdated Canada–United

States civil aviation treaty and to increase American oil quotas were rewarded when the president and the prime minister decided to hold "early talks" on these questions.

The pleasant atmosphere and a natural reluctance among both delegations to jeopardize the success of the meeting inhibited a completely forthright exchange of views on one key question. In outlining his government's intention to address American control over the Canadian economy, Pearson inaccurately assured Kennedy that he would not "penalize United States interests."[14]

For the time being, this hardly mattered. In the weeks that followed Hyannisport, the pace of activity seemed proof positive that "the honeymoon was on and everything which had been sour was sweet."[15] On 20 May 1963, Canada presented the American ambassador, Walt Butterworth, with the promised draft treaty on nuclear weapons. Final agreement on the precise terms of the treaty remained a long way off, but the president and his senior advisors were pleased with this indication of Canada's renewed reliability.[16] Reminded that American proposals for dispersing NORAD air defence squadrons were likely to create an untenable situation for Pearson in Ottawa, Kennedy made it clear that he "did not wish to convey any idea that we are pressing the Canadian Government with this new proposal" and ordered his administration to "immediately desist from initiating any further discussions ... with the Canadians."[17]

The Kennedy administration's willingness to accommodate Canadian sensibilities on defence questions set the tone for the American military establishment and led to a joyous reunion of service representatives at the June 1963 meeting of the Permanent Joint Board on Defence. The two delegations moved quickly through a short agenda that culminated in a discussion of possible new mechanisms for improved communication and consultation. The Canadian representative, Dana Wilgress, characterized the meeting as "the most productive we have had in some time." He assured the secretary of state for external affairs, Paul Martin, "that on the United States side there is a genuine disposition to improve consultative arrangements where this may be necessary."[18]

Elsewhere, the impact of the Hyannisport meeting was equally immediate and substantial. As Pearson had promised the president, Marcel Cadieux, the deputy under-secretary of state for external affairs, led a delegation of senior officials to Washington on 16 May 1963 to brief American officials on Canadian plans to declare a twelve-mile fishing zone. The following day, the United States secretary of labor, Willard Wirtz, flew to Ottawa to meet his Canadian counterpart, Allan MacEachen, in an effort to begin unravelling the Great

Lakes labour dispute. About the same time, Kennedy and Pearson asked the Canadian-born Harvard economist, John Kenneth Galbraith, to investigate poor civil aviation relations between the two countries. Meanwhile, Ottawa moved quickly to convene a meeting with the British Columbia premier, W.A.C. Bennett, in order to secure his complete support for the terms of the Columbia River Treaty before initiating formal talks with Washington on the proposed protocol. The White House was impressed with Paul Martin's speed and finesse in handling the touchy British Columbia premier.[19]

However, not everyone who witnessed the camaraderie of Hyannisport and the impressive flow of business that followed was convinced that bilateral bliss had arrived. Ambassador Butterworth, for example, was sceptical. "I heartily agree that the Hyannis Port meeting augurs well," he wrote, adding that "I am concerned, however, that our recent difficulties in Canada be not viewed as a superficial lapse of customary cordiality now restored by a smile and a handshake. You note that 'on fundamentals they have always been with us.' They were – ten years ago. The important thing to grasp is that our recent differences were over fundamentals."[20]

He was right. While Pearson and Martin had been busy mending fences with Washington, Walter Gordon, the minister of finance, had pressed ahead with his plans to produce a budget within the "sixty days of decision" that the Liberals had promised during the election campaign. Disturbed by their new minister's haste and his unorthodox program to combat American domination of the Canadian economy, senior officials in the Department of Finance unhappily set about drafting the government's first budget.

Placing little confidence in these old-fashioned mandarins, Gordon rejected their initial efforts and brought in three outside consultants. Tension within the Department of Finance, especially over the measures proposed by Gordon's consultants to restrain foreign investment, grew as the budget assumed its final shape. Alarmed officials in the department enlisted the help of Louis Rasminsky, the governor of the Bank of Canada, in an effort to restrain their impetuous minister. Rasminsky met Pearson in late May and warned him that the budget's provisions to stop the growth of foreign ownership were discriminatory and likely to provoke a sharp American reaction, but Pearson refused to act.[21] The Cabinet, too, decided not to intervene after it reviewed the budget's provisions on foreign ownership in early June. On 13 June 1963, the finance minister presented his first budget to an expectant House of Commons.

Gordon's budget was not intended solely to confront the problem of foreign ownership. It sought to meet a number of equally important economic objectives. Only two of these – the attempt to alleviate chronic unemployment, which Gordon defined as "the most serious domestic problem facing Canada today," and the effort to restore a greater degree of Canadian control over the economy – had implications for Canadian-American relations. The government, Gordon asserted early in his presentation, had already begun to combat Canada's unacceptably high unemployment rate. The new department of industry, he informed the House of Commons, had recently initiated discussions with the automobile industry aimed at extending the previous government's efforts to increase the size of the Canadian industry and the number of employment opportunities available to Canadians. Ominously, Gordon promised to explore similar schemes in other industries. "In the search for new employment and increased economic strength we shall not be satisfied with half measures. Wherever major changes in our industrial structure are found to be necessary, we shall energetically promote them." As a further step in this direction, the budget included a provision for an increased capital depreciation allowance for companies with 25 percent Canadian ownership.

Gordon's assault on the unemployment problem necessarily included an attack on the related question of Canada's current account deficit. This was not, however, to be tackled directly, since Gordon well knew that Canada would "continue to need substantial net inflows of foreign capital for quite a few years to come if [the country was] to avoid further exchange rate difficulties and if a reasonable increase in [its] standard of living was to be achieved." Instead, Gordon attacked the general problem of nonresident ownership and control, which, he argued, interfered with the country's natural development as an independent state. It was vital "that industry in Canada ... should operate with due regard to the over-all interest of Canadians and the Canadian economy." Gordon suggested that a 25 percent Canadian equity interest would ensure that a Canadian point of view would be brought to bear on corporate policy decisions affecting purchasing, employment, production, research, and, most important, export sales. The budget included two important measures to increase the proportion of Canadian equity investment. First, it levied a takeover tax of 30 percent on sales by residents to nonresidents of shares of companies listed on Canadian stock exchanges. Second, the withholding tax paid on dividends was increased from 15 to 20 percent effective 1 January 1965 on companies that were not at least 25 percent Canadian owned.[22]

In Canada, the initial reaction to these provisions in Gordon's budget was moderately cheering. "I think this would be a very strong influence in keeping Canadian ownership here and reducing the possibility of the sale of Canadian businesses to foreign companies," remarked Howard Graham, the president of the Toronto Stock Exchange.[23] The *Globe and Mail* reported that the changes in the withholding tax "were generally welcomed by investment men ... as a means of encouraging Canadian ownership of industry."[24]

Within a few days, however, the reaction had turned hostile. The government's problems began innocently enough when the inexperienced minister of finance mishandled a question about the propriety of employing outside consultants to prepare the budget. In the intense scrutiny that followed the first few cries for his resignation, the enormous administrative difficulties involved in implementing the takeover tax and the withholding tax became apparent. It was increasingly unclear how Ottawa would identify the real owners of shares or prevent sales on foreign exchanges or encourage Canadians to buy the shares offered by foreign companies. Any lingering support for these proposals evaporated completely when Eric Kierans, the outspoken president of the Montreal and Canadian stock exchanges, attacked the budget. "Today, our friends in the western world," he announced on 19 June, "will fully realize that we don't want them or their money and that Canadians who deal with them in even modest amounts will suffer a thirty percent expropriation of the assets involved."[25] When Kierans declared that he would tell his friends to sell short, the markets panicked. Pearson and his Cabinet colleagues urged Gordon to retreat. He reluctantly agreed, and on 19 June he temporarily withdrew the proposed withholding and takeover taxes until solutions could be found to the administrative difficulties associated with them. On 24 June the battered finance minister announced that the takeover tax would be withdrawn permanently.

At Pearson's request the White House maintained a discreet silence throughout this tumultuous debate. Nevertheless, the American administration was deeply disturbed at the Canadian action; as soon as the immediate crisis had passed, it lost no time in making its views known. In late June, Griffith Johnson, assistant secretary of state for economic affairs, summoned embassy officials to the State Department. Some of the American anger sprang simply from their surprise. Neither at Hyannisport nor during a subsequent encounter with Dean Rusk, the secretary of state, had Pearson indicated that the budget would have so drastic and so direct an impact on American interests.[26]

There were other, more substantive reasons for American concern. The proposed Canadian measures undermined Washington's international efforts to maintain the principle that offshore investment should be accorded the same treatment as domestic investment. If Canada was allowed to violate this principle, other states where American interests enjoyed a more tenuous tenure might imitate the Canadian example. Moreover, the United States was concerned with the practical effects of the Canadian action. These placed an onerous burden on United States companies that would be forced to offer shares for sale in a depressed market. While Johnson hoped that Canada would take up these points when the budget was considered in greater detail, he concluded his message on a disturbing note. Gordon's budget favoured investment by debt rather than equity capital and so imposed a new burden on the weak American balance of payments position. "Much of the net drain on our balance of payments goes to Canada," Johnson remarked, adding that "we would be reluctant to interfere with the capital markets in New York but it is one of the areas which must be watched. If Canada worsens this situation, then the issue will come to the fore."[27]

Ottawa ignored Johnson's hint that the United States considered the flow of American dollars to Canada to be contributing to its balance of payments problems. Canadian officials and politicians remained confident that the country's need for American capital was well understood and accepted as legitimate in Washington. Pearson had described for Kennedy himself how Canada's trade deficit with the United States actually contributed to a positive American balance of payments position. In early July, Rasminsky had also discussed the bilateral balance of payments situation with the American secretary of the treasury, Douglas Dillon, and with Alfred Hayes, the president of the Federal Reserve Bank of New York. Both men appeared to understand that Canada's need for American capital was more than offset by its current account deficit with the United States.[28]

As a consequence, while the United States administration drafted plans to limit the movement of United States capital to Canada, the Cabinet remained preoccupied with altering the budget to meet American concerns. Faced with stubborn opposition from Gordon and conscious that every retreat further weakened his government, Pearson was reluctant to insist that the budget's discriminatory provisions be removed entirely.[29] Instead, in an acrimonious discussion that stretched out over four meetings in early July, the Cabinet tried to address Washington's concerns by tinkering with the budget's provisions on foreign ownership.[30]

Gordon, abandoned by such staunch allies as Tom Kent, was forced to retreat. The minister was provided with some political cover when Rasminsky suggested a formula for broadening the definition of Canadian ownership under which qualified companies could avoid the 5 percent increase in the withholding tax and benefit from the special capital depreciation allowances.[31] The definition would be met if at least 25 percent of the voting stock was held by one or more Canadians or Canadian-controlled corporations or if no single group of foreign shareholders owned more than 75 percent of the stock. In both cases, at least 25 percent of the directors had to live in Canada.[32] The effort failed to meet American objections. Butterworth and the White House both agreed that the United States should maintain its opposition to the provisions in the budget that interfered with American investment in Canada.[33]

For the moment, however, the United States had more pressing problems to consider. At noon on 18 July 1963, Kennedy announced that he would ask Congress to impose an Interest Equalization Tax (IET) of one percent on capital raised in the United States for offshore investments in order to reduce the outflow of American capital and ease Washington's balance of payments problems.

In Ottawa, where the only prior indication of the American action had been that morning's unusual level of market activity, the government was shocked to learn that the president's measures included Canada. Observers were quick to realize that the new tax threatened the country's capacity to cover its current account deficit and maintain the dollar's value. The market for Canadian securities evaporated, and the dollar weakened significantly during the afternoon of 18 July 1963. Gordon's effort that afternoon to reassure investors in a speech to the House of Commons had almost no impact, and the government was forced to intervene more energetically.

Late in the evening of 18 July the secretary of state for external affairs called in the American ambassador for a talk. In addition to the currency problems created by the American balance of payments program, the media had already begun to characterize the IET as a retaliatory response to the Gordon budget, creating an awkward political problem for a government that prided itself on its capacity to manage the country's foreign policy. The minister, who suspected that the pundits were at least partially right, was in a belligerent mood and complained bitterly of the lack of consultation. He insisted that Washington do something to ease the unfair burden that the measures placed on Canada. Butterworth tried to reassure the minister that Canadian interests had been kept to the fore throughout the decision-making process in Washington and that "there was no element of retaliation in the U.S. programme."[34] Martin was not appeased and hinted darkly that ill feeling over the IET might disrupt continuing discussions of "other important matters." He insisted that the United States exempt Canada completely from the tax. Meanwhile, the government's position might be eased if Rusk made it clear publicly that the IET was not a retaliatory measure.

Martin's entreaties produced one small but gratifying result. At noon the following day a State Department spokesman issued a statement "absolutely" denying that the application of the IET to Canada was in retaliation for the Canadian budget.[35] Robert Roosa, the under secretary of the treasury, delivered a similar message to the Canadian wire services a few hours later. The two statements provided Pearson's government with some welcome protection from its domestic critics but carried little weight with investors and speculators. Pressure on the dollar intensified steadily throughout the second day of the crisis. By the time the markets closed, the Bank of Canada had spent U.S.$104 million supporting the dollar and had been forced to ask the Bank of England to help defend the currency in European markets the next day.[36]

The State Department exploited Canada's discomfort as a useful lesson in North American interdependence. When Charles Ritchie met Rusk and Ball on 19 July to plead for a Canadian exemption, they underlined the ironic aspects of the situation. Ball recalled Washington's restrained response to Gordon's budget, which threatened to harm the United States' balance of payments position by encouraging debt equity, and pointed out to the Canadian ambassador that "the effect of the IET on equity holdings ... was consistent with Canadian budgetary measures directed at increasing the degree of Canadian ownership."[37]

The response from the Treasury Department was much more sympathetic. Distressed by the State Department's indifferent efforts to reassure Ottawa, Roosa made a series of telephone calls on the afternoon of 19 July in a frantic effort to contact senior Canadian officials. Late in the day, he finally reached Alan Hockin, an assistant deputy minister of finance. The American balance of payments program, Roosa quickly explained, had been designed to slow, rather than stop, Canadian borrowing in the United States. Under questioning from Hockin he admitted that Washington had anticipated neither the violent market reaction nor the pressure Ottawa might face for an increase in Canadian interest rates. The Federal Reserve Bank, the under secretary stated helpfully, had already offered the Bank of Canada $10 million to defend the Canadian dollar. In addition, the United States would have no objection if Canada wished to seek some immediate relief in the short end of the market, since securities maturing in less than three years were exempt from the tax. Handed a report of Martin's encounter with Butterworth in the middle of his talk with Roosa, Hockin pressed for an exemption. Without exactly rejecting the Canadian request, Roosa replied ambiguously "that a specific exemption for [Canada] would be very difficult for the U.S. to accept."[38]

The generally cooperative tenor of Roosa's remarks comforted officials in Ottawa. At least in the Treasury Department, there was some interest in addressing the problems that the IET created for Canada. Early on Saturday morning, Gordon instructed his officials to bypass the State Department and appeal directly to the Treasury Department for a formal exemption from the IET before the financial markets opened again on Monday.[39] He asked Rasminsky to head the mission.

Rasminsky was an ideal choice. He knew and liked Americans, and they liked him. As Canada's representative on the IMF during the 1950s, he had developed a broad network of influential contacts in financial and political circles in Washington and New York. American policymakers found him a pleasant colleague, "charming, urbane and sophisticated."[40] More important, they admired his intelligence and were usually ready to hear him out.

The Canadian delegation was met in Washington by the secretary of the treasury, who expressed his considerable surprise at the market's sharp reaction to the tax. Rasminsky admitted that the reaction was exaggerated but insisted that it was "based on a profound truth and [was] basically ... right." Canada's large current account deficit demanded a steady flow of capital imports from the United States. The IET blocked that flow and rendered it impossible for Canada to balance its international accounts.[41]

Rasminsky continued. Canada recognized the balance of payments problems that faced the United States and tried, where possible, to be helpful. During the past year, Ottawa had agreed to Washington's request that it maintain a low level of American reserves and had successfully reduced the gap between American and Canadian interest rates. Canada assisted the United States balance of payments position in one other important respect. As the American dollars borrowed to finance Canada's current account deficit with the United States were insufficient to cover the full deficit, Canada was compelled to finance its deficit through gold production and by importing capital from third countries. Understood in its proper context, the application of the IET to Canada made no sense and would ultimately be counterproductive. Canada should be given a complete exemption.

Dillon acknowledged Canada's past help in dealing with the United States' balance of payments problem. Nevertheless, he remained reluctant to admit that the American action was ill-judged. He questioned Rasminsky's assumption that Canadian borrowing in the United States was influenced largely by differences in each country's interest-rate structure. The most important consideration behind Canadian borrowing was the ready availability of large pools of capital in the United States, and Canada would therefore continue to use the American market. Rasminsky countered: If as little as one-third to one-half of Canadian borrowings in the United States were interest-rate sensitive, then an exchange crisis was inevitable – and imminent. Dillon slowly gave way and admitted that perhaps "interest rate differentials between Canada and the U.S. were much more relevant and important than between the U.S. and others."

Rasminsky was making headway. After consulting Kennedy and Ball, who agreed that the United States might go part way towards meeting the Canadian request for an exemption, Dillon reconvened the conference early Sunday morning. He suggested that the two countries issue a joint public statement in which they acknowledged Canada's genuine need to finance its current account deficit with the United States through the sale of securities in that country. The statement would indicate the president's intention to ask Congress for the power to grant limited and unlimited exemptions to the IET. It would also acknowledge that, as the United States could not be sure of Canada's ability to eliminate an "entrepot trade" in U.S. dollars with third parties and maintain an interest-rate structure that would limit capital inflow, the exemption might reasonably be limited to $500 million annually. The exemption would apply only to new securities.

Rasminsky immediately objected. The $500 million limit would spark a stampede to issue new securities and would do little to alleviate the market's fear that Canada might eventually find itself cut off from the American capital it desperately required. Moreover, the proposed statement, which left it to Ottawa to decide who received a share of the annual exemption, would place the federal government in the impossible position of being forced to limit large provincial security issues. Dillon and Roosa insisted that a complete exemption was simply not possible in view of mounting congressional concern about the extent of Canadian borrowing in the United States.

Again, the United States offered to compromise. Roosa suggested that the statement refer to an "unlimited quota" and to the possibility of reimposing the IET if new borrowings became too large. Rasminsky pressed harder, eventually securing an "unlimited exemption" for new Canadian securities in exchange for an undertaking not to increase Canadian reserves. Dillon and Roosa refused to concede any more ground, and they were supported during the discussions on the Sunday afternoon by Ball, who maintained "that there could not be double legislation which singled Canada as an exception ... [for other] countries would demand similar treatment." Rasminsky continued to press for an exemption that would also apply to outstanding securities, but he was forced to settle for an exemption on new securities alone.

The budget and the IET and its disastrous aftermath shook Pearson's commitment, never deep to begin with, to Gordon's nationalist economic agenda. Increasingly uncertain what course to pursue, the prime minister turned to Rasminsky, who advised him that the IET left Canada with few options. "The main lesson is clear enough," the banker wrote, "Canada cannot count on being able to import capital from the United States in the amounts needed to cover our current account deficit." The solution was equally obvious. Canada must reduce its dependence on imported capital, which in turn meant that government policies must be judged first and foremost on the contribution they made to that objective. For instance, the government might have to delay its promised pension plan lest it reduce Canada's capacity to compete internationally and earn a greater proportion of its required capital abroad. More important, Rasminsky contended, Canada had to develop a larger secondary industry through government intervention along the lines of the small automobile incentive program introduced by Diefenbaker and currently under study by the departments of finance and industry.[42]

Targeting the automotive industry made sense. The highly concentrated industry had been erected behind the high tariff walls of Sir John A. Macdonald's National Policy and was dominated by American branch plants, principally the subsidiaries of Ford, Chrysler, and General Motors. During the 1930s, British Commonwealth preferences encouraged a substantial export trade to Australia, New Zealand, and the United Kingdom. But this trade declined at the end of the Second World War, as American manufacturers established production facilities overseas, and the major Canadian automotive producers focused on supplying the domestic market, importing many of the vehicles necessary to round out their narrow Canadian product range.[43]

Tariffs reinforced the emphasis on the local market. Canada's tariff for most parts and vehicles was set at 17.5 percent, which was remitted if producers maintained a certain level of Canadian content. At the same time, American tariffs were high enough to discourage production for the United States market. The result for Canadian consumers was an inefficiently produced car that cost approximately 30 percent more than in the United States. During the late 1950s, the high price of locally produced vehicles encouraged Canadians to purchase inexpensive imports from Germany, Japan, and the United Kingdom. By 1960 the automotive sector, which accounted for more than $500 million of Canada's $1.2 billion current account deficit, was headed for trouble as unemployment mounted along with costs.[44]

In response to industry and union pleading, Diefenbaker's Conservative government asked Vincent Bladen, dean of arts of the University of Toronto, to investigate the problems crippling Canadian producers. The Toronto economist concluded that short production runs made Canada's automotive manufacturers uncompetitive and suggested several measures to encourage Canadian companies to rationalize production in order to increase their capacity to export. Essentially, Bladen proposed replacing the "duty and content formula" with an "extended content" plan that would allow Canadian manufacturers to avoid import duties – provided they met increased Canadian content requirements that would take into account not only domestic sales but also exports.[45] In October 1962, Diefenbaker's Cabinet decided that Ottawa would collect the normal duty on transmissions but would allow Canadian manufacturers to earn the remission of duties on imported transmissions subsequently incorporated into new exports.

Though it was not clear how effective the program was in stimulating Canadian production, Gordon and his brother-in-law, industry minister Bud Drury, advanced a plan in August of 1963 to extend the Conservative scheme to include most automotive parts. Allowing Canadian manufacturers to earn the remission of duties on each dollar's worth of dutiable imports for every dollar's worth of new exports was expected to generate over $200 million in additional exports annually.[46] Pearson was convinced. So were most of his colleagues, and Cabinet endorsed Gordon's view "that as a government we should state our firm intention of bringing our current account deficit into balance and ... making this the No. 1 priority in formulating our economic policies."[47] Cabinet also agreed that the government should press forward with its efforts to develop a strong secondary industry and to promote a greater degree of domestic control over the economy. Gordon's automotive plan was designed to do just that, unilaterally altering Canada's balance of trade with the United States in Canada's favour.

During the period of adjustment that would accompany these measures, a period the minister optimistically thought might be as short as four years, Canada would remain dependent on imported American capital. As the country sought to establish its economy on a more equal footing with its southern neighbour, Gordon concluded, it was necessary that Washington be made to understand and accept both the rationale behind Ottawa's objectives and the country's critical need for unimpeded access to American capital.[48] The forthcoming meeting of the Canada–United States Ministerial Committee on Trade and Economic Affairs would provide Gordon with the opportunity to convince Washington of the legitimacy of the Canadian program.

Washington attached no less importance to this meeting. Gordon's nationalism angered the Kennedy administration, whose views on the future of North American economic relations were quickly evolving in the opposite direction. Under Secretary of State George Ball was one of a handful of American officials to have firm views on relations with Canada. A committed economic liberal, whose experience reconstructing postwar Europe had convinced him that economic integration represented the most rational, efficient, and practical use of national resources, Ball would later recall: "Canada, I have long believed, is fighting a rearguard action against the inevitable ... Sooner or later, commercial imperatives will bring about free movement of all goods back and forth across our long border; and when that occurs, or even before it does, it will become unmistakably clear that countries with economies so inextricably intertwined must also have free movement of the other vital factors of production – capital, services and labor."[49] In June he asked the Harvard economist and foreign investment specialist Raymond Vernon to lead a series of State Department working groups in a substantial review of bilateral economic relations.

Canadian officials tried but failed to discover what the State Department was up to. Canadian curiosity was stretched to its limits in early September when Ball added an item to the agenda for the forthcoming ministerial meeting designed to "provide an opportunity to devise a philosophical framework which might make it possible to deal with specific issues in Canada–United States relations in a somewhat different manner from that which applies to relations with other countries." The United States, Griffith Johnson assured Canadian embassy representatives, had no specific proposals in mind.[50]

This, of course, was far from accurate. American ideas on the future of North American relations had crystallized in a paper drafted by Vernon. Vernon dismissed the State Department's initial proposals for free trade or a customs union as wildly impractical and likely to revive the spectre of American imperialism. Still, he approached the problem of bilateral economic relations in an almost equally ambitious fashion. In Vernon's view, both the United States and Canada were responsible for the growing number of intractable problems encountered in the relationship. Ottawa was preoccupied with the "alleged u.s. domination of [its] industry" and with its current account deficit with the United States. Washington was increasingly caught up in managing global trade and in addressing its own balance of payments problems. Thus, there was a danger in both countries that positions on bilateral issues might be shaped by these larger considerations. What was absent in both capitals, concluded the Harvard economist, was any consideration of "the general direction of long-run relations between Canada and the U.S."[51]

Vernon suggested that the solution to this problem might lie in having the two governments develop a set of mutually agreed principles that would provide both the basis for a renewed sense of North American partnership and an institutional framework for dealing with bilateral problems as they emerged. The proposed statement of principles would start by recognizing that both Canada and the United States possessed their own "distinct national goals." However, both countries shared the desire "to have the maximum opportunity for profiting from the proximity of the two economies" and agreed that the "long-term desideratum is to increase even further the present easy flow of people, capital and goods across the U.S.–Canada border." Achieving this goal would be complicated. Each country would legitimately wish to pursue distinct policies in such fields as agriculture and energy, bringing about "the need from time to time for the reconciliation of national interests." Therefore, both countries must agree to reconcile divergent national interests "expeditiously ... using special procedures and standards appropriate to the unique interdependence of the two counties."

The statement of principles was intended to provide a rationale for managing the entire economic relationship, but the accompanying mechanisms for resolving disputes were more limited. Vernon suggested creating four working groups to seek solutions for specific bilateral problems. The first, on energy, was to explore how to implement the declaration by Pearson and Kennedy at Hyannisport that the two countries would "cooperate for the rational use of the continent's energy resources." Vernon hoped that it might resolve two issues that had proven impossible to manage: Canadian pressure for relaxed American restrictions on oil imports and Canadian subsidies for domestic coal.

The U.S. economist suggested that the ministerial committee create a second task force to examine how American subsidiaries functioned in Canada. A thorough look at their operations would remove much of the sting from Canadian charges of American domination. The group might also issue a statement urging American subsidiaries to hire Canadian executives, to raise their equity capital in Canada, and to operate their Canadian subsidiaries on purely economic considerations. It might also provide a forum to deal with such related issues as the withholding tax and the proposal to extend the automotive parts incentive scheme.

A third working group was to consider the thorny and technical questions surrounding balance of payments, the impact that each country's measures had on the other, and "any new gimmickry which the

Canadians may have in mind for altering their balance-of-payments sit-uation." A final team would examine the extraterritorial application of American economic statutes. Its terms of reference might try to get Ottawa to agree that these regulations would normally be applied when efforts to achieve the identical objective through the use of the Canadian regulatory structure failed.

The State Department's Office of British Commonwealth and North-ern European Affairs, where the Canadian desk was lodged, thought it unlikely that Canada would be prepared to adopt such a far-reaching set of principles. In pressing ahead, however, Washington had other objectives in mind. The State Department hoped that "the stirring up of an intra-mural discussion among the Canadians would be a good thing ... it may give other Canadian ministers a chance to put a little heat on Walter Gordon; and ... it might even help to bring him around to some modification of his views."[52] More immediately, officials were anxious to refer two of the specific problems that the assembled min-isters would be addressing, balance of payments and energy, to work-ing groups for further consideration.[53]

Both Martin and Pearson had been intrigued by the fragmented reports on American thinking that seeped out of the State Department in July and August.[54] However, the scope of the proposal presented by Ball to the Canada–United States Ministerial Committee on Trade and Economic Affairs in late September was far more than Martin, the head of the Canadian delegation, had ever contemplated. Surprised at the extensive nature of the American proposal, he was especially wor-ried that the task force on the extraterritorial application of United States economic statutes might be an American stalking horse designed to circumscribe Canada's more liberal approach to trade with the Communist bloc. Ed Ritchie, an assistant under-secretary of state for external affairs, shared at least some of his minster's suspicions, prompting Martin to ask for a recess in order to consider the draft statement of principles in detail.[55]

Norman Robertson, the under-secretary of state for external affairs, was much more enthusiastic. Intimately acquainted with the long his-tory of Canada's ineffective efforts to have the United States accept Canada's distinctiveness as legitimate, Robertson immediately recog-nized how far the Americans had come towards meeting Canadian preoccupations: "It strikes me as generally a skilful draft and [a] help-ful presentation incorporating a number of points that we have made to the Americans over the years. The procedural suggestions at the end come as somewhat of an anti-climax to the very impressive introduc-tion, but nevertheless I think we can represent that all the working parties which are proposed deal with highly important matters and that their establishment would be helpful to Canada's interest in the broadest sense."[56]

Martin rejected this advice. Instead, in the final session of the two-day meeting, he claimed to lack the necessary Cabinet authority to agree to such an extensive statement. In any event, he added diplomatically, the declaration might have a greater impact if it emerged in some modified form from a meeting between the president and the prime minister.[57] Ball's ambitious declaration was moribund, at least for now.

The Canadian delegation also failed to achieve its primary objective at the September ministerial gathering. It was unable to convince the Kennedy administration to graciously accede to Canada's determination to exert greater control over its economy. With the Cabinet's decision targeting the current account deficit in his hip pocket, Gordon emerged as the chief spokesman on this issue and made it clear that he spoke with the full authority of the government. Canada was grateful for its exemption from the IET, but it could not afford to be perpetually dependant on American generosity. Anxious to avoid adopting either exchange controls or import restrictions to combat Canada's current account deficit, Gordon emphasized the government's determination to increase the country's exports of raw materials and agricultural and manufactured goods. So much Canadian industry was controlled from abroad and designed to supply the domestic market rather than competing with foreign parents in third-country markets that increasing exports was difficult. The Canadian government was therefore convinced that it must stop the rise of nonresident ownership, while promoting the growth of a distinctively Canadian secondary industry. In concluding his remarks, Gordon recognized that a shortage of Canadian capital would mean a continuing need for regular injections of American dollars during the next twenty to thirty years. In exchange for American patience and understanding, he held forth the promise of a stronger and more self-sufficient Canada that would ultimately benefit the United States as much as it did itself.

The u.s. delegation greeted Gordon's presentation with undisguised hostility. The secretary of commerce, Luther Hodges, was especially outraged. He accused Ottawa of penalizing American investment and, in an oblique reference to the still-unannounced proposals to extend the transmission rebate scheme, of forcing American subsidiaries to export their production against their will. The minister of trade and commerce, Mitchell Sharp, and the minister of industry, Bud Drury, hastened to Gordon's side. They defended Ottawa's decision to target the automotive industry for action. After all, it was the largest single item on the current account deficit, and its homogeneous character meant that any agreed proposal could be implemented with relative ease.

The Americans were unconvinced. Ball hurried to join in the debate as tempers became testy. The under secretary pulled no punches and declared his "fundamental disagreement" with the proposals announced in the Canadian budget to encourage Canadian industry. He denounced these as "short sighted changes in the rules applicable to United States investment and as contrary to the established policies of many international corporations." By interfering with the free flow of capital between the two countries, Ottawa was setting a bad precedent for other countries, encouraging investors to flee Canada, and hindering its own ability to attract the capital needed to fuel industrial development. "[The] USA Government could not acquiesce in such measures affecting USA industry."

With neither delegation able to convince the other of the wisdom of its vision for the future of North American economic relations, the meeting drew to an unhappy and inconclusive end. Despite evidence of Washington's concern, Ottawa's attitude toward its plans for the Canadian automotive industry remained unchanged. The Kennedy administration watched with mounting concern, and in late October, it made a final effort to forestall Canadian action, promising to deal with the problems in the automotive sector "through positive and constructive measures." The American carrot was accompanied by the proverbial stick. Ottawa was reminded that the administration's "forbearance" on such issues as Canada's lumber exports, already besieged by protectionist interests in Congress, was not inexhaustible. Moreover, should any one of the twenty-five thousand American automotive parts manufacturers complain about the Canadian program, the administration would have no alternative under United States law but to impose punitive countervailing duties.[58]

Ottawa refused to retreat. On 25 October 1963 Drury unveiled the details of the extended Canadian automotive rebate scheme in the House of Commons. Henceforth, for every dollar's worth of Canadian components exported, automotive manufacturers would be able to earn the remission of duties on one dollar's worth of dutiable imports.[59] In Washington, Drury's announcement was greeted with considerable apprehension. It seemed to repudiate the economic liberalism that had characterized the postwar continental relationship. Equally important, it was certain to lead to pressure for retaliation, which would upset entirely Kennedy's efforts to place Canada–United States relations on a more stable and secure footing.

The administration in Washington moved quickly to respond to this threat to its Canadian policy. Kennedy himself appeared disturbed by the broader implications of the Canadian action and immediately appointed one of his assistants, William H. Brubeck, "as staff officer for Canadian affairs."[60] Ball quickly tackled the secretary of the treasury, whose department had already received its first formal complaints about the Canadian program and was beginning to limber up its machinery on countervailing duties. He insisted that treasury officials move slowly in applying retaliatory duties, allowing the State Department time to seek a solution with Ottawa. Turning his attention northward, Ball arranged with Gordon for officials from both countries to meet for a preliminary discussion of the Canadian program.[61] Relieved to learn from Canadian officials that Pearson's government had no similar plans for other industries, the administration considered the meeting a moderate success. With the retaliatory machinery temporarily stalled and its political backside protected from any additional Canadian surprises, the White House was ready to tackle the general problem of Canadian economic nationalism.[62]

CHAPTER TWO

A Continental Philosophy:
The Autopact and the Kennedy Round

On Thursday, 21 November 1963, Kennedy began to deploy his administrative resources for a White House assault on Canadian economic nationalism. At his final Cabinet meeting that morning, the president asked the under secretary of state, George Ball, to chair a National Security Council (NSC) subcommittee to reexamine U.S. policy towards Canada.[1]

Kennedy's initiative, like so much else, collapsed after his assassination the following day in Dallas. Neither Lyndon Johnson, bewildered by the sudden change in his position, nor his inherited advisors, unsure of the new president's capacity to govern, were inclined to press forward with a full-scale reassessment of American policy towards Canada. Indeed, for the hesitant Texan, whose political career had been bound up in domestic issues and who lacked any real foreign policy experience, Canada represented a safe certainty in the midst of rapid change. When the Canadian ambassador, Charles Ritchie, met Johnson at the airport as he returned to Washington to take up his duties, the president fastened upon the comfortable old bromides. "Pearson," he said. "Your prime minister. My best friend. Of all the heads of government, my best friend."[2]

As Johnson discovered shortly after moving into the Oval Office, however, relations with Canada were headed for trouble. Congressional opposition to the Canadian automotive incentive plan limited the president's ability to seek a negotiated solution and eventually provoked a direct confrontation with Canada. The American threat to impose retaliatory duties confronted Pearson's government with a clear choice: cooperate with the United States to integrate the North American automotive industry or construct a Canadian automotive industry alone, relinquishing access to the huge and lucrative American market. At the same time, the debate over Canadian trade relations with the United States was joined on the multilateral front, where the prospect of negotiations with Washington under the General Agreement on Trade and Tariffs (GATT) created a similar dilemma. Canada could obtain improved access to the valuable American market, accepting the economic integration that would follow, or it could decline to participate, undermining the government's efforts to increase exports, eliminate the current account deficit, and reduce unemployment. In both instances, Pearson's Cabinet was sharply divided. One wing, led by the nationalist minister of finance, Walter Gordon, hesitated to endorse any measure that would lead to closer economic relations with the United States. A second faction, represented by Mitchell Sharp, the minister of trade and commerce, expressed a more traditional liberal view: as a country whose prosperity depended on international commerce, Canada should encourage those developments that promised to reduce tariffs and improve trade. The debate came to a head in the fall of 1964, when Cabinet agreed in quick succession to accept American proposals for a continental automotive industry and to offer significant tariff reductions at the GATT. These two decisions confirmed and reinforced the North American orientation of the Canadian economy.

For Walt Butterworth, the American ambassador to Canada, 1963 seemed to end pretty much as it had begun: despite Washington's best efforts, relations between the United States and Canada seemed mired in controversy. A new approach to the "Canadian problem" was required, and Butterworth was happy to offer his advice. An astute and imaginative political analyst, Butterworth had enjoyed a successful career as a professional diplomat in a foreign service where most senior positions went to political appointees. During the 1930s he had served in Ottawa as a young man before eventually becoming assistant secretary of state for Far Eastern affairs in 1947. Over the following decade he stayed in touch with Pearson, whom he viewed as a friend, and retained an active interest in Canada, on which he considered himself an expert. He was appointed U.S. ambassador to Canada in December 1962. Blunt and outspoken, a White House official later described this "grand old warhorse of the Foreign Service" as "just the s.o.b. the Canadians deserve."[3]

As Johnson settled into the White House, Butterworth's timing was clearly favourable. In his annual year-end report, which he distributed widely throughout Washington, the ambassador argued for a new departure in U.S. policy. Reviewing the course of Canadian foreign policy since the mid-1950s, he contended that Canadian policymakers were labouring under the naive and idealistic view that "Canada had clean hands, a pure heart, and no axe to grind, a circumstance which would be recognized by both Communists and neutrals if only Canada were sufficiently careful not to damage this treasured image. Moreover, all these notions were seen as somehow compatible with membership in NATO and alliance with the U.S."[4]

In Butterworth's view, it was these illusions that ultimately resulted in the Diefenbaker government's tergiversations over accepting nuclear weapons. Only in January 1963, when the State Department publicly accused the prime minister of misleading Canadians about the nature of the impasse between the two governments, was the issue resolved. The American intervention reinforced Pearson's recent, albeit reluctant, decision to accept nuclear weapons. "The entire process of rejecting Diefenbaker, of choosing Pearson, and of accepting limited nuclear responsibilities was a painful but significant step by Canadians [towards national maturity]."

Butterworth thought that Canadians still held many illusions about the nature of modern Canada. Although the country had come to accept the military obligations imposed by its close proximity to the United States, Canadians showed few signs of coming to grips in a realistic fashion with the increasingly close economic partnership dictated by geography. Consequently, quarrels over the course of North American economic relations were certain to multiply. While Butterworth mused that some kind of "economic union" might ultimately be the best solution, he dismissed this approach as currently "unattainable." Instead, he urged Washington to give the relationship a "sense of direction" by adopting policies that promoted the mutual development of continental resources, encouraged the growth of sectoral free trade, and protected U.S. investment in Canada. The United States had to "place [its] economic relations with Canada on a mature basis, recognizing the depth of both our mutually advantageous interdependence and our mutual independence."

For Butterworth, the major obstacles to achieving a mature bilateral relationship lay primarily north of the forty-ninth parallel. While acknowledging that Canadians were a vigorous and hard-working people, the American official confidently asserted that Canadians "have yet to decide what they want to be." As a consequence, Canadian policy towards the United States was frequently ambiguous. Pleading that history and geography entitled them to favoured treatment, Canadian policymakers chose to cooperate with Washington when it suited their interests but also pleaded a compelling national need to go their own way when it did not. As long as the United States continued to accept the pleadings of Ottawa for a "special relationship," this ambiguity would continue. The solution, concluded Butterworth, was obvious:

It is time, it seems to me, for us to be less ready than we have been in the past to cater to Canadian special pleading. It is time for Canadians to realize that however sympathetic we may be to their problems, we must as a matter of course look first to our own national interests and international responsibilities and to ask a reasonable *quid* for every *quo*. In manner, we should be matter-of-fact, neither clasping them in a suffocating embrace of friendship when they see eye to eye with us nor retreating into petulance when they do not. We should, in short, take greater account of their interests than their sensitivities and help them realize the two are not always the same.

Butterworth's trenchant despatch arrived in Washington in early January 1964, just as an interagency discussion of the new administration's policy towards Canada was drawing to an end. The ambassador's opinions, which differed sharply from the under secretary of state's well-defined views on the future course of bilateral relations, had little impact. Instead, Ball's more conciliatory approach to Canadian affairs emerged as the essential characteristic of Johnson's Canadian policy.

There were several reasons for this. As chairman of the interagency NSC subcommittee on Canada-U.S. relations, Ball was ideally placed to dominate the mechanism through which American policy was created. Kennedy's assassination increased the influence wielded by the Department of State over the policymaking process. Anxious to avoid upsetting its allies, the new administration early on decided to eschew any immediate changes in its foreign policy. Inadequately prepared for his international responsibilities, the new president was inclined to rely heavily on the State Department for foreign policy advice.[5] Indeed, in early December 1963, when Johnson's attention was drawn to the unsatisfactory state of relations with Canada by the secretary of commerce's continued displeasure at the Canadian automotive parts incentive program, he quickly turned to Rusk for guidance. The secretary of state acknowledged the "increasingly sticky" nature of bilateral relations – the inevitable result of the contradiction between Canada's continuing need for American capital and its fear of U.S. economic control – but confidently reassured the president that Ball and his subcommittee would deliver proposals to smooth relations with Canada in plenty of time for Johnson's January meeting with Pearson.[6]

If Rusk expected Ball to produce the kind of extensive review of bilateral relations that Kennedy seemed to have had in mind, he was to be disappointed. When Ball's subcommittee on Canada met briefly in early January 1964, its mood was marked by "a general, though tacit, doubt as to whether the Committee [with Kennedy dead] had any future."[7] As a consequence, its members were perhaps reluctant to devote much time and effort to exploring new ideas for dealing with either the specific problems associated with Canada's automotive incentive plan or the more general problem of Canadian economic nationalism. The committee simply endorsed the Department of State's existing policy on both these key questions.

Despite continuing nervousness among officials from the departments of commerce and treasury about the mounting domestic pressure on the administration for action against Ottawa's automotive parts scheme, the committee agreed with the State Department's view that a nasty confrontation with Canada would complicate bilateral relations: "The application of countervailing duties would ruin the Canadian scheme. It surely would produce a violent reaction in Canada, which would be seriously harmful to political relations, would damage Pearson's standing, and help Diefenbaker."[8] In order to reduce the pressure for precipitate action and to provide time during which the two countries could reassess their positions, the committee agreed with Ball's proposal that the president and the prime minister establish "an intergovernmental committee to explore continental rationalization of the auto industry and report back in six months."[9] Equally important, Ball used the committee to resurrect his earlier project for a statement of principles that would recognize the unique and special nature of the bilateral relationship, while simultaneously checking Canadian economic nationalism.[10] Acknowledging that "we have no easy solutions to problems with Canada other than patience, effort, and good will," the State Department recommended that the president make the quest for a statement of principles the primary objective of his forthcoming meeting with Pearson.[11]

Canada's goal in pursuing an early meeting between Pearson and Johnson was less precise but no less important. While Kennedy's assassination generated no major reexamination of Canadian policy towards the United States, its timing could not have been worse. The emerging dispute over the Canadian automotive incentive plan had already sent ripples of anxiety through Canada's policy-making community. Alerted by Charles Ritchie to the depth of American opposition to the scheme, Pearson had already decided to postpone plans to pass legislation protecting the Canadian magazine industry from U.S. competition when Kennedy's assassination suddenly added more grounds for anxiety.[12]

Although the new president was expected to place American foreign policy in the State Department's reassuring hands, Canadian policy-makers feared that Johnson, who had risen to prominence as a domestic legislator in the Senate, was likely to favour national constituencies and to cooperate with Congress at the expense of American interests abroad. This comparatively unknown Texan was rumoured to be an emotional man who was inclined to perceive issues personally and in terms of the personalities involved. The Department of External Affairs concluded somewhat cryptically that Johnson was "a more familiarly American type of politician than his predecessor ... [which may] ... be a limitation in dealing with the complex problems of the [Western] alliance."[13] Indeed, as the opposition in Ottawa hurried to point out, at least one leader of the alliance – the Canadian prime minister – would no longer enjoy an assured entrée to the president.[14]

Pearson set out to dispel this view. After Kennedy's funeral, he and the secretary of state for external affairs, Paul Martin, had a brief meeting with Johnson. The prime minister sought to establish some common ground with the new president. He described the Great Lakes labour dispute that continued to pose domestic problems for both governments, explaining that he and Kennedy frequently discussed the issue "as one practising politician to another" and that "both understood the practical considerations of each other's position."[15] The prime minister's appeal to the president's essential political character worked. Although White House officials had already urged the over-burdened president to avoid committing himself to a visit from Pearson, Johnson agreed to the prime minister's proposal for an exchange of visits. Pearson would initiate the exchange with a visit to Washington once the president had had a "few weeks" to get organized.

Exploiting this initial success was difficult. Canadian representatives lost little time in approaching their American colleagues in order to plan for an immediate summit with the kind of substantial agenda that would withstand comparison with the Pearson-Kennedy gathering at Hyannisport. With pleasant memories of the New England encounter in the background, the secretary of state for external affairs and embassy personnel in Washington enthusiastically reassured their American contacts that the prime minister "was an informal kind of man."[16] Martin suggested that a casual overnight stay at the LBJ Ranch in Texas might be appropriate, but Rusk objected. The State Department then proposed a lengthy lunch at the White House. Canadian officials, who had hoped for an overnight stay at Camp David at least, were dismayed. Only after considerable discussion and debate did the president finally agree to a two-day visit that included dinner at the Canadian ambassador's residence followed by formal meetings the next day. Far from soothing Canadian uneasiness about the new administration, the effort to secure even this limited victory hinted at a foreboding future. Indeed, as one Canadian official remarked after yet another inconclusive scheduling meeting with American officials, it seemed clear "that we don't have very many heavy-weights pulling for us in the tug of war for influence here."[17]

This was not an altogether accurate assessment. Given the opportunity, the Johnson administration proved anxious to signal its willingness to accord Canadian problems the degree of attention they had traditionally enjoyed in the postwar White House. When Johnson was asked by Pearson in late December to veto a Congressional bill that would effectively inhibit the import of British Columbian softwood lumber, the president agreed.[18] "This bill," he explained to Congress, "would aggravate our relations with Canada at a time when we are trying to improve those relations at every level."[19] Still, on the eve of Pearson's visit to Washington, Canadian misgivings lingered.

For the most part, these apprehensions retreated during the course of the two-day visit. Pearson and his entourage, who were warmly received at the White House on the morning of 21 January 1964, later remarked with evident relief on the "relaxed atmosphere which characterized the whole visit."[20] Relations between the two leaders at the start of the visit, however, were "brittle [and] not very comfortable." Already preoccupied with the deteriorating situation in Vietnam, which he had observed with interest while serving as Kennedy's vice-president, Johnson lacked "any feeling for Europe." In contrast, Pearson was inclined to celebrate his North Atlantic identity. At dinner that evening, which began poorly when the prime minister presented the bemused Texan with an English-style RCMP saddle, the differences dividing the two men were evident. While Pearson gossiped with Rusk about their experiences at Oxford, Johnson grew quiet and withdrawn. "The general effect on Johnson was to make him feel uncomfortable," recalled Canada's minister-counsellor Basil Robinson. "You could see it happening – you could feel it. Johnson was trying to give up smoking. He had a cigarette in his mouth but he would not light it [and] there he was, having to listen to these guys talking about their fun and games in England."[21]

Things improved once dinner was over. Sticking close to his briefing notes, Johnson drew Pearson aside for a short discussion of France's recent decision to recognize Communist China. He repeated this manoeuver, which was intended to flatter and impress the Canadian prime minister, the following day at the formal meeting. For over an hour, the two men strolled through the White House gardens and exchanged opinions on a range of international and bilateral questions.

Pearson, reassured by his discovery that the president was inclined to adopt a "calm and moderate approach to cold war problems," declared the trip a success: "It was a good talk. Once or twice the President flattered me by throwing away diplomatic proprieties and using language which showed he felt very much at home!"[22]

Johnson shared Pearson's judgment. The president thought that the visit had gone "extremely well." According to the White House, Johnson "had liked the prime minister, found him easy to talk to, and was particularly pleased to find that he could talk politics with him."[23]

The president had at least one reason to feel contented; the Canadian had responded positively to his suggestion that the two countries begin work on Ball's projected statement of bilateral principles.[24] However, Johnson had failed to persuade the prime minister to strike a bilateral committee to examine the Canadian automotive incentive program and the prospect of rationalizing the industry on a continental basis. Alarmed by the congressional furore that followed the decision by the American automobile manufacturer, Studebaker, to relocate its North American operations to Hamilton, Johnson raised the problem with Pearson twice during the prime minister's visit. Armed with a cabinet decision reaffirming the government's determination to proceed with the program, Pearson refused to agree to the suggested committee.

Inside the White House, Ball adopted a tougher line when he discussed this issue with Martin. As long as the automotive program continued to cause the administration problems, there was little hope that other troubling bilateral issues could be put to rest. He made it clear, for instance, that Canada's desire to amend the Canada–U.S. double taxation treaty in order to reflect the changes necessitated by Gordon's budget would "be approached in the context of other problems in the financial and economic fields, e.g. the withholding tax and the auto policy."[25] He described the Canadian automotive scheme as "a considerable problem," which had resulted in "active Congressional interest" and "a crescendo of complaints." Ball repeated American warnings that countervailing duties remained a distinct possibility but promised to delay their implementation if Canada agreed to suspend its program while a joint working group was established "to examine the auto industry on a continental basis, to see what might be done of a broad and general nature."[26]

Martin side-stepped Ball's proposition. Although consultation was unobjectionable, he explained disingenuously, he had not discussed this possibility with the responsible minister, Bud Drury. In any case, there was little chance that Canada would agree to amend the program, since it had already begun to operate. Ball subsequently appealed directly to Pearson, but the prime minister refused to be drawn. Martin intervened more firmly and insisted that Canada had exhaustively studied the possible alternatives and was convinced that the current program was the only one that would achieve the results desired by the government. There would not be any change to the program. Obviously frustrated, the American under secretary grimly noted that there would certainly be some excitement in Congress and that someone would eventually insist on a formal investigation. He concluded ominously that "there was a real possibility that the courts in the United States might find that there was [a subsidy involved]."

Johnson found it difficult to understand the Canadian refusal to assist the administration in seeking a bilateral solution to the automotive problem. Having vetoed the lumber bill, the president was "puzzled as to why Canada was giving him trouble just after he had done something for Canada."[27] He was not alone. Officials in the State Department, the Department of Commerce, and the Treasury Department were also disturbed at Canada's steadfast refusal to seek a bilateral solution to the continuing impasse over automotive parts. Sceptical of Ottawa's categorical assurances that it had no intention of extending the plan to other industries, U.S. officials were increasingly determined that the automotive parts incentive plan should not be allowed to stand as an example of Canadian unilateralism. When the Modine Manufacturing Company of Racine, Wisconsin, asked the Commission of Customs to apply countervailing duties against imported Canadian radiators in mid-April, the need for action became acute.

The meeting of the Canada–United States Ministerial Committee on Trade and Economic Affairs in April 1964 provided the Johnson administration with another opportunity to resolve the dispute without imposing countervailing duties. The chair of the American delegation, Douglas Dillon, the secretary of the treasury, adopted a sympathetic tone. He acknowledged Canada's desire to develop its secondary industries but explained that the current program exposed the administration to a steady increase in Congressional pressure and raised the spectre on Capitol Hill of "lay offs and industrial and political unrest." Since both countries agreed on the desirability of rationalizing continental automotive production, it seemed counterproductive to carry on arguing at cross-purposes. The solution to the current impasse, he contended, lay in the president's suggested bilateral study group. At the very least, the group might persuade Modine to withdraw its complaint or delay further action.[28]

Gordon, armed with a recent Cabinet decision, which again endorsed the existing program, refused to budge.[29] The American proposal to explore the rationalization of the North American industry "seemed practical only in the context of a greater degree of integration than existed at present." He doubted that such integration would be healthy for the Canadian economy and drew the discussion to an abrupt close.

In early May, Philip Trezise, deputy assistant secretary of state for economic affairs, made one last effort to draw Ottawa into negotiations. He suggested a number of modifications to the Canadian plan that would reduce the political pressure on the administration and could form the basis of talks between the two countries. First, since American replacement parts exported to Canada were not covered by the program and were subject to full duty, he proposed that Ottawa eliminate the credit earned on the export of replacement parts to the United States. More substantially, he contended that parts made in Canada and then shipped to the United States for incorporation into larger components should count as part of the Canadian-content requirement necessary for duty-free entry. The list of parts currently admitted duty-free to Canada should also be frozen rather than shrinking as the range of Canadian-produced parts increased under the scheme, and automotive parts imported duty-free by the United States under the provisions of the Defence Production Sharing Plan should not qualify for remission of duty.[30]

Canadian officials tried to buy time, conscious that the longer the program continued in its present form, the harder it would be for Washington to alter it. Responding to Trezise's overture, Ed Ritchie, assistant under-secretary of state for external affairs, indicated that the American's ideas could be taken up later that summer as part of the Kennedy Round GATT consultations. The proposals regarding Canadian content requirements were in any case bound to the United States under the GATT. The letter hinted at a possible concession on the defence production sharing problem and indicated Canadian willingness to explore the problems of replacement parts. This did not, however, signal a Canadian retreat. Ritchie made it quite clear that Trezise's proposal to freeze the current duty-free list would strike at the heart of the Canadian program and was simply not acceptable.[31]

The State Department dismissed Ritchie's letter as a delaying tactic. In late May, it summoned Canadian representatives for a short lesson in American civics. The White House harboured a "large store of goodwill towards Canada ... right to the top" and was reluctant to see countervailing duties imposed, both because of their impact on Canadian-American relations in general and because of the unfortunate precedent it would set for American protectionists. Nevertheless, even the White House could not ignore congressional pressure indefinitely.

The administration was forced to allow the Modine petition to proceed and would publish the official notice of the investigation the following week. The enquiry's terms of reference, the State Department remarked almost casually, would include not only radiators but all Canadian automotive parts exported to the United States.[32]

Canadian officials, who had been convinced that the initial investigation would focus only on the Modine complaint against the importation of radiators, were momentarily uncertain of the significance of the American decision to target the entire Canadian industry.[33] For Walter Gordon, the full import of the American action was immediately obvious. As the American investigation dragged on, new investment in Canadian plant would grind to a halt, new orders would be delayed, and the heart would be torn from the Canadian program. He denounced the American action to the first member of the administration he could find and threatened to build a "people's car" if the Canadian program was frustrated.[34] Washington's response was just as firm. The United States would not back down. Gordon concluded grimly that "having proceeded with this show of strength, they probably feel they have us at a disadvantage. And this is true."[35]

While Gordon set finance officials to work examining Canada's possible options, the Americans moved steadily ahead in a preemptive effort to establish the agenda. Trezise, accompanied by Bill Brubeck, the Canadian expert in the White House, met with Canadian embassy staff in early June to discuss how to "pick up the pieces." They suggested that the two countries might try either to slash Canadian and American tariffs on automobiles and automotive parts on a most-favoured-nation (MFN) basis or to create "a limited customs union between Canada and the United States covering the automotive field."[36]

Senior Canadian officials in Ottawa reacted with scepticism to both these ideas. Simon Reisman, the combative assistant deputy minister of finance who had created the original automotive parts incentive scheme, doubtfully described the idea of a customs union as "pretty bold and unrealistic (unless [it included] carefully worked out conditions and guarantees as to Canadian output)."[37] However, as Canadian officials explored the options open to Canada over the course of the next few days, the American notion of a customs union seemed increasingly viable. Retaining the present program and fighting Modine through the courts was certainly not practical. Even if the courts sided with Canada, the lengthy delay involved would frustrate Ottawa's objectives. Negotiating with the United States on the basis of the proposals presented by Trezise in May would also destroy the Canadian program.

Finance officials wondered whether it might be possible to develop an entirely new program that would encourage Canadian automotive manufacturers to capture a larger share of the domestic market. But this approach had its disadvantages. The cost to consumers would increase, and the government would have to restrict American automotive imports, which was difficult since Canadian tariffs on these imports were bound to the United States under the GATT and could be altered only by negotiation. Only one option remained – a negotiated settlement "based on the concept of rationalization within the North American market, but not involving remissions and thus not risking countervailing duty."

Drawing together the various issues each side had emphasized during their periodic discussions of the issue – "rationalization through exports, avoiding the risk of countervailing duty, and the United States preference for a settlement of this issue as part of the Kennedy approach" – Canadian officials proposed working towards what was a carefully qualified variant of Tresize's "limited customs union." Under the general terms proposed, the United States would agree not to oppose Canadian efforts to secure "a certain minium production of automobiles and parts in Canada." The minimum would be defined as "that share of the North American market which is now produced in Canada, plus that production for export which Canada could reasonably have expected under the present programme and, of course, an appropriate share of the growth of the market." Specifically, the United States would let Canada use the threat of import controls to ensure that the automotive industry agreed to produce a certain share of their total output in Canada. The United States would also cut its tariffs on automobiles and parts by 50 percent in the Kennedy Round. In exchange, Canada would dismantle its present automotive parts incentive program, reduce its tariffs on cars and parts, and reexamine Canadian-content provisions.[38]

The Cabinet Committee on Finance and Economic Policy seemed less disposed to compromise. Gordon deeply resented the American attempt to thwart the existing Canadian program. As chairman of the committee, which also included Drury and Sharp, he dominated discussion and convinced a majority of members to give the official-level paper a much harder edge. Although the committee resolved to seek a mutually agreeable solution, it authorized Canadian negotiators to make it clear that the only alternative to "an arrangement based on rationalization and increased two-way trade" was a protectionist "inward-looking policy designed to accord Canadian producers a larger share of the domestic market." Officials were instructed to threaten "that Canadian support for the Kennedy Round of tariff negotiations would inevitably be affected by the United States attitude toward the objectives of the Canadian automotive policy."

In adopting a firm line, Gordon was influenced partly by tactical considerations. As he later acknowledged in his memoirs, he was anxious to convince the United States of Canadian resolve.[39] Equally important, however, Gordon was by no means fully resigned to a continental solution, and he refused to abandon completely his plans for a self-reliant Canadian automotive industry. His committee instructed officials to begin detailed work on the protectionist option, which would be designed to reserve the domestic market for Canadian producers.[40]

It was clear that the committee's recommendations were not unanimous. Sharp had served as a senior official in C.D. Howe's Department of Trade and Commerce during the 1940s and 1950s when Canada pursued as forcefully as possible a liberal multilateral trade order. A free trader by inclination, Sharp was also a pragmatist who recognized the need for Pearson's government to promote secondary industry in Canada. However, he was disturbed by the unyielding attitude adopted by Gordon's committee, and he led several ministers in questioning its recommendations when they were discussed by the full Cabinet on 11 June.

Worried that the deliberately antagonistic approach adopted by the committee was designed to torpedo the negotiations, Sharp insisted that Canadian officials might accomplish more if they refrained from threatening their American counterparts. Instead, they should stress Canada's genuine desire to seek a joint solution to the automotive problem. Any Canadian threats should be carefully veiled. Along with amending the cabinet committee's instructions to take Sharp's views into account, the assembled ministers insisted that officials prepare two detailed reports on the options available to Ottawa – one outlining the elements of a negotiated settlement and a second describing a protectionist solution.[41]

This more temperate approach seemed to pay immediate dividends. On 7 July, when Canadian and American officials met in Ottawa for the first exploratory discussion, the two sides quickly came close to overcoming most of their differences. Led by Reisman, the Canadian delegation made it clear from the start that it was prepared only to consider alternative arrangements that would "ensure trade, investment and employment benefits for Canada at least equivalent to those that would result from the present system." Trezise, who spoke for the United States delegation, readily acknowledged the importance the government attached to the automotive program and Ottawa's determination to achieve its objectives. He indicated that Washington was ready to consider new arrangements to meet these goals, even "if under such new arrangements Canada should receive a more than proportional share of new investment." Trezise emphasized that the United States questioned only the methods of the current program and suggested that the two countries replace it by rationalizing the North American automotive industry through tariff reductions. Already authorized to cut tariffs by 50 percent under Kennedy's Trade Expansion Act, the administration was ready to ask Congress for authority to make further cuts in order to satisfy Canadian requirements.

Canadian officials were clearly intrigued by the American suggestion. However, simply reducing tariffs, which would allow the industry to rationalize production in only one country if it so wished, was obviously not the whole answer. Reisman proposed some kind of "conditional" free trade agreement. After extensive discussions, the two sides agreed on four basic provisions that would necessarily underlie this agreement. First, both countries would reduce tariffs. Second, the United States would explicitly accept the objectives of the existing Canadian program and inform the industry in both countries of this understanding. Third, there would have to be on-going bilateral consultation to ensure that measurable progress was being made towards its objectives. Fourth, the United State would have to acknowledge Canada's right to restrict automotive imports if, within a reasonable time, its industry had not grown at a satisfactory rate. With the fundamental principles of an agreement apparently in place, the two delegations agreed to meet again in mid-August. In the meantime, they would consult their respective automotive industries and governments.[42]

To the chagrin of the bureaucrats, the Cabinet Committee on Finance and Economic Policy was ambivalent about the apparent break-through.[43] It eventually agreed to the approach, but not without dividing sharply over the steps to be taken in the event that the talks collapsed. Again, a majority tried to commit the government to an industrial strategy freed from American influence. Gordon's committee asked Cabinet to acknowledge that "if a solution ... designed to achieve greater efficiency on a continental basis proved unacceptable to the United States, an alternative approach would have to involve measures to reserve a larger share of the Canadian market for the Canadian industry."[44] A smaller group of ministers thought that "it would be premature for the Cabinet to commit itself" to an alternative approach at this stage. The full Cabinet agreed, and for the moment Canada remained committed to a continental solution.[45]

The 17 August meeting of experts was disappointing.[46] In confidential corridor conversations, Trezise confessed that the administration had been unable to withstand growing congressional pressure in an election year and had been forced to abandon the approach the two groups of officials had sketched out in July. Although American officials expressed their sympathy with Canada's desire to increase the production of cars and parts in Canada through rationalization, they rejected the idea of a bilateral agreement that guaranteed Canada a precise share of the North American market. The administration, Congress, and the industry would not support this kind of a settlement. Nor could the United States agree to waive in advance its right to retaliate should Canada find it necessary to restrict imports in order to achieve the desired market share.

In any event, the American delegation contended, the automotive industry knew exactly what the Canadian government required of it. If the two countries negotiated a settlement that eliminated tariffs and included a general statement of the program's objectives and the consultative mechanisms to be used if they were not realized, Canada would naturally achieve an increased share of North American production. The accord could also include an escape clause that would allow either government to terminate the agreement if, after an initial period, its objectives were not being achieved.

The American counterproposal was clearly unacceptable. With no precise definition of the Canadian share of the North American market in place, Canada was being asked to undertake a "colossal gamble." Since it would be impossible to reverse the process of integration once it had started without staggering political and economic costs, the escape clause was meaningless. When further exchanges confirmed that it would be impossible to negotiate a set of precise objectives, the discussions were broken off and an impasse declared.

Despite this disappointing conclusion, a slender hope remained in some quarters that Canadian objectives could still be achieved through a less precise agreement. During the August talks, Canadian and American officials had toyed briefly but inconclusively with the notion of a tripartite accord that would bind the two governments and the automotive industry to an agreed set of objectives. Francis Linville, the counsellor for economic affairs at the United States Embassy, suggested to Reisman over drinks that Canada's need for assurances might be met if the individual automotive manufacturers voluntarily undertook to expand their production in Canada in exchange for a reduction in duties.[47] Trezise agreed and urged Ottawa to invite the industry to join the talks and help develop a program to rationalize the North American automotive industry.[48]

The American suggestion was welcomed in the Department of Finance, where officials had begun to develop new proposals to overcome the objections raised by the American delegation in August. The first and recommended course of action envisioned a bilateral agreement recording in general terms both governments' desire to see that Canada achieved a more equitable share of the North American automotive industry. Ottawa would subsequently obtain precise indications from the motor vehicle producers of the steps they would take to realize their share of new production and exports during the next three-year period. If these steps met the objectives of the current program – $260 million worth of new production annually by 1968 – the United States and Canada would agree to reduce or eliminate tariffs on vehicles and original parts. If the automotive manufacturers failed to meet their objectives, the government could terminate the agreement and adopt other, less palatable policies to achieve these objectives. To protect the inefficient Canadian parts manufacturing sector, only bona fide Canadian motor vehicle manufacturers were to be eligible to import parts and vehicles duty-free.[49]

Because it was still not clear that Gordon could be persuaded to endorse a course of action that committed Canada to increased economic integration with the United States, officials prepared two additional options. Neither of these "made-in-Canada" solutions was very attractive. The first amended the existing duty-remission plan. This approach advocated the remission of duties for Canadian vehicle and parts manufacturers who achieved "greater rationalization, improved efficiency and expanded investment and production in Canada." Since exports were only one of the criteria taken into consideration, the new scheme would not be liable to American countervailing duties. By the same token, while it would help increase employment in the industry, it would do little to reduce Canada's trade deficit with the United States.

The second option – a package of technical measures adjusting tariff and Canadian content regulations – promised to reserve a bigger proportion of the domestic market for Canadian automotive manufacturers. Its most important innovation, however, involved the imposition of an excise tax high enough to discourage the sale of imported luxury cars in Canada, encouraging economies of scale in smaller and medium-sized cars. The drawbacks associated with this option were manifold. It would not reduce the current account deficit; it did not allow Ottawa to predict the amount of new production; and, most important, it was certain to raise the ire of both American automobile manufacturers and Canadian consumers.

While these options awaited ministerial consideration, a renewed sense of urgency was beginning to grip the administration in Washington. Luther Hodges, the secretary of commerce, was "dismayed" by the collapse of the August talks, which he blamed on Canada's unreasonable demands "for assurances that would, in effect, make a free trade scheme practically riskless for them."[50] He urged Rusk to remain firm, convinced that there was no feasible alternative to the imposition of countervailing duties. Dillon agreed, and in mid-September he prepared a memorandum for the president that recommended that retaliatory duties take effect on 1 November 1964.[51] Aware that this recommendation would soon have to be made public, the administration was under tremendous pressure to act. Rusk, in a meeting with Martin in Windsor on 14 September, and Johnson, in a brief encounter with Pearson three days later in British Columbia, raised the matter with their Canadian interlocutors.[52] Though neither Pearson nor Martin needed to be reminded of the importance of this issue, the American interest was duly reported to the Cabinet Committee on Finance and Economic Policy when it met on 15 September to consider its options. The committee and the full Cabinet readily agreed that Canada, the United States and the automotive industry should negotiate a tripartite agreement to overcome the present stalemate.[53]

A meeting between the Canadian and American negotiating teams was arranged in Washington for 24–25 September. Ball and McGeorge Bundy, the national security advisor, had meanwhile convinced Dillon to delay any further action until the results of the meeting were known.[54] From the Canadian perspective, the results of this third exploratory meeting were "reasonably satisfactory."[55] The American negotiators exhibited a "lively interest" in the Canadian proposal. They seemed to accept the scheme in principle and appeared ready to bring the agreement into force as quickly as possible.

There seemed to be a substantial basis for continuing to talk as long as – and the Canadian negotiators were very emphatic about this – the United States refrained from imposing countervailing duties. After consulting their respective cabinet ministers and automotive industries, the two groups met again in early October and late November to consider the Canadian proposal in greater detail.[56] Convinced that the Canadian scheme represented a means to defuse the threat posed by the existing automotive incentive scheme to the administration's domestic and bilateral fortunes, Ball's NSC subcommittee on Canada approved a recommendation from Trezise that the United States finalize a deal along the lines of the Canadian proposal. Ball was genuinely pleased with the shape of the agreement, which would enable Canada and the United States to avoid a nasty trade war, to rationalize production, and to move towards still closer commercial relations after several years of bickering. The cost to the United States – a "modest increase in Canadian automotive production" – was "not unreasonable." Johnson agreed.[57]

As the final touches were placed on the automotive parts agreement, Canada and the United States were about to embark on an equally important set of trade negotiations – the Kennedy Round of the General Agreement on Tariffs and Trade (GATT). Preparations for this set of GATT negotiations had been in the works for several years. In 1961 ministers of the member countries of GATT had agreed that the traditional item-by-item technique used to negotiate tariffs had become too complex and was no longer adequate. They recommended that some form of broad, across-the-board linear tariff reductions be adopted. This approach was given added impetus in January 1962, when Kennedy asked Congress to approve legislation whose principal provisions gave the administration the authority to cut tariffs by 50 percent and remove completely those tariffs that were under five percent. For the Kennedy administration, launching a new GATT round of tariff reductions was important both as a trade liberalization measure and as part of Kennedy's "grand design," a program to strengthen "the unity and coordination of the free world."[58]

For the most part, Canada shared Washington's view of the Kennedy Round, welcoming the president's efforts to use the GATT to reduce economic divisions within the North Atlantic Alliance. More important, the United States administration was prepared to reduce its tariffs as never before, with obviously important implications for Canada, which sent over 50 percent of its exports to the United States in 1962.[59] At the same time, Washington was determined to use its bargaining power to improve access to the European market and seek an international settlement on grains and wheat, where surpluses from the mid-1950s and European import restrictions had resulted in cut-throat competition among the major exporting nations. At the GATT session in November 1962, Canada joined with the United States to call for a ministerial meeting to prepare for the new round and promised "to play an active role in the negotiations, offer important concessions, and pay fully for tariff concessions by others of benefit to Canadian exporters."[60]

Despite their general support for the Kennedy Round, there was widespread agreement among Canadian officials and ministers that the linear approach was not suitable for Canada. Maurice Schwarzmann, assistant deputy minister of trade and commerce, put it well: "Since we import about ten times more manufactured goods than we export, a linear cut in Canadian tariffs to match a similar cut in the tariffs of our major trading partners could clearly be out of balance in terms of compensating benefits received and given by Canada, as well as being out of all proportion in terms of the degree of adjustment that would be required in Canadian industry as compared with the mass production industries of the u.s. and Europe."[61]

Canadian officials repeatedly outlined this position, but with little apparent effect. The United States, which wanted to secure a strong expression of Canadian support in order to help convince the reluctant Europeans to participate, was not convinced by the Canadian argument. Schwarzmann cautioned from Washington in late April 1963 that "Canadian reservations about [the] linear approach are regarded with great suspicion and are interpreted more as an attempt to get a 'free ride' or to cater to protectionist groups in Canada."[62] The administration insisted that Canada's concerns were "exaggerated" and reflected "an unduly 'static' and short-term assessment of [the] benefits accruing to Canada." The Department of Commerce thought that Canada should place more emphasis on the benefits to be achieved by a general expansion in world trade than on a simple calculation of reciprocity. Washington insisted that the Canadian position could be met "through special devices or procedural modifications in the linear formula," rather than by rejecting the linear proposal out of hand.[63]

To contain these differences over the linear approach, Kennedy sent his special representative for trade negotiations, Christian Herter, to Ottawa only four days after Pearson's election. Herter was to seek assurances that Canadian hesitations about the linear approach "would not be highlighted" and that Ottawa would avoid "explicit reservations."[64] In exchange, the United States would accommodate the unique Canadian position. Although the government had yet to determine its detailed approach to the Kennedy Round, Herter's meeting with Pearson, Gordon, Sharp, and Martin went smoothly. The Canadian ministers continued to insist on the unsuitability of linear cuts for Canada but made it clear that they were "very willing to look for a formula which would enable [them] not to attack the u.s. position on linear cuts." Herter was convinced that the Canadians did "not want to be free riders" and that Ottawa "may well come up with some proposal that [Washington] felt was acceptable without sacrificing their secondary industry."[65] A few days later, Pearson himself reassured Kennedy at Hyannisport "that if there is to be a failure at Geneva it won't be [the] Canadians' fault."[66]

Led by Sharp and Jake Warren, an assistant deputy minister of trade and commerce, the Canadian delegation to the May ministerial meeting went to Geneva armed with instructions not to endorse the linear approach. At the same time, however, it was also told to "avoid ... impairing or prejudicing u.s. efforts to obtain agreement on such a negotiating procedure for countries for which this technique is appropriate."[67] The meeting, Sharp later reported, was "very difficult."[68] Much of the problem stemmed from differences between the United States and the European Economic Community (EEC), which feared that the linear approach would reduce its relatively low tariffs to meaningless levels while leaving the protective effect of higher American tariffs intact. At the last minute, after agreement was reached with the Americans, the EEC turned on Canada and forced Sharp to explain why Canada should be exempt from the linear approach. With American support the Canadian exemption survived unscathed, and the ministers agreed that the next round of negotiations would formally begin in May 1964. Special provisions were made for those countries with a "trade and economic structure such that a linear cut by them would not yield reciprocity."[69]

The May ministerial meeting also established a Trade Negotiations Committee (TNC) and a host of subcommittees and commodity groups to elaborate the rules and procedures that would govern the trade negotiations. Though progress was difficult and painstakingly slow, by April 1964 there were signs that the two principal antagonists, the United States and the EEC, were moving slowly towards an agreement. The TNC consequently turned its attention to the rules governing Canada's participation in the Kennedy Round. A recent decision by Japan and the low-tariff Scandinavian countries to adopt the linear approach left Canada almost alone in its opposition to these cuts. Ottawa was increasingly worried that without explicit recognition by the TNC of its unique pattern of trade and economic structure, Canada would come under pressure at the May ministerial meeting to adopt the linear approach.[70]

The United States, which could count on little support from either the EEC or the United Kingdom, was worried that the Canadian offer would be disappointingly small and further undermine the Kennedy Round. American officials in Geneva therefore pressed for a greater Canadian commitment to the negotiations. They asked that Canada table its offer at the same time as the other participating countries listed their "exceptions." To avoid a "token offer" from Canada, the Americans insisted on an explicit statement that the offer would be "designed to pay for all the concessions Canada expects to receive." In addition, Washington asked Canada to agree to consult with its trading partners both before and after the offers were announced. These were all reasonable demands, and in April 1964, at the meeting of the Canada–United States Ministerial Committee on Trade and Economic Affairs, the assembled Cabinet ministers again reiterated their support for the rough arrangement that made close bilateral cooperation at the GATT possible. The United States would continue to recognize Canada's unique position, while Canada agreed to make the kind of forthcoming and realistic offer that would help advance the Kennedy Round.[71]

At the TNC meeting in May, Canada was formally identified as a nonlinear country. In exchange, Sharp, as head of the delegation, assured his international counterparts of Canada's determination to play a substantial role in the negotiations. "I wish to reaffirm that from the beginning, Canada will be a full and active participant over the whole range of these negotiations," he announced. "We regard the Kennedy Round as a unique opportunity to help raise world trade to new levels and thus to contribute to higher levels of economic activity and employment in our countries. We see it as a stimulus to a more effi- cient world economy. Canada will seek improved terms of access for Canadian products in all markets, and we are prepared to pay fully in exchange for benefits received."[72]

Throughout the summer of 1964 work on the Canadian offer pro- ceeded in Ottawa under the direction of Norman Robertson, who had been appointed chief negotiator in February, and his deputy, Hector McKinnon, the former chairman of the Tariff Board. The two men, who had been closely involved with efforts to liberalize the interna- tional trade system since the late 1930s, crossed the country through- out the spring and summer of 1964, holding over forty-five sessions with a range of Canadian businesses. Despite the qualms expressed by the Canadian Manufacturers' Association, many of the submissions received by Robertson's Tariffs and Trade Committee were positive. One informal press survey reported that the Canadian negotiators would probably "have a strong free-trade mandate."[73] Sharp con- curred. Many industries and businesses, he told the House of Com- mons in April 1964, were ready "to forgo at least part of the protec- tion afforded them by the Canadian tariff ... provided the concessions requested are forthcoming."[74]

While this was certainly true, there was also a great deal of nervous- ness in Ottawa. Gordon and some of the more protectionist officials in the Department of Finance were reluctant to engage in a tariff-cutting exercise that would diminish their capacity to use protective tariffs to shelter Canadian industry and to create a strong, domestically con- trolled manufacturing sector. As the government began to consider the draft offer drawn up by Robertson and McKinnon, the minister of finance forced it to retreat from the relatively liberal position adopted by Sharp in Geneva. In late October, officials began exploring the possibility that Canada might make only some form of "token offer," delay the offer, or even withdraw from the tariff negotiations.[75]

Robertson was appalled. He warned the prime minister and Gordon Robertson, the clerk of the privy council, not to retreat. A vague statement, which promised a more precise offer later, would not suffice. "It would not be regarded as satisfying Canada's previous undertakings," the chief negotiator explained, "and would leave us open to charges that we were impeding the progress of the negotiations."[76] Robertson argued that at a time when Franco-American and Franco-German differences were calling into question postwar cooperative arrangements in the Western alliance, it was important for Canada that "there should be some positive movement forward in at least one significant area, the Kennedy Round."[77]

Pearson was persuaded and agreed to proceed with the offer largely as drafted, although the government decided to hold back its concessions on a number of sensitive products until later in the negotiations. To defuse any American criticism, he telephoned Johnson and assured him that the Canadian offer would be "good and reasonable."[78]

It was. Canada offered to impose a general ceiling on its tariffs at a moderate level, with some exemptions for especially sensitive items. On items below the ceiling, Canada offered to reduce its tariffs by 50 percent on a broad range of semi-fabricated products and to remove duties on most industrial raw materials. It also offered to reduce its tariff on fish by 50 percent (provided there was a reciprocal offer) and to go free on some agricultural products, while cutting duties by 50 percent on others. In return, Canada wanted the main industrial countries to cut their tariffs on all industrial items of actual or potential interest to Canada and to include agricultural products as part of the negotiations.[79]

With the tabling of offers the ground was set for serious negotiations to begin. During the next six months these negotiations proceeded slowly as the linear participants explored their offers and justified their exceptions. Throughout these discussions, which lasted until February 1965, the Canadian role was "necessarily somewhat passive."[80] Robertson had a number of exploratory discussions with the American negotiators, but serious negotiations were not expected to begin until at least late April. Negotiations with the EEC and Japan, which would have to wait until the results of bilateral talks with the United States, remained a long way off. Still, by the spring of 1965 the Kennedy Round was beginning to take shape. Plans were adopted for informal discussions in the pulp and paper, textile, chemical, and metal sectors, where the most important industrial talks would take place. At the same time, the EEC declared that it had reached internal agreement on wheat pricing and was finally prepared to begin to negotiate a commodity agreement on cereals.

During the spring and summer of 1965, Canada and the United States conducted an "item-by-item" review of bilateral trade, clearing "the ground for the substantive negotiations."[81] These discussions confirmed that in addition to the great number of items of interest to Canada in Washington's initial linear offer, the Americans were prepared to grant free entry for Canadian fish, lumber, and metals if the two could agree on additional Canadian concessions. However, real negotiations were suspended when the EEC, on whose offer much of the United States linear offer depended, was forced to withdraw temporarily from the talks following a confrontation between the French president, General Charles de Gaulle, and the European Commission over the community's agricultural policies.

Only in July 1966, then, did Canada and the United States begin to come to grips with the differences dividing them. Following an extensive review of the two offers, during which the delegations reconciled Canadian and American statistics, they agreed that the offers were uneven. While the Canadian offer applied to U.S.$1.2 billion worth of imports from the United States, the American offer would reduce duties on more than U.S.$1.45 billion worth of Canadian exports. The exercise reinforced the growing conviction among members of the Canadian delegation that their offer would have to be improved. At the same time, they were hopeful that this review demonstrated to the United States how small a gap separated the two positions.[82]

There were additional reasons for strengthening the Canadian offer at this time. Talks between the United States and the EEC had gone poorly during the summer, and it was widely expected that the United States would begin to withdraw parts of its offer in the autumn. By improving its offer to the United States, Canada might be able to influence which products the United States decided to withdraw. Moreover, Canada would improve its general negotiating position and, not least of Ottawa's considerations, "strengthen the hand of the U.S. negotiators who are working for the best available Kennedy Round and who are reluctant to withdraw offers if this can be avoided, well aware this could provoke general withdrawals."[83]

In October the Canadian offer was substantially improved with the addition of important concessions on chemicals and machine tools. Machine tools alone represented almost U.S.$400 million worth of American exports to Canada.[84] The United States delegation was not appeased. It admitted that the amended Canadian offer removed the imbalance in the trade coverage but maintained that the American offer, which provided for a 50 percent reduction in tariffs, was much better. Moreover, while only U.S.$333 million worth of Canadian exports to the United States were not covered under the American offer, almost u.s.$1 billion worth of exports were excluded from the Canadian offer. Michael Blumenthal, the tough, no-nonsense chairman of the u.s. delegation, demanded reductions on another u.s.$500 million worth of goods, threatening to withdraw u.s.$180 million worth of concessions from the original American offer.[85] On a more positive note, the American negotiator offered to go free on fish (worth u.s.$82 million) and indicated that he was also authorized to go free on additional low-tariff items. Sydney Pierce, who had replaced an ill and tired Robertson in June 1965, rejected the American's "arithmetical balance sheets" and argued that it was not the depth of the cut that was important but the tariff level over which trade flowed.

The two delegations agreed to leave aside the question of the overall balance of the two offers when they met again in early 1967. Instead they focused on examining the Canadian offers on chemicals and machinery. While the two countries argued over exactly how the reduction in duties on machine tools was to be computed, Pierce was confident that a bilateral agreement would emerge from Geneva. Its principal features would include a 50 percent reduction in a wide range of industrial products of interest to Canada, as well as the complete elimination of American tariffs in the lumber, fisheries, and agricultural sectors. By mid-April, the task of reconciling the overall balance was all that remained.[86]

The outlook for negotiations in the cereals group, which began to meet regularly in the fall of 1966, was not as optimistic. International grain sales were an especially difficult problem for Ottawa in its relations with the United States. During the late 1950s and the early 1960s, grain production soared, while the major markets, the EEC, the United Kingdom, and Japan, reduced imports in favour of domestic producers. This led to fierce competition among wheat exporters for market share and rendered international efforts to stabilize the market through the International Wheat Agreement (IWA) ineffective. The immense American economy gave the United States a distinct advantage in this struggle as successive administrations pursued greater market share for subsidized wheat by large grants of food aid, concessional sales, and deep price cuts. Although Canada and the United States had consulted regularly since the mid-1950s on wheat prices, these discussions had grown progressively less fruitful, as the United States became more and more determined to seize a larger share of the market. Canada's search for price stability and a viable return on its growers' investment seemed irreconcilable with Washington's determination to increase its market share. It was by no means certain that the United States and Canada could find a basis on which to cooperate in the GATT discussions on wheat, where agreement was regarded in Geneva, Ottawa, and Washington as essential for the successful conclusion of the Kennedy Round.

The first real test came in October 1966, when the four major exporting countries – Canada, the United States, Australia, and Argentina – tried to forge a common front for their negotiations with the main importers. Sharp differences emerged over prices and market-sharing proposals. Canada, with support from Australia and Argentina, suggested that the exporters begin by offering a minimum price of U.S.$1.85 per bushel for No. 2 Hard Winter, ex-Gulf, retreating if necessary to U.S.$1.77. The United States refused to go higher than U.S.$1.70 per bushel for No. 2 Hard Winter, leaving a difference of 7¢. "Unless this gap was closed," the Canadian representatives threatened, "there appeared little possibility of Canada being prepared to proceed with the cereals negotiations in Geneva."[87]

Canada and the United States were also divided over the price differentials to be applied to different grades of wheat. Ottawa sought fixed differentials that would apply to every grade of wheat at every price level, while the United States favoured a more flexible system. In addition, the two countries differed over American proposals for market sharing. The United States wanted exporters to agree in advance on the market share each country would get for various grains when trading was at or near the minimum price. Market share would be regulated by raising prices, withholding wheat, or turning down sales. Ottawa could go this far, but the United States wanted more. It believed that exporters could avoid the minimum price trigger altogether by agreeing in advance to share the international wheat market at all times.[88]

The Washington meeting uncovered the profound differences dividing the two countries and set alarm bells ringing in Ottawa. The ministers of trade and commerce, finance, and agriculture and their officials were inclined to ask Pearson to take up the issue with Johnson. This idea was scotched when the two countries' differences over Communist China and Washington's unresolved request to station nuclear weapons at Argentia were considered.[89] It was left to Australia to approach the United States "at the highest political level" and secure assurances that Washington would support the proposal for an initial minimum price of U.S.$1.85 per bushel for No. 2 Hard Winter. Informal telephone discussions between Warren and Herter's deputy in Washington, William Roth, revealed that the United States was ready to moderate its position in other respects as well in order to achieve exporter unanimity. It accepted reluctantly the idea of fixed differentials. Roth also agreed that the American market-sharing proposals would operate only at the minimum price level. Although Canadian

officials doubted that importing nations would agree, they promised to
support the concept when the United States advanced it at Geneva. The
two trade officials also reached agreement on the amount of wheat that
the EEC, the United Kingdom, and Japan would be asked to import,
and on a 10-million ton multilateral food aid program involving a
Canadian commitment of $75 million.[90]

The Canadian-American agreement was confirmed by the full group
of exporters in early November, although the exact value assigned to
each grade of wheat was still to be negotiated among importers and
exporters in Geneva. Similarly, the precise details of the market-sharing arrangement were left undefined so that the discussions with
importing nations could begin at once.[91] This tactic allowed the
exporters only a short respite from their differences. By February 1967,
two months after their offer was tabled with the GATT secretariat, discussions in the cereals group had ground to a halt as the importers
waited for exporters to elaborate their views on differentials and market sharing. This proved no easier in Geneva than in Washington.

After several weeks of additional effort, Canada and the United
States remained divided on both differentials and market sharing.
Pushed hard by their Department of Agriculture, the American
negotiators adopted an "unyielding and somewhat belligerent
approach." They clung tenaciously to proposals that called for
export restrictions and permitted exporters to breach the minimum
price in order to retain their traditional markets. These suggestions
undermined the very concept of a minimum price, and Schwarzmann rejected them out of hand. In response, Blumenthal and Roth
threatened to table the American proposals alone, a step that would
effectively destroy the common front on minimum price levels. The
American posture, with its rigid and unfamiliar unilateralism, worried the Canadians: "We are concerned and puzzled about real
inwardness of USA position. While USA support is essential to our
objectives, conflicting pressures and motivations behind their
approach make them an unpredictable partner. This has been
reflected in their delays in resuming exporter negotiations and in
their intransigence in moving from extreme positions."[92]

It also worried the Australians, who helped work out a compromise
in the final weeks of February. This was achieved only after "difficult
and protracted negotiations" between Canadian and American representatives, discussions marked by "misunderstanding and suspicion."
The new market sharing arrangements would come into effect when a
certain volume of wheat sales was concluded at prices close to the minimum. At that time, a "prices consultative committee" would meet and
adjust prices so that traditional trading patterns were maintained. If

this did not result in "equitable market sharing" after sixty days, the committee would take "additional measures."[93]

Despite the agreement on market sharing, the United States and Canada remained far apart on the price differential between various grades of wheat. It was becoming "clear that as long as the issue of quality differentials remained unresolved between Canada and United States, we were in daily risk of the split among exporters being exposed and of the USA moving off [the] price position."[94] The Canadian concern was shared by American negotiators, who suggested as a compromise that differentials should be fixed only for the highest and lowest grades of wheat. This would effectively establish reference levels that could be used to work out prices for other grades as they were traded, provided that the exporting countries accepted "close arrangements for cooperation."[95] In early April, Canada and the United States agreed on a schedule of "indicative minimum prices for a number of major grades," supplemented by procedures for consultation "which would provide, or at least not exclude a breach in the minimum [price] if agreement is not reached." As well as solving the differentials problem, this new pricing system replaced the market-sharing arrangements concluded in February.[96]

During the last few weeks of April 1967, importers and exporters hurried unsuccessfully to reach agreement. Although exporters reduced their minimum price to U.S.$1.80 per bushel, importers refused to increase their offer beyond U.S.$1.69 per bushel. Similarly, the two groups were divided over access commitments. The EEC would agree only to maintain its ratio of imports to consumption at 11 percent, while the exporting countries wanted it fixed at 13.4 percent. (The United Kingdom insisted on maintaining this ratio at 28 percent; exporters wanted it fixed at 37.6 percent.) The access question was complicated by an additional United States demand for access guarantees for coarse grains that was firmly rejected by the EEC. Finally, there was no agreement on a multilateral food aid program. Japan rejected it entirely, while the EEC and the UK accepted it only in principle. As a result, in late April, Eric Wyndham White, the long-time secretary general of the GATT, concluded that "as matters stand at this time, there is no basis for agreement."[97]

Against the background of White's statement and a declaration by the U.S. delegation that a "cereals agreement was essential to the successful conclusion of the total Kennedy Round," the GATT's steering group met on 29 April to assess the progress of the round. It was a gloomy session.[98] The impasse over cereals was duplicated in the chemical sector, where the United States and the EEC were deeply divided. In early May, Robert Winters, who had succeeded Sharp as trade minister after the

1965 election, departed for Geneva and a final round of negotiations, worried that "the Kennedy Round was in danger of failing."[99]

In the final two weeks of intensive negotiations, the elements of a trade deal fell into place. In a surprising change in policy, the United States abandoned the demand for access guarantees. The cereals negotiations were quickly focused on the more malleable questions of price and food aid.[100] Meeting day and night, the cereals group finally agreed on the central elements of a new international grains agreement. Prices were established on a range of wheat, with the bench-mark minimum price for u.s. No. 2 Hard Wheat set at u.s.$1.73 per bushel, and a prices review committee was authorized to reduce price levels further when necessary. The group also agreed on a multilateral food aid program of 4.5 million tons.[101]

Resolving the differences between the United States and Europe over chemicals was even more difficult, but eventually a compromise emerged.[102] Throughout these last-minute negotiations with the EEC, the United States put the finishing touches on its bilateral negotiations with Canada. This was not as straightforward a task as it might once have appeared. In a late-April meeting, Blumenthal insisted that the Canadian and American offers were not balanced. He asked for additional concessions on various agricultural products and threatened to withdraw agricultural offers worth $27.5 million. The American also requested additional concessions on the industrial side. Although surprised by the strength with which the United States put forward its case, the Canadian delegation was not entirely unprepared. It had anticipated a last-minute stiffening of the American position as a bargaining tactic and had held back almost $100 million worth of Canadian concessions. With the incidence (or overall impact) of the tariff on machinery still to be resolved, Canada was well armed for the final round of negotiations.[103]

The two delegations made steady progress, and by the time the Kennedy Round concluded at the end of June, they had agreed on a package affecting almost $3 billion worth of bilateral trade. The United States agreed to abolish duties on Canadian exports valued at $1.92 billion. Tariffs of 5 percent or less were eliminated on $560 million worth of Canadian exports, effectively introducing free trade for lumber, paper, and some fisheries products. Agricultural tariffs were removed on exports valued at $28.6 million. Duties on another $1.06 billion in exports were reduced by 50 percent, while smaller reductions were made in tariffs on an additional $298.3 million worth of exports. In return, Canada reduced its tariffs on $1.09 billion worth of u.s. imports; the reductions involved a range of products that affected almost every sector of the tariff. The treatment Canada agreed to accord machinery was especially important. Canada eliminated the 7.5 percent tariff on machinery "not made in Canada" and reduced the tariff on machinery "made in Canada" from 22.5 to 15 percent, agreeing that the overall impact of the tariff on machinery would be reduced to 9 percent.[104]

Canada generally welcomed the results of the Kennedy Round. The *Winnipeg Free Press* enthusiastically proclaimed that "the riches opened up to Canadian industry by the Kennedy Round of tariff reductions are almost impossible to exaggerate. In return for incredibly minor concessions to the products of other countries, this already prosperous and favoured land has been offered opportunities which are limited only by the willingness of its people to exploit them and by the vigour and competitiveness of its business community."[105] Together with the new automotive agreement, the tariff changes negotiated during the Kennedy Round were to have a profound and lasting effect on Canadian-American trade relations. In the words of the trade analyst Michael Hart, "Canada and the United States took a giant step towards reducing barriers between them."[106] Historian J.L. Granatstein agrees: "It was not quite free trade, but to a substantial extent tariffs were now becoming almost inconsequential."[107]

The impact of the two agreements on Canadian-American trade was striking and immediate. Bilateral trade in automotive products alone rose from $1.2 billion in 1965 to $3.5 billion in 1967 to $6.7 billion in 1969.[108] Spurred on by the Kennedy Round, trade between Canada and the United States soared. Total bilateral trade rose steadily from $15 billion in 1967 to $20.5 billion in 1969 to $26.2 billion in 1972.[109] Goods shipped to the United States rose as a share of total Canadian exports from 55.4 percent in 1963 to 67.7 percent in 1968.[110] Despite its professed intention to reduce Canada's economic dependence on the United States, the Pearson government was responsible for a dramatic and significant increase in North American economic integration. For the first time since 1911, the possibility of North American free trade entered the political debate in Canada as a defensible policy option. It was surely no accident that the Liberal Party endorsed free trade at its national convention in 1966.[111]

Most important of all, however, the automotive agreement and the Kennedy Round negotiations represented the triumph of Ball's continentalist vision. This, perhaps, was not always apparent to Canadians, as opposition to the Vietnam War and American consumerism provoked a nationalist backlash north of the border. But American observers were more perceptive. In 1968, even as he denounced Canada for selling the United States short in Vietnam and railed against Gordon's nationalism, Butterworth knew that the Pearson and Johnson governments had decided the future shape of North American relations:

Growing interdependence with the u.s. was a characteristic of other aspects of u.s.-Canadian economic relations during the Pearson Government's tenure. Our most important single negotiation in the Kennedy Round was with Canada and virtual free trade has been achieved in industrial raw materials, fossil fuels, forest products, fish, some agricultural commodities, farm machinery and automotive products. The Automotive Agreement was a major achievement. Our mutual automotive trade has increased in fantastic proportions ...

What is most significant about these developments is their thrust toward economic interdependence. They are evidences, hopefully, of a nascent, pragmatic approach to the sharing of the resources of a continent which would accept a continental philosophy where such can be seen to be in the interests of both countries.[112]

CHAPTER 3

Converging Currencies: Financial Relations

Despite Kennedy's decision to adopt the Interest Equalization Tax (IET) in July 1963, American balance of payments figures showed little substantial improvement. Indeed, by the summer of 1964 the administration was forced to expand its effort to staunch the drain of American capital. This intractable problem preoccupied the White House for the rest of the decade as a strong international economy, the war in Vietnam, and attacks on the status of the dollar as a reserve currency weakened the U.S. exchange position. Like the negotiations with the United States over the automotive incentive plan and the GATT round, Washington's increasingly severe balance of payments measures raised fundamental questions about Canada's future economic orientation.

Although President Johnson's administration acknowledged Canada's legitimate need for unrestricted access to American capital, it was under constant pressure to remove inequities in its various balance of payments programs. Congress viewed growing Canadian reserves with suspicion and urged the White House to tighten up regulatory loopholes that Canadian banks and American subsidiaries in Canada used to circumvent restrictions on the movement of United States capital. As Washington pressed Ottawa to regulate American dollars flowing to Canada under its exemption from the IET, the choice for Canada was clear: it could either assist the United States, which would reduce its capacity to shape financial policy independently, or it could refuse, accepting a devalued Canadian dollar, higher interest rates, and stagnant economic growth. The public and private discussion of

this choice pitted economic nationalists against so-called continentalists. Although the Pearson government was forced to acknowledge
nationalist demands and arguments, there was little doubt that it
would accept the American constraints in exchange for continued economic growth.

While the legislation necessary to impose the IET wound its way
through Congress during the spring and summer of 1964, the American balance of payments situation continued to worsen. By the fall of
that year, the Treasury Department was no longer certain of the wisdom of its decision to exempt new Canadian securities from the tax.
The passage into law of the IET and the Canadian exemption in early
September 1964 immediately released over $700 million worth of new
Canadian securities onto the New York market. The size of this
demand, which was twice as large as Treasury Department officials
had anticipated and an apparent increase in the level of Ottawa's
reserves, created considerable concern in Washington.[1] By late October, American officials had completed a full-scale review of the Canadian exemption and concluded that Canada's current account deficit
had been declining steadily since 1960. The rising level of Canadian
reserves suggested that Canadian borrowing in the United States was
no longer directed exclusively towards covering the current account
deficit. Canada, in this traditional Treasury Department view, was
becoming an important part of the American balance of payments
problem. Lisle Widman, director of the Treasury Department's Office
of Industrial Nations and the author of the study, suggested that Canada's exemption should be limited or even eliminated.[2]

In late November, Robert Roosa, the under secretary of the treasury,
and Paul A. Volcker, his deputy, invited Wynne Plumptre, an assistant
deputy minister of finance, to meet with them in Washington to review
Canadian reserve levels and new security issues. In vain, Plumptre tried
to calm American fears. He pointed out that the recent burst of activity in Canadian securities was simply the result of the pent-up demand
that had accumulated between July 1963 and September 1964, when
the United States market was effectively closed to Canada while Congress debated the legislation giving effect to the IET and the Canadian
exemption. Current interest-rate spreads were low, he added, and were
unlikely to attract any extra funds from the United States during the
next year.

More fundamentally, Plumptre rejected the notion that Canada's
current account deficit was declining. Without a special sale of wheat
to the Soviet Union in late 1963, the current account deficit would
have risen from $750 to $900 million between 1963 and 1964. While
the Canadian economy continued to expand and import more machin-

ery, the current deficit was expected to grow to $1 billion in 1965. The assistant deputy minister emphasized that the agreement of July 1963 related only to the level of reserves, not to the volume of new securities issued. He rejected the Treasury view that these reserves had increased. The American figures included the $275 million that Ottawa had recently repaid the International Monetary Fund (IMF) for its emergency loan of 1962. This was unfair and unreasonable. Canada would never have agreed to the exemption if it had thought for a moment that its debt to the IMF would be counted as a credit in the calculation of its reserve levels. He was not very hopeful, however, that he had eased Washington's distress: "It was, of course, quite impossible for me to allay, in a matter of hours, doubts and worries that have been building up for weeks, even months."

Plumptre was right. American concerns were far from dissipated, and he, with R.W. Lawson, the executive assistant to the governor of the Bank of Canada, returned to Washington a week later for another round of talks with Roosa. The administration was planning to ask Congress in the spring of 1965 to extend the IET until 1967 and was especially worried about fourth quarter borrowings. Roosa probed deeply into the nature of the recent flurry of securities and the borrowing pattern expected during the coming year, in an effort to persuade the two visitors to admit that the exemption should be tightened. The response involved the delicate task of convincing the Americans that Canada continued to require an unlimited exemption, while sounding vaguely hopeful that the actual amount required from the United States would not be too high. Fearing quotas or limits, Plumptre refused to admit that the current account deficit might be lower than expected. It could be anywhere from $600 million to $1 billion, though most of his colleagues were inclined to accept the higher figure as the most probable. There were some hopeful signs. The proposed Canada Pension Plan would reduce the country's need for foreign financing, while recent cuts in the federal budget would result in declining federal government cash requirements. Plumptre added that the interest-rate spread was expected to narrow in the near future.[3]

The Americans were not convinced. Roosa admitted that the interest rate spread was indeed narrowing and agreed that the IMF loan should not be included in the Canadian reserve position. However, the new pension plan would not ease Canadian borrowing, for it would only move savings from private to public accounts and would not change the actual savings rate. More important, there was the growing problem of short-term flow from the United States to Canada and onto the Euro-dollar market. This "pass-through" problem threatened to

undermine the entire balance of payments program. Roosa acknowledged the difficulties that Canada would face if the United States limited the exemption but reminded Plumptre and Lawson that Congress
was not about to give the president a "blank cheque." It would insist
on some American control over the flow of its currency. Although he
promised to explain the Canadian position to Congress, Roosa made
it clear that the problem remained on the bilateral agenda.

The United States launched a renewed effort in early 1965 to convince Canada to reduce the flow of American capital to Europe. During a February meeting in Washington, the under secretary of the
treasury, Frederick Deming, assured Plumptre that there was no question of touching the Canadian exemption. The administration recognized that reducing Canada's ability to cover its current account
deficit with the United States would force Canadians to limit American imports. As the White House prepared to extend the IET and
expand it to cover bank loans, however, the size of the Canadian
exemption was likely to give rise to concern in Congress, and the
administration wanted Ottawa's help in limiting it. Deming had four
general objectives in mind that represented a rough "working agreement" for managing the IET exemption during 1965. First, although
aware that Ottawa could not control the level of provincial borrowing, the United States wished to receive "some reasonably firm assurances" that new Canadian issues would total no more than $500 mil-
lion in 1965. Second, the administration wanted Canada to use its
interest rates to decrease short-term flows from the United States.
Third, Canada must ensure that Canadian banks would not "actively seek" additional United States dollar deposits. Fourth, Canadian
banks should not withdraw funds from their United States operations
to make loans in Europe.[4]

Canadian officials tried to be helpful. Plumptre reviewed Ottawa's
recent efforts to convince the provinces to reduce their borrowing,
noting "that moral suasion was being used in Canada more extensively at the present time than at any time since the war." Acknowledging the difficulties that the administration might encounter in jus-
tifying the Canadian exemption to Congress, Plumptre announced
that Gordon would happily visit Washington in order to convince sen-
ators and congressmen of the importance of the Canadian exemption.
The Canadian government was also ready to retire early two outstanding Canadian securities from the late 1950s worth about $100
million. Lawson assured Deming that Canada was aware of its
responsibilities under the 1963 agreement and would use its interest
rate structure to ensure that there was no abnormal flow of United
States dollars to Canada. However, on the major point around which

the discussion revolved for two days – the total volume of anticipated Canadian issues during 1965 – Plumptre and Lawson refused to yield. The deficit on the current account for 1965, they insisted, was expected to reach $1 billion, and this would need to be covered by an inflow of United States capital.[5]

Disappointed with the discussions at the official level, Treasury Secretary Douglas Dillon asked the president to intervene directly with Pearson. Johnson was urged to avoid any discussion of specific objectives and to focus on convincing the prime minister to reaffirm "the existing Canadian commitment to avoid excessive borrowing from the u.s." In a telephone conversation with Pearson, Johnson asked him to approve, for inclusion in the president's forthcoming message to Congress on the administration's new balance of payments program, a carefully worded sentence designed to help the administration "avoid heavy pressure ... to set a strict dollar limit for Canadian borrowings": "To stop the excessive flow of funds to Canada under its special exemption from the Equalization Tax, I have sought and received firm assurance that *the Canadian government will take the steps needed to hold these outflows to levels consistent with that special exemption.*" The president told Pearson that "this language merely affirmed the existing earlier Canadian undertakings."[6]

Neither Gordon nor Louis Rasminsky, the governor of the Bank of Canada, nor Gordon Robertson, the clerk of the privy council, was convinced by Johnson's claim. When Pearson consulted them on the language employed in the American draft, they revised it in order to remove the implication that the present level of borrowing was excessive and that the Canadian government had failed to police the agreement of 1963: "To prevent any excessive flow of funds to Canada under its special exemption from the equalization tax, I have sought and received firm assurances that the policies of the Canadian Government are and will continue to be directed toward limiting such outflows to levels consistent with the stability of Canada's foreign exchange reserves."[7] After slightly altering the paragraph's final phrase, Dillon accepted the sentence as amended. Whatever the actual language employed in the president's message, it was now clear on both sides of the border that Ottawa would need to be much more vigilant in monitoring the flow of American dollars to and from Canada.

The slate of measures that Johnson unveiled on 10 February 1965 to remedy the United States balance of payments problems had little immediate impact on Canada. The 1963 exemption for new Canadian securities protected it from the major component of the program, the decision to extend the IET until July 1967. Canada was also exempted from the Department of Commerce's new program asking American corporations to restrain their direct foreign investment voluntarily. Canada was not exempt from the extension of the tax to long-term bank loans and the creation of a voluntary program to limit short-term bank loans, but these channels were not routinely used by Canadians to raise large sums of money in the United States. Similarly, the reduction in the $100 duty-free allowance enjoyed by returning American tourists was expected to have only a comparatively small impact upon the flow of capital to Canada.[8]

Canadian ministers and officials understood the full implications for Canada of the renewed American drive to slow down the outflow of U.S. capital. In order to retain its exemption from the IET, Canada would have to adopt tough measures to ensure that it did not become a gap in the American defences. Within days of the president's statement, Gordon secured cabinet's approval to warn the Canadian banking community not to exploit the new American regulations. The new restrictions placed on foreign lending by United States banks created the possibility that Canadian financial institutions might use their own United States dollar balances to take over some of the business given up by their American counterparts. Gordon warned that this "would frustrate the declared intention of the President ... and would undoubtedly raise questions between the U.S. and Canadian Governments." He advised Canadian bankers to "be very careful not to put themselves in a position where any charge of this sort could be levelled against them."[9]

The major Canadian banks seemed ready to heed the minister. One was already reported to have stopped soliciting deposits from residents of the United States and expected its American liabilities to decline sharply.[10] Meanwhile, Canadian and American officials began to explore how to stop Canadian banks and other financial institutions from using the IET exemption to "pass-through" funds from the United States to third countries where the IET would normally apply. The United States, explained Volcker, hoped that as their liabilities to American residents came due, Canadian banks would meet these payments partly by liquidating some of their American assets and partly by liquidating their overseas assets. As Merlyn Trued, the assistant secretary of the treasury for international transactions, put it, the United States wanted "an undertaking that Canadian banks will not shorten their U.S. position."[11]

Canadian officials objected to the American suggestion. The government had no legal authority to intervene in Canadian banking operations to that extent. More important, contended Alan Hockin, who succeeded Plumptre as the assistant deputy minster of finance responsible for this portfolio, the banks' assets in the United States usually represented their most liquid American dollar resources. They would want to protect this liquidity by drawing down funds in Europe to meet "some or all of any decline in their dollar deposits from the u.s."[12] It was precisely this liquidity and its potential for transfer outside the United States that was the problem. This potential gap in the American regulations could be overcome by advising "Canadian banks to the effect that, at a minimum, any decline in their assets in the u.s. should not exceed any decline in their liabilities to u.s. residents."[13] Officials from the Bank of Canada and the Department of Finance tried to develop a formula that would preserve for the banks some measure of liquidity in their u.s. assets, but this proved too difficult, and they agreed to accept the American proposal.[14] In early April, Gordon asked Canadian bankers to ensure "that the net position in u.s. dollars of your head office and Canadian branches vis-à-vis residents of the United States is not reduced below the position which existed on December 31, 1964."[15]

The American desire to tighten up the Canadian exemption had a second important consequence. In mid-February the United States renewed its suggestion (first presented in September 1963 as part of George Ball's package of reforms designed to integrate the two economies) for a joint committee, at the assistant deputy minister or under-secretary level, to keep balance of payments questions under review. "An important aim of the committee," noted Francis Linville, economic counsellor at the American Embassy in Ottawa, "should be to prevent problems from arising insofar as possible through regular full discussions and exchanges of views, rather than by depending, as we have done in the past, on ad hoc meetings after problems have arisen."[16]

The reaction in Ottawa to this suggestion was far from enthusiastic. Officials in several departments worried that the committee might give the United States too much influence on Canadian fiscal and monetary policy. They especially feared that such a committee might allow the United States to survey closely Canada's capital account and reserves and that it implied a commitment to consult Washington before taking any decisions that might affect Canada's balance of payments position vis-à-vis the United States. In addition, officials were inclined to question the committee's usefulness in view of the two countries' very different payments outlook: while the United States would tend to dwell on the outflow of dollars to Canada, Canadian officials would focus on their country's current account deficit.[17] Nevertheless, Ottawa realized that it could not oppose the American request without jeopardizing its IET exemption, and it reluctantly agreed to accept a committee broadly charged "to review developments in the balance of payments of the United States and Canada and to discuss problems of mutual concern which may arise therefrom."[18]

The balance of payments committee met for the first time in Washington on 26 July 1965 and provided both countries with an opportunity to review the situation. The outlook was not reassuring. American officials were worried by their figures for the remainder of 1965. Johnson's February payments program had succeeded so quickly that there was little room left for further improvements in the second half of the year. To complicate matters, Canadian officials admitted that Canada's current account deficit for 1965 might possibly exceed $1.2 billion.[19]

By early fall American concern had reached new heights. United States officials hinted at potential bilateral trouble in discussions with the Canadian delegation to the annual IMF meeting in early October.[20] The extent of Washington's concern, which was compounded by growing evidence that the pass-through problem was greater than ever, was revealed in late October. Meeting with Steven Handfield-Jones, the Canadian Embassy's economic counsellor, Widman announced that the Treasury Department had examined the deteriorating balance of payments situation and attributed a good deal of the blame to Canada, whose reserves had increased by $200 million in the third quarter alone. This figure, which was expected to grow in the final quarter, underestimated the impact of Canadian transactions on the United States payments position, since Canadian insurance companies, exempt from the IET, had developed a lucrative business in the pass-through field.

Widman emphasized the importance attached to this whole problem in Washington. The Treasury Department was reviewing Canada's exemption from the guidelines on long-term securities issued by American nonbanking financial institutions and reexamining the priority given to Canada in the overall guideline targets. Still more disturbing, the United States had begun to explore scenarios in which the Canadian IET exemption might be withdrawn altogether. While this review proceeded, Widman insisted that something must be done immediately.[21] In order to remove any lingering doubts in Ottawa about the seriousness with which the United States viewed the situation, Johnson asked Rusk to call Pearson to urge immediate bilateral discussions.[22]

On 28 October 1965 Hockin and Handfield-Jones met with a strong delegation from the Treasury Department that included Deming, Joseph Barr, the special assistant to the secretary of the treasury, and Stanley Surrey, the assistant secretary of the treasury for tax policy.

Barr and Deming briefly reviewed the deteriorating American balance of payments situation, which they felt had been exacerbated by the unexpected volume of new Canadian securities and the continuing pass-through problem. Aware of the difficulties created by the Canadian election scheduled for 8 November, the United States did not wish to explore Canadian-American balance of payments in detail. The real need was for immediate action to salvage fourth-quarter figures. The United States suggested that Ottawa join it in asking Canadian borrowers to defer any new issues until the new year. Hockin agreed that a sixty-day deferment might be possible and was certainly "preferable to action of a more open-ended nature." Ominously, the Treasury Department declined to indicate what further, long-term changes in policy might be necessary to ease the American balance of payments problem.[23]

Although willing to accede to the American request, both the prime minister and the minister of finance were anxious that balance of payments questions not become an election issue.[24] On 1 November 1965 the Conservative Party leader, John Diefenbaker, had attacked the government for its July 1963 agreement on reserve levels, a charge that still echoed through the Department of Finance. Gordon worried that an approach to Canadian borrowers might raise doubts about the stability of the U.S. and Canadian dollars and spark a currency crisis in the final week of the election campaign. Henry Fowler, the secretary of the treasury, agreed, and he accepted Gordon's claim "that he would be in a better position to bring his influence to bear next week immediately after the election."[25]

With the timing settled, Gordon agreed to help persuade the "larger Canadian borrowers" to defer their new securities on the understanding that the deferral was only temporary and that the United States would take no action that would prevent them from issuing new securities in early 1966. The American undertaking, which was confirmed the following day in a conversation between Deming and R.B. Bryce, the deputy minister of finance, was not as unequivocal as the Canadian authorities might have wished. "[I]n general," Deming commented, the United States "did not contemplate any new action aimed at Canadian new issues. There is nothing in the mill of that nature there." There was no question, however, of delaying the project while this was resolved. Although Deming was "friendly and understood the difficulties involved in this operation," the under secretary "was firm about [its] necessity." He even insisted that Ottawa approach "relatively small borrowers ... including municipalities."[26]

The operation went almost perfectly. Over the weekend of 5–6 November, Rasminsky and Bryce put the finishing touches on a complex plan to ensure short-term bridging funds for the Canadian borrowers who were to defer their issues. On Tuesday, 8 November Gordon called the assorted borrowers, while officials from the Bank of Canada approached Canadian securities dealers.[27] The deferment exercise appeared to satisfy the United States, whose preliminary third-quarter balance of payments figures were much better than anticipated. While the Treasury Department continued to study how to strengthen the balance of payments guidelines – examining the Canadian exemption on direct investment as well as the continuing pass-through problem – American officials reassured the Canadian Embassy "that the IET exemption was not being questioned."[28]

The outlook changed completely within days. On their way to the November meeting of the balance of payments committee, Trued and Andrew Brimmer, an assistant secretary of the treasury, met privately with Hockin and Ed Ritchie, an assistant under-secretary of state for external affairs. After reviewing the American balance of payments situation, the two Washington officials revealed that they were contemplating a new series of balance of payments guidelines. Two measures, on which they wanted Ottawa's comments, would have a direct impact on Canada. The general guidelines on direct foreign investment were to be replaced by ones with "explicit targets" for individual companies. American corporations would be allowed to increase their direct foreign investments in 1966 only by a limited percentage over a base period. The existing guidelines, which encouraged the repatriation of profits and short-term assets, would be included in the amended regulations, and Canada would no longer be exempt.[29]

This was bad enough, but changes contemplated in the rules governing the purchase of new securities with an initial term to maturity of over ten years were even more disturbing. The United States planned to restrict the volume of new securities purchased by individual financial institutions in the United States. Each company would be allowed a certain percentage increase, which was nontransferable, beyond a base period. The total effect would be to reduce portfolio investment outside the United States by $200 million. The impact of this reduction would not be uniform. American officials expected that countries like Canada, which were exempt from the IET and were therefore attractive destinations for American capital, would receive most of the allowable increase and emerge untouched. Western Europe, on the other hand, would experience a net loss in American portfolio investment.[30]

In Ottawa, where this information was a closely guarded secret, the reaction was profound shock. The guidelines on direct investment were burdensome, but they could be absorbed without too much difficulty. The restrictions on new securities seriously threatened the

Canadian economy, however. Although Washington had clearly tried to keep the Canadian need for capital in mind while it drew up its payments measures, it failed to understand (as it had in July 1963) that any limit, however hypothetical, on the amount of new Canadian issues might provoke doubt among investors about American willingness to support the Canadian dollar. Rasminsky and Bryce speculated that the decision to limit new securities was "very likely to cause immediate and serious trouble in our capital markets with the possibility of an exchange crisis such as we suffered in July 1963."[31] Ritchie alerted his minister, Paul Martin, to impending trouble. "While it would be in Canada's interest to cooperate as far as practicable in supporting efforts to maintain the strength of the United States' dollar, the proposed new measures would seem to be asking too much."[32]

Over the weekend Pearson and Sharp, who replaced Gordon as minister of finance following the 1965 election, decided to send Bryce and Rasminsky to Washington on Monday morning to outline the Canadian problem to Deming, Trued, and William Martin, chairman of the Federal Reserve Board. As a matter of tactics, they agreed that the two men would object to the guidelines on direct investment but that they would not press this point. Bryce and Rasminsky would concentrate instead on the limits to be placed on long-term foreign investment by nonbanking financial institutions. They would also underline the danger to the Canadian dollar and review the reasons why the United States had agreed to give Canada an unlimited exemption from the IET in the first place.

There was, agreed the small group of officials and politicians in Ottawa, a better and safer way for the United States to meet its objectives. In exchange for assurances that "access to u.s. markets of Canadian issues exempt from the IET would be permitted without restriction, and that investors could buy such Canadian issues in accordance with ordinary market judgements," Ottawa was prepared to buy from American holders enough Canadian securities held in the United States to keep its reserves at an agreed level. To sweeten this deal, Bryce and Rasminsky were to offer several other concessions. As additional help to the United States and as "visible evidence of our confidence in the dollar," Canada would sell Washington $200 million worth of gold from its reserves at the official price of u.s.$35 per ounce. At the same time, Ottawa would refrain from purchasing American gold during 1966. The government would also ask Parliament to permit it to hold short-term United States dollar bonds issued by the International Bank for Reconstruction and Development in its Exchange Fund in order to relieve even more of the pressure on Washington. Finally, the two

Canadians would offer to reduce Canada's reserves from the agreed level of $2.692 billion to $2.6 billion.[33]

The meeting with senior officials from the Treasury Department and the Federal Reserve Bank went well. Bryce and Rasminsky reviewed the initial justification for the unlimited exemption from the IET and met no opposition from the American delegation. As soon as Bryce revealed that the government was prepared to purchase outstanding Canadian securities held in the United States in order to maintain reserves at an agreed level, the two groups of American officials appeared to fall into line. Indeed, Bryce later reported to his minister that "it was evident that we were likely to get what we wanted without mentioning our intentions with regard to gold."[34] Still, to be on the safe side, he offered to sell the United States $200 million worth of gold over the next six to eight months. The two sides concluded their discussions by agreeing that Canada would try to reduce its reserves from $2.692 billion to $2.6 billion during 1966.

The government was sanguine when the revised American balance of payments program was announced on 5 December 1965. In addition to securing an exemption from the new measures on securities, the Department of Finance had (as it had the previous February) played a role in drafting the statement's references to Canada. American investors were specifically reassured that they could continue to purchase new Canadian securities "on the basis of market considerations."[35] Moreover, as it turned out, the measures governing direct investment for the two year period of 1965–66 were sufficiently generous that Canada would probably not even need the limit allowed it for 1965. When he responded in public to the American announcement, Sharp therefore emphasized the government's success in securing continued access to the American capital market. He complained only in the most guarded tones about the direct investment guidelines, noting that they were generally consistent with the government's own policy of reducing the level of American direct investment in Canada.[36]

Ottawa's moderate response to the new guidelines on direct investment, though appreciated in Washington, underestimated the growing concern in some Canadian quarters over the price being paid for unimpeded access to American capital. Eric Kierans, Quebec's minister of health and its acting minister of revenue, contended that the guidelines represented an extraterritorial extension of American jurisdiction. After studying the American program for two weeks, in an interview with the *Globe and Mail* on 24 December Kierans denounced the federal government for selling Canada short. "Instead of boasting about how much they managed to salvage, they should have told the Americans to go ahead and impose their tax."[37] Rasminsky tried to reason with Kierans in a lengthy telephone conversation, explaining that the government had accepted the guidelines to ensure access to American capital and arguing that "you people in Quebec should know we are doing this particularly for you."[38] Kierans was not convinced by this reference to recent Hydro Quebec bond issues and told a friend "that he regarded this issue as the greatest threat to Canadian independence since the War of 1812."[39]

Kierans opposed the measures for two reasons. In the first instance, they directed American subsidiaries operating abroad to raise capital locally whenever possible, instead of seeking money in the United States. This placed an added burden on the already overloaded Canadian capital market. In addition, to the extent that American subsidiaries followed the guidelines in raising capital or in repatriating profits, they would no longer be acting as independent businesses but as arms of the United States government. On 4 January 1966 the combative Kierans complained directly to the American secretary of commerce, J.T. Conner, that this "program would have 'an impact' on Canadian and Quebec priorities ... Subsidiaries in Canada and Quebec are Canadian and as such are subject to our laws and are expected to collaborate in the attainment of Canadian and Quebec economic objectives ... It has always been understood ... that foreign capital and corporations are subject to the political authority and direction of the host country not of the home government."[40]

Kierans' letter was immediately the centre of controversy. The prime minister was livid. He publicly berated the Quebec minister and described his letter as "highly irregular."[41] Nevertheless, there was considerable support in some parts of the country for the substance of Kierans' argument. The *Toronto Star*, for instance, pointed out that "Mr Kierans had something pertinent to say, and he has said it with more clarity and force than the Pearson government has lately been able to muster on the subject of foreign investment and the conduct of foreign-owned companies in this country."[42]

The IET exemption was also under attack on a different front. The Canadian economy had expanded steadily throughout 1965, and by midsummer there were already signs that it had reached its capacity in some parts of the country and that inflationary pressures were becoming a problem. The consumer price index, for example, rose from 136.9 in January 1965 to 140.2 in November. During the same period, the seasonally adjusted national unemployment figures declined from 4.3 percent to 3.6 percent. The decline was more precipitous in industrial Ontario and British Colombia and in the booming Western provinces, where the spectre of a labour shortage loomed by the end of the year.[43] In contrast, the American economy grew more slowly and the Federal Reserve Bank continued to set low interest rates to stimulate growth.

Bound by the agreement of 1963 on reserve levels, the Bank of Canada was unable to increase its interest rates to curb the inflationary pressures in the Canadian economy without attracting United States dollars and adding excessively to its reserves. The time had come, argued at least one influential observer, for Canada to free its monetary policy from this American albatross. In his annual address to his shareholders Earle McLaughlin, the president of the Royal Bank of Canada, called upon the government to surrender its exemption and use the resulting freedom to pursue a monetary policy that would combat domestic inflation.[44]

The government flatly rejected McLaughlin's prescription. His assumptions – that Canada would continue to have free access to American capital and that Ottawa could add to its exchange reserves (as appropriate in an inflationary period) – were dead wrong. If Canada gave up the exemption, maintained the assistant deputy minister of finance, Canadian borrowers in the United States would not only be subject to the original IET but would, under the latest guidelines, face actual limits on the amounts of money they could borrow. These conditions would almost certainly spark a stampede to the American market and "very unstable conditions in the Canadian market." In addition, the United States was unlikely to allow Canada to build up its exchange reserves, and, as a result, "the central bank would still need to implement monetary policy with regard to the capital flows between Canada and the United States." In any event, the recent decision to buy and sell Canadian securities in order to keep reserves at the agreed level would reduce the government's dependence on interest rates and give it some modest room to adjust monetary policy if necessary.[45]

It was less easy for the government to dismiss the arguments advanced by Kierans and his nationalist allies. Cabinet ministers moved quickly to reassure Canadians that the guidelines would have very little impact. Sharp, admitting that the government agreed with some of the points made by Kierans, promised to act quickly if the American guidelines threatened "to affect Canadian industry and our balance of trade."[46] At the same time, the minister of trade and commerce, Robert Winters, asked the heads of sixteen of the largest American subsidiaries operating in Canada to meet with him to discuss the potential impact of the guidelines on their operations. The meeting provided the government with another opportunity to reassure the public. In a press statement released after the gathering, Winters said that the discussion had produced "no evidence that to date the application of the guidelines by u.s. parents ... had impinged on the Canadian companies' normal pattern of procurement and trade."[47]

While this was certainly true, the meeting also revealed that there was a great deal of uncertainty among the representatives about the future impact of the guidelines. The government's growing unease over the guidelines was reinforced by the wide-spread attention that Kierans' views continued to attract across the country. During a visit to Washington in mid-February, Martin complained about the "extra-territorial flavour" of the guidelines and reminded Rusk that their application to Canada would not improve the United States balance of payments position, since "a change in the flow of capital must be offset by a change in our trade balance." The Canadian foreign minister made it clear that the guidelines would be discussed again at the forthcoming meeting of the Canada–United States Ministerial Committee on Trade and Economic Affairs.[48]

The United States did not approach the tenth joint ministerial meeting with quite the same degree of interest. "The u.s.," a State Department briefing paper noted, "has, at the moment, no trade or economic problem with Canada that is of major importance and has, therefore, little of a concrete nature to gain from this Meeting."[49] Nevertheless, the United States was still anxious to resolve the continuing pass-through problem, which it had raised again briefly at the November 1965 meeting of the balance of payments committee. At that meeting, Trued had provided Canadian officials with a confidential Treasury Department study of the question. The United States had no idea of the exact size of the problem, but its officials had unearthed a long list of strategies involving Canada that were being used to circumvent the IET. These strategies ranged from simple transactions through which American corporations ostensibly borrowed money in the United States for their Canadian subsidiaries to more complicated arrangements in which American pension funds deposited money with Canadian nonbanking financial institutions, which in turn invested that money in Europe.[50]

As Canadian officials studied the pass-through difficulties, the Treasury Department tried to curb the problem unilaterally. In mid-January, the Department of Finance learned that the United States had warned the Sun Life Assurance Company against investing its reserve of United States dollars in Euro-dollars.[51] In view of the persisting furore over the guidelines on direct investment, this evidence of Washington's continued interest in eliminating the pass-through added to Sharp's anxieties: "I find this troublesome. For the u.s. government to direct a Canadian company in the investment of its own funds even if they are held in the u.s. is a provocation which if it were known could arouse protests in Canada and might lead to demands that we should direct Canadian subsidiaries on the investment of their reserves accumulated out of their Canadian operations."[52]

Ottawa was more directly apprised of Washington's desire to solve this problem a few days later when Trued asked the Department of Finance to stop Canadian companies from selling their holdings of United States corporate securities and using the proceeds to invest in securities issued by American subsidiaries in Europe. "This would amount to requesting these institutions," he wrote, "not to shorten their position vis-à-vis the United States."[53] Hockin was prepared to comply immediately with the American request because in his view it was relatively narrow in scope and did not ask Canada to influence "the investment of funds which have not hitherto been invested in u.s. dollar securities in the u.s."[54] However, in the Department of External Affairs, Ed Ritchie suggested delaying a response until ministers had discussed the guidelines at the forthcoming ministerial meeting. The minister of finance agreed, recognizing that the American request provided Canada with some slight leverage in its fight against the guidelines on direct investment and suggested that Canada might "be willing to agree to issue guidelines to Canadian firms in return for an exemption for Canada from US guidelines."[55]

At the meeting of the United States–Canada Committee on Trade and Economic Affairs in March 1966 , ministers and officials from the two countries patched together an informal arrangement that permitted both governments to avoid any further bilateral and domestic difficulties over the American guidelines. The basis of the deal was largely worked out by Canadian officials in the week before the March meeting. Canadian ministers undertook to stop the pass-through, although the government's effort was designed to look as if it was protecting the Canadian capital market from the effects of the American guidelines rather than the exchange market. On his return to Ottawa, Sharp asked Canadians to restrain their borrowing abroad in the national interest: "To help ensure that Canadian savings are available to meet the present large demands for capital in Canada, the Government is asking all Canadian investors, including financial institutions such as the banks, life insurance companies, and trust and loan companies, as well as other corporations, pension funds and individuals, not to acquire securities, denominated in Canadian or u.s. dollars, which are subject to the u.s. Interest Equalization Tax if purchased by u.s. residents."[56]

In exchange for this gesture of support in combating the pass-through problem, the United States agreed to include in the ministerial meeting's final communiqué an interpretation of the guidelines that would help Ottawa deflect the kind of criticism levied by Kierans and other nationalists. The communiqué noted that "the u.s. government was not requesting u.s. corporations to induce their Canadian subsidiaries to act in ways that differed from their normal business practices, as regards the repatriation of earnings, purchasing and sales policies, or their other financial and commercial activities ... [and] re-emphasized the view that u.s. subsidiaries abroad should behave as good citizens of the country where they are located."[57]

At the end of March 1966, the minister of trade and commerce unveiled an elaborate set of "guiding principles of good corporate behaviour."[58] Winters also planned to ask large and medium-sized subsidiaries to provide confidential information on their operations and financing. The government's guidelines were well received across the country and neatly took much of the sting out of nationalist charges. The *Montreal Gazette*, for example, pointed out that Winters' principles "nullif[ied] the American ones" and made "it plain that as far as these companies are concerned it should be Canada first."[59]

For the remainder of 1966 and well into 1967, the reserve agreement worked smoothly and provoked little domestic criticism. However, faced with the escalating costs of the Vietnam War, it was becoming increasingly difficult for Washington to stem the pressure on the dollar in an orderly fashion. On 18 November 1967, the British pound, under siege since late 1966 amid rumours of Britain's retreat from "East of Suez," was devalued. As speculators jumped into the international gold market in the hope that the United States would sever the link between the American dollar and the official gold price of u.s.$35 per ounce, the United States dollar was placed under enormous strain. During the final six weeks of 1967, Johnson wrestled with the speculative tide. He conferred at length with congressional leaders in order to determine the price they would extract for a domestic tax increase. Deming was hastily sent to Europe in an effort to garner support for the dollar and the gold pool. By mid-December, the White House was forced to conclude that the payments deficit "threaten[ed] to turn the year into a disaster."[60]

To stem the exodus of American dollars, Johnson sent another balance of payments message to Congress on 1 January 1968.[61] Hastily concocted in secret by Fowler and opposed by a number of his senior officials, the measures were substantially tougher than the earlier versions. The voluntary direct foreign investment guidelines for American corporations were made mandatory, and the levels of allowable investment reduced. American direct investment in Canada was limited to 65 percent of the amount invested during 1965–66. The regulations tightened the restraints on lending abroad by banks and other financial institutions, limited foreign travel, and decreased Washington's expenditures overseas. Canada's exemption from the IET, however, protected it from most of these measures.

The president also included in his message a set of measures to improve the competitive position of the United States economy. A small domestic tax increase would supply the administration with greater fiscal capacity. At the same time, inflationary pressures would be curtailed by new wage and price controls. More important, the administration threatened to impose a border tax in retaliation for the European Union's new value-added tax (VAT) system, which harmed American exports.[62] In addition, Johnson announced a series of measures to encourage American exports.

The administration's program was not a complete surprise to Canada. On the eve of the president's message to Congress, Anthony Solomon, assistant secretary of state for economic affairs, briefed the prime minister, who was vacationing in Florida, before heading to Ottawa to inform Sharp and Canadian officials about the new measures.[63] Solomon carried with him a warm letter from the president. Johnson reviewed the tumultuous events of the past year, which he characterized as "marked by our traditionally close consultation and cooperation at all levels of government." He drew particular attention to Canada's work in NATO and in the Kennedy Round and underlined his gratitude for Canadian efforts in November and December to limit the damage that followed the devaluation of sterling. "I have been particularly gratified by Canada's staunch support and cooperation at that time." These efforts had not gone unnoticed in the White House, where Canada's need for American capital had been fully understood and taken into account: "In making my decisions, in which you and your country have a vital interest, I want you to know that the effects on Canada are very much on my mind. Your need for a high rate of investment is well understood here, and we have done our best to minimize the effects our new measures will have on your economic progress and development."[64]

The immediate Canadian reaction was positive. In a statement that he subsequently described to the president as "generally helpful," Sharp cautiously welcomed "these further measures to strengthen the United States balance of payments, stop speculation, and maintain confidence in the United States dollar." He praised American efforts to take into consideration Canada's unique position and reassured investors that the country retained its exemption from the IET and its unlimited access to American capital. The mandatory guidelines on American direct investment, he added, were not likely to reduce U.S. direct investment in Canada and would permit American subsidiaries to conduct their business "in accordance with normal commercial practices."[65]

During the first few days of the new year, as officials in Ottawa studied the u.s. action in more detail, they discovered no real reason to revise their initial assessment. However, there were aspects of the American actions that bore watching. The Department of External Affairs was worried by the extraterritorial overtones in the mandatory character of the new guidelines on direct investment. While the regulations did not have an extra-territorial quality from a strictly legal point of view, Marcel Cadieux, the under-secretary of state for external affairs, worried that they might cause some American firms to act in a manner that ran counter to government policy and that would effectively diminish Ottawa's jurisdiction.[66]

It was also becoming clear by the end of the first week of January that Johnson's plan to impose a border tax had important implications for Canadian-American trade. As Washington's largest trading partner, Canada would be profoundly affected by the American action: even a small border tax would damage the bilateral balance of trade, upset the country's balance of payments, and weaken the Canadian dollar. Should the United States proceed with its plan, Canada would need to take immediate compensatory action to harmonize its custom and excise regime with Washington's.[67]

The international implications of Washington's proposed tax were even more disturbing. It would almost certainly cause the European Union to retaliate and might spark an unraveling of the tariff negotiations agreed to during the Kennedy Round. Indeed, Canadian officials argued that "there is a very great danger that the proposed usa action might disturb irreparably the international trade and payments systems developed since 1945."[68] Bilateral consultations in the middle of January provided little comfort. Solomon explained to a senior level Canadian delegation, which included Ed Ritchie, now ambassador to the United States, and Maurice Schwarzmann, the deputy minister of trade and commerce, that the European Union would not dismantle its vat, despite the threatened American border tax. As a consequence, the White House was actively considering a tax adjustment. The assistant secretary of state thought that Europe would probably accept the American action and would take no retaliatory measures. He added ominously that the United States would regard any retaliation as "a declaration of war."[69]

The inflexible American attitude disturbed Canadian officials, who thought that neither the United States nor the European Union fully understood the other's position or the issues at stake. The imposition of a border tax, the Department of External Affairs concluded after taking its own soundings in Europe, was likely to provoke "a very strong reaction."[70] Canadian officials advised the prime minister to ask the American president to delay acting on the border tax until world-wide balance of payments problems could be considered in their proper context. Isolated from its allies by its pursuit of the unpopular war in Vietnam, the United States seemed in danger of losing touch with world opinion. "In the present international circumstances there does not appear to be any other government in a position to speak frankly to the American Government about their potential effects."[71] Pearson and his colleagues in cabinet were initially reluctant to advise the White House, but, as the situation worsened, they agreed to act. In the final week of January, Pearson advised Johnson to seek an international solution to his balance of payments difficulties: "I hope that, if you determine that some action by the United States is required, you will place proposals before the appropriate international bodies for consideration before taking such action. I believe that in this way we can avoid a cumulative process of action and counter-action whose consequences would be very damaging not only to the gains achieved through the Kennedy Round but also to the whole system of international trade and payments created under United States leadership since the war."[72]

Canadian officials continued to monitor the White House's deliberations on this issue, but there was no additional action that Canada could take. In any event, Canadian ministers were increasingly preoccupied with Canada's own developing exchange crisis. There were several reasons for the weakening Canadian dollar. The American guidelines were partly at fault, as United States subsidiaries began repatriating capital. The looming possibility of border taxes also increased the dollar's instability, as American importers refused to negotiate long-term contracts with Canadian suppliers. More important, the government's failure in the budget of November 1967 to address the inflationary pressures that threatened Canada's competitive position left the dollar exposed, just as nervous international investors were rebounding from the devaluation of sterling.[73] These several factors contributed to a gradual, but steady, decrease in the value of the dollar. Despite the Bank of Canada's efforts in late 1967 and early 1968 to sustain it (an effort that cost $350 million), the dollar slipped to u.s.91.76 cents by 18 January, its lowest level since 1951.[74] When the market closed for the week, investors began to speculate that the government was planning to devalue the dollar.

Sharp quickly denied this rumour, but he realized that some more concrete gesture of support for the dollar was necessary. Over the weekend he and the prime minister agreed to ask Washington for an exemption from the direct investment guidelines. The United States secretary of the treasury, however, refused the Canadian request. After consulting several American corporations with subsidiaries in Canada, Fowler reasonably concluded that there was "no evidence that the pressure on the Canadian dollar was attributable to the direct investment regulations."[75] In the circumstances, he would agree only to issue a statement reminding United States companies that there was no reason for their subsidiaries in Canada to engage "in abnormal transfers of earnings or withdrawals of capital."[76]

With the American statement as a starting point, Sharp and Rasminsky tried to shore up the dollar before the markets opened. On Sunday evening the Bank of Canada increased its interest rate from 6 to 7 percent. It also asked Canadian chartered banks "to discourage the use of bank credit to facilitate abnormal transfers of funds abroad by Canadian subsidiaries of foreign companies" and to block attempts by subsidiaries "to meet requirements in Canada which have in the past been met by parent companies."[77] The minister of finance addressed the House of Commons early Monday morning, making clear the government's determination to take whatever steps were necessary to defend the dollar.[78]

These measures helped stabilize the dollar during the following week. Nevertheless, the market remained tense and, as the parliamentary secretary to the minister of finance observed, "everyone, including Mike [Pearson] seemed to have the jitters."[79] For the government's nationalist wing, the fate of the dollar provided an opportunity to pursue the enduring debate over American control of the Canadian economy. Its Cabinet representative, Walter Gordon, the president of the privy council, had come to share the view of some nationalist economists that the government would increase its capacity to pursue made-in-Canada economic policies if it adopted a floating exchange rate. By allowing the value of the dollar to float down by 2 or 3 percent, the government could pursue its expansive domestic economic policy by encouraging exports at the expense of imports. Gordon, who had pressed Pearson to consider this idea several times during the preceding six months, returned to the attack. At lunch with the prime minister on 31 January, he urged him to convene a small group of senior officials and ministers to consider carefully the "pros & cons of devaluation, or devaluation under IMF auspices & control vis-à-vis a floating rate." Pearson agreed.[80]

Gordon, however, was already being outmanoeuvred. Rasminsky, who had been one of the original architects of the fixed exchange rate in 1962, met the prime minister and a small group of ministers in early February to discuss the crisis. Gordon was not invited. Rasminsky was clearly "very worried." The Bank of Canada's exchange losses in January alone totalled $350 million, or 15 percent of the country's reserves. The central bank could not continue to sustain losses at that rate. "We have shot our bolt and no more help is to be looked for from monetary policy." It was up to the government "to restore confidence that its overall policies will be coherently directed towards arresting erosion in the value of money."[81]

Some ministers questioned the program of budget reductions and domestic tax increases favoured by Rasminsky to strengthen the dollar and wanted the government to adopt a floating exchange rate. Rasminsky easily dominated the discussion. The United States, he warned, would certainly not continue to exempt Canada from the IET if the Canadian dollar was allowed to float and to disrupt an important market for American exports. If the dollar continued to weaken, the government should ask the United States to guarantee the Canadian exchange rate.[82]

While the prime minister weighed the conflicting advice that he had received from Gordon and Rasminsky, the dollar continued to weaken. Figures showing a decline in Canada's reserve levels were released at the end of January and triggered a brief flurry of speculation against the dollar. The defeat of the government's anti-inflationary tax bill on 19 February and the appalling lack of leadership on the government benches sparked a second speculative stir. Although neither event provoked an immediate and large outflow of U.S. dollars, the cumulative cost to the Bank of Canada of these depredations was beginning to mount. By 23 February, it had spent U.S.$750 million in support of the Canadian dollar, or just over 30 percent of the country's foreign exchange reserves.[83]

Two days later, as the financial crisis gathered momentum, Rasminsky met again with Pearson and a few select ministers and officials. Gordon was not present and again Rasminsky dominated. The banker insisted that the government could not go on defending the dollar indefinitely. The time had come for remedial action. For good reasons, he rejected either devaluing or floating the dollar. Domestically, both courses would lead to sharp increases in the cost of living and to "serious economic dislocation."[84] These steps might also provoke other countries to devalue their currencies, renewing pressure on the U.S. dollar and threatening the entire international balance of payments system.

The crisis confronting the government reflected the market's collapsing confidence in the Canadian dollar. Rather than blaming the United States, whose balance of payments program was only a small part of the problem, Rasminsky pointed the finger at Ottawa. The government's own fiscal policies and its inability to address the inflationary pressures in the domestic economy were important factors in the current difficulties. The government needed to reduce expenditures, pass the defeated tax bill, and take steps to control wages and prices. It should also ask Washington to exempt Canada from its balance of payments guidelines on direct foreign investment or, at least, establish Canada as a separate category with a quota of 100 percent of the base period. This would have the effect of further integrating the two capital markets, he emphasized, as Ottawa would need to ensure that the exemption had no impact on the United States balance of payments situation by rigorously adhering to the reserve agreement. Finally, the Bank of Canada might also need to seek a substantial international line of credit.[85]

Rasminsky's advice was noted and, for the moment, ignored. During the last week of February, the government continued to drift. Neither Sharp nor Pearson wanted to attract the ire of nationalists by appealing to Washington for help. They were equally reluctant to adopt Gordon's floating exchange rate. The government was finally forced to act, however, when the Bank of Canada lost u.s.$100 million defending the dollar on 1 March.[86] Sharp, who was in Washington for a meeting with the United States secretary of the treasury to reiterate Canada's opposition to the proposed American border tax, asked Fowler for help. He suggested that the United States either exempt Canada from the balance of payments guidelines or establish a separate category for Canada. Fowler admitted that the problem was serious, but he and the White House remained reluctant to exempt Canada completely from the guidelines. While the administration waited to see how the crisis developed, the Treasury Department began to line up international credits for Canada and explore the possibility of issuing a "statement of intent that we would re-examine our investment guidelines for Canada *if* they were proving to be a serious problem."[87]

The American response to Sharp's entreaties was clearly not going to solve Canada's financial problems. On Sunday, 3 March, Rasminsky, Sharp, and Pearson together with their senior officials gathered once more at the prime minister's residence to discuss the situation before the markets opened.[88] Rasminsky recommended that the government send him to Washington to negotiate a full exemption for Canada or at least a special category for Canada with a direct foreign investment quota of 100 percent of the 1965–66 average. He suggested that, in exchange, Ottawa should offer to police the pass-through problem rigorously and to hold its reserves in a form that would not constitute a liquid claim on the United States. This time, Rasminsky was authorized to proceed to Washington.[89]

On 6 March, after explaining the Canadian position to American and European central bankers for two days, Rasminsky was invited to Washington to meet with Fowler. He reviewed with him the domestic and international factors that lay behind Canada's current financial crisis. If Canada's reserves, which stood at only $1.7 billion when the talks opened at 3:45 P.M., fell to $1.5 billion, Rasminsky said that Ottawa would have no choice but to allow the dollar to float. Citing the Bank of Canada's recent decision to increase interest rates and the government's determination to seek legislative authority for additional tax revenue, he assured the American cabinet official that the government was actively wrestling with the domestic causes of the crisis. These steps would matter very little, however, if it were not possible to put to rest fears that Canada would not be able to fund its persistent current account deficit by borrowing in the United States. This could be achieved, argued Rasminsky, only if Washington was to grant Canada a complete exemption from its balance of payments guidelines.

The need for action, he insisted, grew more urgent by the hour. With a sharp sense of the dramatic, Rasminsky announced immediately after dinner that Canada's reserves had dropped that afternoon to $1.6 billion. When the discussion resumed at 8:30 P.M., Fowler quickly agreed to grant Canada its exemption provided Ottawa would take steps, as Rasminsky promised, to solve the pass-through problem and to hold its reserves in a form that did not represent a liquid claim on the United States. Having achieved his victory, the Canadian banker cautioned that there were limits on how far he was prepared to go to accommodate the American program: "We would not regard this offer as implying that we were harnessing our wheel completely to the American chariot. If they thought, for example, that the price of this exemption was that we would duplicate the United States balance of payments programme, I had to say that I would not recommend to the Canadian Government that the offer should be accepted."[90]

Nevertheless, Rasminsky's proposals to eliminate the pass-through problem were extensive. Ottawa promised to institute regulations allowing it to control the participation of Canadian banks in the Euro-dollar market and stop Canadian corporations from borrowing in the United States to raise capital for investments elsewhere. The government would also make sure that American subsidiaries in Canada did not use the exemption to invest in third countries, where the IET would normally apply. Fowler and Eugene Rostow, under secretary of state for political affairs, were delighted with these suggestions; over the course of the next few hours (the talks dragged on until 3 A.M. the following morning) the final touches were placed on the deal.[91]

During the spring of 1968, Ottawa drafted rules and regulations to control the flow of American dollars to Canada, effectively establishing "a form of continental common market for capital."[92] Butterworth observed that the new system recognized that the two countries had developed "a new dimension in financial interdependence."[93] The arrangement worked reasonably well and responded to Canadian requirements until the two countries simultaneously dismantled it when the IET was eliminated in 1974. The continuing struggle to secure an exemption from the interest equalization tax, however, left its mark on officials in Ottawa. Increasingly, they came to hold the view that the Canadian economy, which continued to require unfettered access to American capital (and American markets), could not depend on the kind of ad hoc consultative mechanisms used in the 1960s. It was dangerous to rely on the capacity of Canadian officials to explain to Washington how interdependent the two North American economies were every time the United States acted without considering the impact on Canada. This lesson was driven home in August 1971, when Canada failed to win an exemption from a 10 percent surcharge imposed by President Richard Nixon on imports to the United States. Increasingly, for many Canadian policymakers Canada's uncertain experience with the IET and the August surcharges pointed to one obvious conclusion: in order to respond quickly and effectively to American policies that might have an adverse impact on Canada, Ottawa needed to pursue an even closer and more formal economic partnership with the United States.

CHAPTER FOUR

Defending the Deterrent

During the summer of 1963 much of the old intimacy returned to defence relations between Canada and the United States. From May until September delegations from both countries worked steadily to carry out the promise Prime Minister Lester B. Pearson had made at Hyannisport to accept nuclear weapons for Canada's NATO squadrons and to store nuclear warheads in Canada for American forces. The two sides accepted almost without change the draft agreement of 1961 that negotiators for Prime Minister Diefenbaker and President Kennedy had concluded two years earlier. Nuclear warheads for Canada, it was agreed in mid-August 1963, would be held in American custody and released only following authorization from both governments.[1] With this agreement as a starting point, Ottawa and Washington concluded negotiations in late September on the terms and conditions governing the storage of nuclear warheads in Canada for American detachments at Goose Bay and Harmon Field. These weapons would also remain in American hands and would normally be used only when authorized by both governments.[2] The agreements committed the two governments to define as soon as practical the exact conditions governing "authorization and consultation."

Even as the Pearson government completed this piece of unfinished business, there were growing pressures for changes in Canada's defence policy. The government's campaign commitments to a host of new social programs – old age security, medicare, and regional development – sparked a scramble for money that left the budget of the

Department of National Defence exposed just when the possibility of détente and superpower stalemate in Europe made Canada's small contribution to Western defence seem insignificant and expendable. Budgetary pressures, however, were only part of the equation. Several cabinet ministers, including the prime minister, and influential officials in the Department of External Affairs were anxious to carve out a more distinctive and independent international role for Canada as the likelihood of conflict in Western Europe receded. The dangerous instability in the developing world that followed the collapse of European colonialism promised plenty of scope for independent activity when diplomatic initiative was combined with innovative defence policy.

The Pearson government announced its new defence policy in the 1964 *White Paper on Defence*. Although the paper confirmed Canada's continued commitment to NATO and NORAD, it emphasized Ottawa's growing interest in peacekeeping. During the following two years Canadian resources and attention shifted towards peacekeeping and related aid activities in the developing world. At the same time, the government's reluctance to completely integrate North American defence and its support for a less rigid and more accommodating Western alliance irritated the United States. Some American officials, including Washington's bombastic ambassador to Canada, Walt Butterworth, were inclined to view Canadian defence policy as increasingly "neutralist" and untrustworthy. Others, conscious that Canada's interest in peacekeeping and in the developing world was at least partly the result of American encouragement, suggested that the real problem with bilateral relations in this sphere stemmed from Washington's uncertainty about what it wanted from its Canadian ally. There was widespread support for this view in the American capital, and by the spring of 1967 the State Department and the Department of Defense had reassessed Canadian defence policy and set out some modest objectives for Canada's contribution to Western defence. However, by then the relentless conflict in Vietnam had undermined popular support in Canada for sharing the Western burden in NATO and NORAD, and had transformed these American expectations into remote and politically difficult goals for the Pearson government.

When the Liberals promised during the 1963 election campaign to establish a special parliamentary committee to examine Canadian defence policy, no one expected the kind of searching review that was eventually undertaken. Pearson's ambitious minister of national defence, Paul Hellyer, who had clearly developed ideas on both the administration and the make-up of the armed forces, saw the review as his opportunity to make his mark. It afforded the minister the chance to realize his desire for a more flexible, mobile, and conventionally armed military and allowed him to begin modernizing the administration of his department. Disgusted by the waste and duplication he had witnessed as a noncommissioned officer during the Second World War and armed with a recent report by the Royal Commission on Government Organization that attacked the bureaucratic structure of his department as "unsuited" and "uneconomic," Hellyer was determined to complete the process of integration that had begun in the 1950s. Thus, while the special parliamentary committee held public hearings in the summer of 1963, the minister asked R.J. Sutherland, chief of operational research for the Defence Research Board, to undertake a confidential and more extensive study of Canadian defence policy.[3]

In August 1963, as the parallel reviews gathered steam, Pearson and his Cabinet began to examine closely their spending priorities for the next fiscal year. This process would also have a profound impact on the government's defence policy. Determined to repair the damage that his reputation had suffered in the wake of his first budget and effectively prevented from addressing the question of foreign ownership by Washington, the minister of finance, Walter Gordon, turned his attention to the domestic agenda. In order to balance the budget and find the money required to fund the government's ambitious plans for pension reform and medicare, he systematically went over government spending. Given the apparent easing of international tension that followed the Cuban missile crisis and the signing of the Nuclear Test Ban Treaty in August, the defence budget was an obvious target, and in early September, Hellyer and Gordon agreed tentatively to freeze defence spending at $1.5 billion for the next three years.[4] Thus, even before the public and private defence reviews were complete, the government was forced to cancel existing plans to procure frigates for the Royal Canadian Navy (RCN) and CF-101 and CF-104 aircraft for the Royal Canadian Air Force (RCAF).[5]

Hellyer was confident that the armed forces would be able to limit the impact of this budgetary ceiling by streamlining their administration. Indeed, from his perspective the decision to cap defence spending and to cancel existing purchasing programs freed the government to adopt radically new policies. However, the initial drafts of the white paper were quite orthodox in their view of Canadian foreign and defence policy. The first draft, which Hellyer himself wrote out in longhand and began to circulate in early December 1963, was singularly unimaginative and politically inept.[6] Intended to justify defence policy for the next ten years, it emphatically rejected the possibility of East-West détente and dismissed as unimportant developments in the newly emerging states of Asia and Africa. While Hellyer allowed that Canada might play a role as a peacekeeper in these regions, his paper rejected suggestions (advanced more than once by the prime minister himself) that Canada maintain part of its military forces specifically for peacekeeping duties as impractical and poorly conceived. The country's primary military function for the next decade lay in Western Europe and the North Atlantic. The North Atlantic alliance's new determination to ensure that it had the capacity to respond with conventional weapons to limited Soviet aggression when appropriate – the doctrine of flexible response – made Canada's role in Western defence clear: to enhance the conventional deterrent in Europe.

Hellyer suggested that Canada maintain its existing brigade in West Germany while improving the mobility of its two Canada-based brigades, which might serve as reinforcements in the event of a European conflict. This would be done by stockpiling large amounts of equipment in Europe over the next ten years in preparation for eventual deployment and by investing in a large fleet of air transports. In addition, a fourth specially trained brigade would be created for service with either the United Nations or NATO. Two assault ships, one stationed on either coast, would provide this brigade with enhanced mobility. The RCAF's nuclear attack role in Europe would be phased out and replaced with eight squadrons of "high performance" tactical aircraft capable of providing ground support to the four Canadian brigades. Canada would maintain its traditional antisubmarine role in the North Atlantic, a mission strengthened by the purchase of two nuclear-powered submarines.

The purchase of new equipment would be financed largely by the savings that the minister confidently predicted would result from his proposal to integrate and then unify the three branches of the armed services. Hellyer also forecast significant savings in North America. He proposed phasing out at the end of their operational life the three squadrons of CF-101s committed to NORAD. Canada would rely instead on the United States and its anticipated antiballistic missile system.

The reaction in Ottawa to the draft white paper was uniformly hostile. The Department of Defence Production, whose minister, Bud Drury, was also responsible for implementing the government's policy of reducing Canada's current account deficit by expanding its manufacturing sector, was disturbed by the paper's complete disregard for the interests of Canadian industry.[7] Gordon, too, was upset by Hellyer's plans for continued large-scale defence spending and renewed his suggestion that the government channel its defence budget into more socially useful domestic spending. He reminded the prime minister of the unique set of circumstances that had initially produced Canada's postwar role in Europe and contended that as Western Europe was now able to defend itself, "Canada's commitments there should be substantially reduced."[8]

Although neither Pearson nor Martin agreed with Gordon's desire to drastically reduce Canada's commitment to Europe and NATO, they shared his view that the international circumstances in which Canadian foreign and defence policy were made had changed profoundly since the 1950s. In the Department of External Affairs, where officials agreed that altered international conditions merited some adjustment in Canadian policy, Hellyer's paper was seen as a welcome opportunity to secure formal government approval for the department's struggle to shift the focus of Canadian efforts for collective security from NATO and the North Atlantic region to United Nations peacekeeping operations and the dissolving empires of Asia and Africa.[9] Martin and his senior officials criticized the draft for emphasizing Canada's function in NATO while failing to take into account Western Europe's renewed capacity to undertake its own defence. More important, the proposals paid insufficient attention to the threat that decolonization represented to international order and the role that Canada had already begun to assume in response to this threat:

The omission of adequate emphasis on one of the most important developments of the postwar period – the vast increase in the numbers of newly independent and unstable nations as a consequence of the closing of the colonial era – seems to neglect a factor which is having a significant effect on the military requirements for the effective maintenance of international peace. This has led to a downgrading in the paper of the role of the United Nations and the significant contribution which Canadian armed forces have made to its peacekeeping activities. Indeed, throughout the paper, there is a basic misconception of the role performed by the United Nations as a versatile instrument for the preservation of peace and security.[10]

Martin also pointed out that any assessment of Canada's future defence requirements should take into consideration "the changing nature and locale of the continuing struggle for influence between Communist and non-Communist worlds" that was the product of the East-West stalemate in Europe and of decolonization.

Pearson shared the interest of the Department of External Affairs in international peacekeeping and was alert to the implications of decolonization and European renewal for Canadian defence policy. He was "appalled" by Hellyer's effort. When interested ministers gathered at the prime minister's residence for an informal meeting to discuss the paper in February 1964, Pearson led the attack and insisted that the paper be completely rewritten. In addition to shifting its focus away from Europe, the redrafted paper must emphasize integration and unification and must avoid specific long-term financial commitments.[11] Kent and officials from the Privy Council Office quickly rewrote the paper to meet the prime minister's objections.[12]

The final version of the *White Paper on Defence* was approved without difficulty by the full Cabinet on 25 March 1964 and tabled in the House of Commons the following day. The initial response to the paper's proposal to integrate the three branches of the armed forces as the "first step towards a single unified defence force" was positive.[13] At a time when innovation and change were becoming popular watchwords, Canadians were intrigued by this experiment in military organization. The country was also gratified by the far-sighted and imaginative perspective that this version of the paper adopted on Canada's role in world affairs. Unlike Hellyer's initial draft, it outlined a flexible and adaptable defence policy that suited an international environment in the midst of dramatic and rapid change. Though détente was not yet a reality, the paper welcomed the possibility as real and speculated that "increasing importance will probably now be attached to the quest for security through negotiations." While tensions in Europe would persist, the white paper argued that communist pressure would focus on "fermenting and support[ing] so-called "wars of liberation" in less-developed areas." As the resulting instability called for "containment measures which do not lend themselves to Great Power or Alliance action ... the peacekeeping responsibilities devolving upon the United Nations can be expected to grow."[14]

In this kind of uncertain international situation, nations were naturally required to maintain the forces necessary for their defence. The bulk of Canada's military forces were, as in Hellyer's first draft, generally reassigned to their existing roles in NATO and NORAD. Canada would maintain an infantry brigade in West Germany, supported by two additional brigades stationed at home. The eight squadrons of the Air Division would also remain in France and Germany, although their CF-104s would slowly be replaced by an unspecified "high-performance aircraft" capable of providing Canadian ground forces with direct support. These aircraft would also be available for the defence of North America, where they would eventually replace the CF-101s employed by the three squadrons currently assigned to NORAD. The white paper assumed that the primary role of the navy would continue to be its long-standing NATO antisubmarine mission in the North Atlantic.

In contrast to Hellyer's initial proposals, each of these missions had a new built-in element of mobility and flexibility that was designed not only to fulfil alliance roles but also to ensure that Canada was able to play a larger part in United Nations peacekeeping operations. For instance, the white paper explained that the two reserve infantry brigades would no longer be "ear-marked primarily for the European theatre." Instead, they would be "re-equipped and re-trained as a mobile force," so that they might be deployed "in circumstances ranging from service in the European theatre to UN peace-keeping operations." In addition, the air force and the navy were both given new missions to develop the capacity to move troops and equipment quickly "to any trouble spot where their presence might be valuable to maintain peace or assist in the limitation of local outbreak [sic]."

The evolution of Canadian defence policy in the first six months of the Pearson government's mandate was observed carefully and with mounting concern by the United States. In early January 1964, Butterworth speculated that the review may "reflect the hope of avoiding any additional direct involvement with nuclear weaponry" and warned that the "reappraisal may substantially alter the Canadian contribution to NATO ... [and] force us to make a careful new appraisal of our future defence requirements for the use of Canadian real estate."[15] Butterworth's suspicion that the defence review was in part an exercise designed to allow Pearson's government to abandon its commitment to nuclear weapons – a view that was strengthened later that month when the prime minister remarked on television that he hoped Canada would reduce and eventually abandon its nuclear role – reinforced Washington's determination to ensure "that the revised defence policy does not impair Canadian commitments to [the] joint defence of North America and NATO."[16] Butterworth, the State Department, and the Department of Defense agreed to use the next meeting of the Permanent Joint Board on Defence (PJBD) to remind Ottawa that the "maintenance of [an] effective deterrent to aggression against North America or members of the North Atlantic alliance will continue to be fundamental to Canada's defence policies and programs."[17]

With the publication of the *White Paper on Defence* much of this concern evaporated. The white paper exceeded Washington's expectations. It not only reiterated Canada's support for NATO and NORAD, reported Butterworth, but it seemed to go out of its way to signal Ottawa's willingness to remain a reliable member of the Western alliance. The ambassador, whose report was soon cited authoritatively in the State Department, emphasized the limited prospects for détente that the paper outlined and pointed out that it provided a justification for the acquisition of nuclear weapons "in terms of the western alliance's realistic defense needs rather than in terms of the necessity to

honor 'commitments' entered into by the previous government."[18] Butterworth mistakenly interpreted the policy statement as a clear indication that the Canadian government "views its forces primarily as components of the Western alliance with UN peacekeeping in a secondary
role."[19]

Although the minister of national defence thought this, it was not
clear that the rest of the government, especially Martin and Pearson,
agreed. In the months following the release of the white paper, several
developments forced the American ambassador to reevaluate the relative weight that Ottawa attached to its peacekeeping and related activities. As if to emphasize the importance the government attached to
peacekeeping, Pearson sent Canadian troops to maintain the peace in
Cyprus when Turkish and Greek militants threatened to go to war over
the small island in the spring of 1964. The day after the UN mission
was launched, the prime minister exclaimed with evident delight that
"this was the kind of thing I like to see Canada doing."[20]

The crisis in Cyprus reinforced the prime minister's longstanding
interest in some kind of permanent international peacekeeping
machinery. As he pointed out in an important article in the popular
magazine *Maclean's*, if the United Nations was unable or unwilling to
establish such machinery, there were others who could assume this
responsibility. "As a leading middle power, with a well-known record
of support for the United Nations peace-keeping operations," wrote
Pearson, "Canada is in a unique position to take the initiative. It is
prepared to do so." In November 1964, as a step towards establishing this kind of international force, the prime minister invited twenty-
two major peacekeeping nations to discuss the technical issues
involved in peacekeeping.[21]

At the same time, Cabinet approved a program of military assistance
to the developing world. The possibility that Canada might establish
this kind of program had been debated sporadically in Ottawa during
the late 1950s and early 1960s, only to reemerge in the summer of
1963 when Tanzanian prime minister Julius Nyerere asked Pearson for
help with establishing a national air force. This request and a subsequent Malaysian petition for assistance in its confrontation with
Indonesia confirmed the established Canadian view that military train-
ing assistance represented an important contribution to international
stability and collective security. In addition to enhancing the strength
of local police and military units, forces that Ottawa characterized as
"usually ... good influence[s] for law and order," Western aid usefully
displaced destabilizing Communist bloc assistance.[22]

The United States did not object to Canada's growing role as an
international peacekeeper. The president himself encouraged Pearson

to undertake the Cyprus mission.[23] Washington also welcomed the Ottawa peacekeeping conference and praised Ottawa's efforts to establish a military assistance program.[24] Still, by the end of 1964 American authorities were beginning to worry that Canada, with its limited resources, might find itself spread too thinly and become anxious to reduce its role in NATO and NORAD in order to maintain its international peacekeeping activities. The government's new five-year, $1.5 billion procurement program, which Hellyer announced on 22 December, gave Washington real grounds for concern. The program included no funding for equipment designed exclusively for nuclear weapons or warheads. It made no provision for replacing the aging fleet of CF-104s and indicated that the government would buy the cheaper and simpler F-5, rather than the more sophisticated and expensive Phantom F-4 fighter-bomber as the "high performance tactical aircraft" promised in the white paper.[25] Whether these decisions actually anticipated a reduction in Canada's commitment to NATO and NORAD was, as Butterworth noted in his annual year-end report, "unclear." However, the American was clear on what the wavering Canadian policy meant for the United States: "Canada's self-chosen UN peace-keeping role is ... of singularly constructive help, to the West and to world order, but its pursuit should not be at the expense of Canada's part in the Atlantic and North American communities. Canada may well see the Western alliance and participation in UN peace-keeping operations as posing a choice, a political as well as a military choice. Many Canadian leaders already find more purity and more opportunity for influence in the 'neutral' role. The United States should not hesitate wherever and whenever to remind Canada of its basic political and military commitments."[26]

Butterworth's exhortation to his colleagues to persist in their efforts to convince Canada to assume its full share of the Western defence burden was timely. By early 1965 Washington had become increasingly frustrated at its inability to convince Ottawa to adopt its priorities in NATO and NORAD. From Washington's perspective, the two nuclear agreements negotiated in August and September 1963 were only the first steps in a more extensive program to fully integrate continental defence. As early as Pearson's meeting with Kennedy at Hyannisport, the United States had made it clear that the defence of North America called for two additional major bilateral projects. First, in order to reduce the damage that a Soviet first strike might inflict on NORAD's capacity to defend North America against a bomber attack, the United States wanted to disperse forty-four squadrons of interceptors across nine remote Canadian bases. Second, Washington insisted that Canadian and American naval units serving on Canada's east coast required nuclear weapons in order to carry out their antisubmarine warfare (ASW) mission effectively.

At Hyannisport, Kennedy had accepted Pearson's plea that he lacked the political support to move ahead on these two issues and had agreed to defer them for the time being.[27] With the agreements on nuclear weapons for Canadian and American forces in place by the fall of 1963, the United States began to press for action on the question of dispersing American interceptors in Canada and equipping ASW operations with a nuclear capacity. At the meeting of the PJBD in October 1963, the American delegation outlined the argument in favour of providing nuclear weapons to Canadian and American naval forces stationed in Canada and alerted the board to its determination to pursue this topic "at an appropriate moment."[28] The United States, armed with a military assessment by Admiral Thomas H. Moorer, the Supreme Allied Commander, Atlantic (SACLANT), outlining NATO's need for a nuclear ASW capability in North America, announced at the next meeting of the PJBD in February 1964 that it wished to begin negotiations on this subject as soon as possible.[29]

Later that spring, as preparations began for the first meeting of the Canada-United States Ministerial Committee on Joint Defence since 1959, the White House decided to make an effort to resolve all outstanding nuclear weapons questions. In early April, the National Security Council reversed Kennedy's prohibition on discussing the interceptor question and asked Ottawa to put it and the ASW problem on the agenda of the meeting. At the same time, President Lyndon Johnson suggested to Pearson that the two countries begin to negotiate the terms of the agreement for consulting on and authorizing the use of nuclear weapons that was promised in the exchange of notes in August and September 1963.[30]

The prime minister had been carefully assessing the domestic political costs associated with meeting the American requests for further nuclear facilities for some time. Hellyer, to whom Pearson had turned in late February for political advice on the question of the American interceptors, was reassuring. Although a small but vocal minority would oppose the deployment for idealistic reasons, most Canadians would be more forgiving. Hellyer assured Pearson that the "economic advantages of allowing the U.S. dispersal would be applauded by the majority [of Canadians] ... Our experience in the recent [defence] cuts indicates very clearly that, in most cases, individuals and communities place economic considerations above all others."[31]

Hellyer's advice was far from decisive. The prime minister's own inclination to avoid any extension of Canada's nuclear role was strengthened by the opposition to nuclear weapons expressed by sev-

eral Quebec Cabinet ministers during the Cabinet's discussion of the
White Paper on Defence in March 1964.[32] Thus, while Pearson agreed
to discuss the procedures for consultation and authorization, he asked
the president to defer consideration of the proposals to disperse American interceptors and to store ASW nuclear weapons in Canada. Johnson, who "did not want to risk politically embarrassing Prime Minister Pearson," agreed, and the two items were promptly removed from
the agenda of the joint ministerial meeting.[33]

The president's decision left the problem of consultation and
authorization as the only substantial issue for ministerial consideration. Negotiations at the official level, which began in Washington
the week before the ministers gathered, ended in deadlock. Having
accepted nuclear weapons for Canadian forces, Ottawa was determined to transform NORAD into a genuinely shared command. Canadian negotiators, led by Ross Campbell, an assistant under-secretary
of state for external affairs, proposed making the deployment of
NORAD's nuclear weapons by the alliance's American commander-in-
chief (CINCNORAD) anywhere in North America subject to joint
authorization by the two governments. When there was time, consultation, either in person or by telephone, would precede authorization.
In an emergency, CINCNORAD would be authorized to use nuclear
weapons anywhere in North America on his own authority. (An
emergency included an attack against North America that CINCNO-
RAD judged "strategic" or an imminent or actual attack against
Alaska where "delay might seriously prejudice the defense of the area
involved.")

While American negotiators readily accepted the conditions under
which the two countries would normally consult, they were reluctant
to accept the idea that CINCNORAD would not be free to deploy the
nuclear forces at his command anywhere in the continental United
States and Alaska without prior Canadian authorization. The U.S.
joint chiefs of staff explained that the United States might need to act
alone, in a hurry, if Alaska was attacked. When Canadian negotiators
offered to draft a special provision addressing this eventuality, American resistance stiffened. The Pentagon objected in principle to the concept of a joint command and refused to surrender its freedom to
employ United States forces in the United States as it wished.[34]

While the ministerial meeting on defence failed to resolve the deadlock, it did make some progress. The Canadian delegation continued
to insist that authorization and consultation arrangements should be as
uniform as possible throughout NORAD's operational area. The American secretary of state, Dean Rusk, who was anxious to make the meeting as successful as possible, was conciliatory. He maintained the

American position, suggesting that it might be better to focus efforts on the problem of authorizing the use of nuclear weapons in Canada alone, but agreed that the two negotiating teams should meet again to see if the Canadian proposals could be amended to satisfy the American position.[35]

By late July provisions that met United States military requirements had been drafted. Under the terms of the draft agreement, the United States was allowed to deploy in the United States nuclear weapons normally under the operational control of CINCNORAD without authorization from Canada. In addition, the draft permitted both countries to use NORAD command and control facilities for national purposes, but only "to the extent necessary for the effective employment of the national forces." The State Department, worried that ongoing opposition to the Canadian proposals would give Pearson (and his French Canadian colleagues) an excuse to abandon Canada's nuclear role, was prepared to accept Ottawa's terms. The Pentagon, however, continued to resist and refused to sanction the draft agreement. Rusk eventually appealed to the White House. Following the 1964 elections, during which consideration of the potentially awkward problem had been suspended, Johnson concurred with the State Department, and the Canadian proposal became the basis for an agreement that was eventually signed in September 1965.[36]

If the White House hoped that this forthcoming gesture would soften attitudes in Ottawa towards nuclear cooperation in North America, it was soon disappointed. During the winter and spring of 1965, Canadian delegations to PJBD meetings refused to address either the dispersal problem or the issue of nuclear ASW weapons storage, forcing the United States to change its approach.[37] In preparation for the June 1965 session of the board, the Pentagon abandoned its search for nuclear weapons storage for both Canadian and American antisubmarine forces; instead, it asked for storage facilities in Canada for American ASW detachments only.[38]

While this suggestion awaited a Canadian response, the United States amended its tactics for dealing with the interceptor problem. Partly on the basis of advice received from David Kirkwood, the secretary of the Canadian section of the PJBD, the United States carefully reexamined its need for dispersal in Canada and concluded that, rather than nine bases, it only required four.[39] In September 1965 the Americans hinted casually that formal notes asking for these facilities would soon be presented. This development, warned Dana Wilgress, chairman of the Canadian section of the PJBD, signalled a stiffening of Washington's attitude and its growing lack of patience with Canada. "This matter, having been dormant as long as the U.S. considered it necessary to be extremely cautious in their nuclear relations with us, will soon again require consideration."[40]

American pressure mounted gradually during the fall of 1965. During a visit with Hellyer in September, Moorer referred to the American request for nuclear storage facilities for ASW weapons, prompting the minister to conclude by mid-October that "we could no longer delay satisfying U.S. wishes."[41] However, for the time being Hellyer alone prodded the prime minister. Despite advice from his officials, Martin refused to join in urging the prime minister to agree to the American request in the face of the opposition expressed by some French Canadian members of Cabinet.[42] Wilgress attended the next meeting of the PJBD in February 1965 with instructions to avoid committing Canada.

On his return from the PJBD session, Wilgress again warned the prime minister that American patience was wearing thin: "I believe that you would wish to know that at the meeting our United States colleagues clearly required the dispersal proposal as being in principle compatible with the general commitment to integrate the air defences of the continent which we undertook in the NORAD agreement. They also felt that somewhat similar considerations applied with respect to the ASW proposal, both in a NATO and a continental defence context."[43] Pearson continued to seek refuge in delay; Washington continued to press. At the meeting of the PJBD in May 1966 the American delegation warned again that the United States would soon ask Ottawa formally for permission to disperse its squadrons in the Canadian north and to store nuclear ASW weapons in Canada. Wilgress maintained that the United States, in threatening to force a response from Canada, was fully aware of Pearson's political difficulties. Irritated by the unrelenting pressure and the American decision to use the PJBD as a lobby platform, Pearson received Wilgress' report with uncharacteristic pique. "I think," he minuted Martin in frustration, "we should have an assessment of the value of the PJBD in present circumstances."[44]

The prime minister's frustrations over defence relations were shared south of the border. Indeed, by the spring of 1966 they were perhaps felt more acutely in Washington than in Ottawa, for in addition to Pearson's hesitations over NORAD, the United States had had to cope since the fall of 1963 with Canada's increasingly restless attitude towards NATO. Europe's economic recovery and growing integration made the North Atlantic alliance much less amenable to American domination. While the United States assumed the "western burden" in former European colonies like Vietnam and the Congo, decolonization offered Europe new freedom. The gradual emergence of détente in the wake of the Berlin and Cuban missile crises added to strained relations among the allies as they increasingly disagreed on how to deal with the Soviet Union. These structural obstacles to allied unity were exacerbated by growing divisions over NATO's strategic posture. The doctrine of "flexible response," for instance, raised questions about the willingness of the United States to risk its own security in defense of Europe. American efforts to resolve these divisions by promoting closer North Atlantic economic relations and by giving each member of the alliance some share in its nuclear planning through projects like the Multilateral Nuclear Force (MLF) were unsuccessful and stretched relations between Washington and Paris almost to the breaking point.

Although firmly committed to NATO, Pearson and Martin assumed office conscious of the need to address the growing tensions within the alliance. Sensitive to Soviet advances and disappointed over the lack of political consultation, the prime minister saw the pursuit of détente as a new and politically invigorating role for the alliance. In contrast, Martin saw the alliance as an important arena in which Canada could further develop its relations with France and forestall Quebec's efforts to develop its own international personality. Martin was also convinced that Canada was uniquely qualified to mediate between France and the United States. As he pointed out on more than one occasion, "we have a French population in Canada, [and] we think it helps us to understand the French ... the Americans have not understood sufficiently well how to handle the French effectively. It was not reasonable to expect a man like President Johnson to understand General de Gaulle."[45] Although the Canadian objectives – a renewed alliance and closer relations with France – sometimes collided uncomfortably, they had one thing in common: both goals irritated Washington, which suspected the government in Ottawa of subordinating Canada's international responsibilities to its domestic interests.

The government's concern with the future of France's relations with NATO grew throughout 1964. At the December ministerial meeting, Martin proposed and secured support for an exercise designed "to establish a set of principles or general guidelines which could form the basis for an examination of the future of the Alliance."[46] The minister also used the meeting to demonstrate to France that Paris was not alone in its opposition to American plans to meet European demands for a nuclear role through a revived MLF. The State Department, which had overcome its doubts about Martin's earlier initiative – "a proposal which is so vague and could lead to platitudes or premature discussion in NAC [the North Atlantic Council] of fundamental differences between member states" – in order not to offend Canada, was livid about Martin's verbal sallies at American expense.[47] The White House was also concerned. Although the United States was aware of Canada's practical objections to the MLF, Johnson had been led by Pearson's remarks at Hyannisport to believe that Canada's opposition would be muted and that he could hope "for as much understanding and support from Canada as possible." When McGeorge Bundy, the national security advisor, outlined the president's anxieties to Charles Ritchie, the Canadian ambassador to the United States replied that the United States must realize "that Canada was torn between her fervent belief in Atlantic integration and her necessary concern to avoid seeming to join in isolating France." He promised, however, to bring the White House's interest to Pearson's attention.[48]

Procedural bickering and the continuing controversy over the MLF and arrangements for nuclear sharing effectively postponed any discussion of Martin's initiative until the fall of 1965. By then, NATO's relations with France, which was rumoured to be preparing its own proposals for restructuring the alliance, were so strained that the exercise was quickly shelved as too divisive. However, as Washington and the other members of the alliance grew increasingly impatient with de Gaulle, the minister remained anxious to appease France. When de Gaulle abruptly announced his decision to withdraw France from NATO's integrated military structure in March 1966, Martin ensured that Canada's position was among the most moderate in the alliance. Cabinet agreed that Canada should seek "to limit the damage to the unity and effectiveness of the Alliance ... [and] accept without rancour and seek constructive adaptations to France's considered positions, even where they are in conflict with our own." Canada should "continue to demonstrate confidence in France as an ally ... leave the door open for the eventual return of France to full participation in the collective activities of the Alliance ... [and] continue, in spite of the NATO crisis, to develop our bilateral relations with France."[49]

To achieve its primary objective – the preservation of alliance unity and the maintenance of some form of French participation within NATO – Canada tried to moderate both the procedural and substantive positions for negotiating with Paris suggested in a British aide-mémoire that was circulating with the support of most other NATO delegations. Canada agreed with the general principles and future objectives as laid out in the British paper, but two aspects of the British position were worrying. Implicit in London's approach was the idea that Paris be presented with the minimum demands of the "fourteen," a tactic that seemed designed to provoke a confrontation with France. In discussions with the British, Martin counselled a more circumspect approach,

explaining that "it was particularly important for us in Canada to fos-
ter continued French association with the Alliance, otherwise we
would be misunderstood if we did not."[50]

More important, the British paper failed to address the problem of
East-West relations in a manner that would unite the alliance by
addressing France's desire to accelerate détente. Martin instructed
Canadian representatives in London, Washington, Brussels, and Bonn,
where governments were known to have the United Kingdom paper, to
make clear the Canadian view that "the political advantages of producing a good statement on [détente], and of having the statement
appear in the communiqué in the name of the Alliance as a whole justify a special effort both on what should be said and on obtaining
French concurrence. In this way the continuing solidarity of NATO will
be most effectively demonstrated, and at the same time de Gaulle's
effort to appropriate to himself the initiative in the field of East-West
relations will be contained and controlled."[51]

At the end of March 1966 Cabinet agreed that Canada should
strive to draft a ministerial statement on East-West relations that
would signal NATO's determination to address détente and constitute
a basis for compromise between the "fourteen" and the French. A
draft paragraph along these lines acknowledged that NATO was more
than simply a military alliance and welcomed any development that
might lead to improved relations with the Soviet bloc. It attempted to
reconcile the views of France, which insisted on its independent right
to pursue relations with the Eastern bloc, with those of the United
States, which favoured a collective approach to the problem of East-
West relations. Ottawa urged the members of NATO to "accept that
diversity of approach need not be a source of weakness. Their common objectives in the field of East-West relations can be pursued in
various ways including both bilateral and collective exchanges with
the Eastern countries. Continuous consultation in the alliance concerning developments in this field ensures that the collective interests
are fully protected."[52]

Canada's mediatory efforts were far from exhausted. Although the
American, German, British, and French foreign ministers reached the
major decisions on the procedures governing France's withdrawal
without substantial Canadian help, Martin frequently intervened in
the discussions. At the ministerial meeting in June 1966, he convinced
the "fourteen" to postpone a decision on moving the North Atlantic
Council from Paris to Brussels, thereby temporarily retaining a symbol of France's continuing political relationship with NATO.[53] The fate
of Canada's proposal on East-West relations, which was incorporated
in the final communiqué, was similarly gratifying.[54] Uppermost in

Martin's mind, as the American delegation noted with irritation, were the domestic considerations: "Persistent theme from Martin ... was his insistence that 14 must make no moves to pre-empt France in any decision not already taken by France. He insisted that Canadian Government, Parliament and people would not understand if there was any failure on the part of 14 to make every effort to salvage every possible French link with NATO."[55] In pursuing such a prominent and unpopular role, Canada incurred the wrath of most of its NATO allies. Rusk, whom the White House credited with holding the "'family of fourteen' together despite the stubborn sogginess of the Canadians," was especially irked and characterized Martin's approach as "being more royalist than the king." Canada, he concluded, would "require some special bilateral attention in the weeks to come."[56]

In this atmosphere, Pearson's decision to use a speech in Springfield, Illinois, to speculate about NATO's present problems and future directions was decidedly impolitic. In bemoaning the alliance's failure to evolve with the times, he seemed almost anxious to endorse de Gaulle's actions. He raised questions about Washington's leading role in the alliance and suggested that Europe's renewed strength might allow American and Canadian forces in Europe to be deployed elsewhere.[57]

The speech, which invited expressions of concern from several American officials, sent Canadian diplomats scrambling to develop a line of interpretation that would render Pearson's comments less harmful. Governor Averell Harriman, one of Johnson's stable of international trouble-shooters, quickly arranged to see the prime minister. He was pleased to learn that the speech reflected speculative thinking on Pearson's part but pointedly reminded him of the dangers of speaking his mind in public. In late June an assistant under-secretary of state for external affairs, H.B. Robinson, travelled to Washington to review NATO developments in more depth with Harriman and a high-powered American delegation that included senior officials from the State Department and the Pentagon. As the report from Washington made clear, the theme of the wide-ranging discussion was "burden-sharing." "There is a pervading consciousness in Washington of the heavy burden of responsibility now being carried by the United States," Robinson observed. "This stems predominantly from Vietnam but spills over into other fields, such as external aid and NATO ... the U.S. would need continuing and increasing support from its friends if the Administration were to be successful in persuading Congress to carry on even with the present U.S. efforts abroad. They feel very keenly that U.S. capacity and willingness to share generously in the burdens of providing global security may be circumscribed

by the unwillingness of its allies to accept responsibility for a proportionate share."[58]

Although Harriman levelled no specific charges against Canada, it
was not surprising that he should strike this note. The governor was
not alone. In view of the differences over peacekeeping, NORAD, and
NATO that had emerged between Ottawa and Washington since 1963,
several State Department officials had already started to consider how
Canada might best contribute to the defence of the free world. The
answers, however, were not as apparent as one might suppose. John
Leddy, head of the State Department bureau responsible for Canada,
first tackled the question in September 1965. Obviously, Ottawa's
frozen defence budget, Canada's ill-equipped military forces, and the
country's reluctance to accept its nuclear responsibilities constituted
damning evidence that "in terms of Free World foreign policy aims, as
the U.S. sees them, Canada's performance leaves something to be
desired."[59]

This analysis, however, was only one side of the equation. On most
major foreign policy questions, Leddy contended that "Canadian
hearts are in the right place." What American policymakers needed to
understand was that there were sound domestic political reasons why
Canadian leaders were instinctively and unconsciously reluctant simply
to echo American foreign policy. Not least, he pointed out, was the
desire of Canadians, particularly English Canadians, to use foreign
policy to assert Canada's uniqueness. "As Canada is a nation without
heroes or unique institutions ... foreign policy appears to [them] to be
one of the few vehicles which [they] can use to raise a distinctive voice
both at home and in international councils."

In order to develop and maintain a distinctive foreign policy, Canada was inclined to assume roles and responsibilities that, even though
they met American objectives and were frequently encouraged by
Washington, allowed Canada to operate in a more independent fashion. Canada's commitment to the United Nations, for instance, was
"whole-hearted," and its extensive peacekeeping duties were undertaken with "good grace." Moreover, under Pearson Canadian foreign
aid had shown "considerable improvement ... in the amount of aid and
its form." Canada also supplied considerable military assistance to
Tanzania and Malaysia. If the United States was dissatisfied with
Canada's effort on behalf of the free world, part of the problem lay in
Washington's unwillingness to recognize and account for the factors
that determined Canadian foreign policy. The search for a solution,
concluded Leddy, would need to begin in Washington: "Obviously
Canada can do more to support Free World objectives, but before we
as a Government seek ways of persuading them to do more ... we ought

to take a careful look at what roles, in the large sense, we wish Canada to play. For example, should its armed forces emphasize peace-keeping or NATO? Are nuclear-capable weapons in Canadian hands important to the defense of the West or not? Should Canada be encouraged to play a larger role in the Commonwealth, where they could be grateful for the absence of the U.S. ... or should Canada devote more of its attention and money to, say, Latin America?"

In his annual report for 1965, Butterworth adopted a similar theme. The time had come for Washington to review its approach to bilateral defence relations. Throughout 1965 the United States had faced obstacles in securing cooperation in NORAD, and Canada's commitments to NATO remained only partially fulfilled. Moreover, complained the ambassador, the prime minister seemed anxious to withdraw Canadian troops from Europe. "In short," concluded Butterworth, "no likelihood was seen in 1965 that Canada might eventually assume a proportionate share of the military burden of the Western Alliance. The emphasis in Canada's present defence policy continues to be participation in UN peacekeeping operations."[60]

Butterworth thought that the United States should continue to press Canada to assume its share of the cost of Western defence, but he wondered "whether our policy is fully up-to-date and realistic." As the two countries adopted increasingly different defence priorities, it was more important than ever before that Washington "know precisely what we want the Canadians to do and that what we ask is necessary and reasonable." Did it make sense to alienate Canadian authorities by pressuring them to purchase a costly follow-on aircraft to the CF-101 fighter when the United States was in the midst of cutting back its own defences against manned bombers? Would NATO really require Canadian aircraft in a nuclear strike role by the time the CF-104 was obsolete? Perhaps there were other roles for Canada? These questions underlined the need to review "our policy with respect to Canada's contributions to NATO and NORAD. We are going to have difficulties with Canadians in defense matters in any case, and I consider it urgently essential that we have the most up-to-date, persuasively realistic defense policy to pursue here which it is possible to devise if we are to accomplish our purpose."

Butterworth's recommendations were received warmly in the State Department. The question of renewing the NORAD agreement, which was due to expire in 1968, lent added urgency to the review that finally got underway in August 1966. On the whole, the completed study, which was drafted by James Goodby of the State Department's Policy Planning Council with help from the European branch and the Department of Defense, was optimistic about future bilateral defence relations: "There are reasons enough ... to be apprehensive, if not down-right discouraged, about the future. This paper concludes, however, that current trends in Canadian defense policy are not likely to be reversed. And it is suggested not only that the United States can live with these trends but also that Canada's defence policies may turn out to be good for us as well as good for Canadians."[61]

In support of this conclusion, Goodby began by explaining to his American readers the fundamental tensions that threatened Canada's existence. Close economic and cultural ties with the much larger and overwhelming United States, as well as continued French-English tensions, "undermined the psychological foundations of Canadian nationhood." Postwar Canadian politicians, Liberal and Conservative alike, have tried to counter these domestic strains by pursuing "an independent and influential role in world affairs." Canada's defence posture has been directed, in NATO and especially at the UN, "toward providing the means for an active foreign policy."

The final result of this search was the 1964 *White Paper on Defence*. In Goodby's view the promised reorganization of Canada's forces into mobile and flexible units that were suited more to peacekeeping than to Canada's traditional roles in NATO and NORAD reflected "a significant shift in Canada's view of its proper role in the world, generally in the direction of a peculiarly Canadian, nationalistic approach to defence questions." At the same time, a very low ceiling was placed on the Canadian defence budget as the federal government tried to resolve Canada's domestic tensions by directing more money to the provinces and into social programs. As these two developments reflected deep-rooted pressures within the Canadian federation, they would not and could not be swept away. The implications for the United States seemed obvious. Rather than trying to "induce the Canadians to return to the kind of comfortable junior partnership arrangement which has been typical in the past ... the United States may find that it must be more selective in what it asks Canada to do in the defense field and that [it] must become more accustomed to 'leading from the rear.'"

Washington should begin to accommodate Canada's new defence and foreign policy postures by acknowledging frankly that while the two countries have a mutual interest in a number of different defence relationships, they accorded these partnerships different priorities. Washington maintained that Canada and the United States shared a common interest in defending the North American continent, in deterring Soviet aggression in Western Europe, and "in encouraging social, political, and economic progress in the developing areas of the world while avoiding the violence and disorder which might bring major powers into collision with each other." Canada, however, reversed the order Washington assigned these three priorities.

Developing a working and successful defence partnership, Goodby pointed out, would mean working with Ottawa's priorities and exploring how Canada could contribute to American objectives on its own terms. Washington should recognize that Canada's plan to reorganize its military into mobile and flexible units could be a source of American and Western strength. After all, Goodby reminded his readers, "this Canadian philosophy fits neatly with our own perception of the kind of wars that are most likely in the future ... [and] a military posture which appeals to the special Canadian outlook and which could augment our own limited war and peacekeeping capabilities especially for use where a U.S. presence might not be desirable, ought to be as important to us as it is to the Canadians."

Rather than press Ottawa to strengthen its forces to meet Soviet aggression (especially when Washington was not able to convince the Europeans to augment their defences), the United States ought to encourage Canada's new defence posture. Washington should also press Ottawa to fulfil the promises it made in the 1964 white paper to equip these forces properly. Over the long run, the United States should encourage Canada to play a military role that extended beyond simply peacekeeping for the UN. Canada might be persuaded to supply a mobile force to extinguish a "brushfire" war in a Commonwealth country or to restore order at the behest of an established government in the developing world. There were limits implicit in asking Canada to assume a greater share in policing the world's trouble spots: "Naturally, we will not convince Canada that its interests are everywhere the same as ours, but there should be enough instances of overlapping viewpoints to make a Canadian peacekeeping role outside the UN an important adjunct to our own efforts."

Having accepted that a substantial part of Canada's military effort would be directed towards peacekeeping, the State Department's study further acknowledged the need to accept adjustments in Canada's contribution to NATO and NORAD. The United States could easily afford to allow Canada to opt out of its nuclear role in NATO and should stop regarding "the acceptance of nuclear weapons ... as a test of Canada's fidelity to the United States." Instead, as questions were raised in Canada about the Canadian presence in Europe, Washington should concentrate on encouraging Canada to maintain its brigade group in West Germany. From a military perspective, the departure of the Canadian brigade would substantially weaken NATO's forces on the North German Plain and "would reinforce the tendency of the smaller European countries to cut back their contributions." In turn, this would promote American-German bilateralism and weaken the alliance as a whole. Washington should exploit Canada's interest in maintaining "its political membership and influence in NATO" and make the Canadian government aware that anything smaller than a brigade "would hardly be noticeable in either military or political terms."

Goodby's study adopted similarly reduced expectations about Canada's contribution to NORAD. It was no longer clear that the United States required nuclear storage facilities in Canada or that Canada's contribution to North American defence required the use of nuclear weapons. Indeed, the study dispassionately concluded that a host of technological changes might even eliminate the need for NORAD altogether. Improved long-range interceptors, for instance, would soon reduce the need for forward air defence bases in northern Canada. The diminishing Soviet bomber threat also lessened the need for interceptor aircraft and bases. Moreover, while it might be helpful to have Canada's assistance in watching for the new threat posed by Soviet and Chinese missiles, it was no longer necessary. Missiles could be tracked from bases in the United States and from airborne warning and control systems (AWACS). An antiballistic missile (ABM) system could probably be stationed successfully in the United States alone. Finally, improvements in nonnuclear ASW weapons would soon render the need for American nuclear ASW storage facilities in Canada obsolete. Goodby concluded that "the only absolutely essential requirement we ... have to levy on the Canadians would be use of their air space. Everything beyond this would appear to be a bonus ... pleasant to have but not at the price of cutting back Canadian efforts in other fields." Nevertheless, with this fairly flexible bottom line in mind, there were good reasons why the United States should pursue NORAD's renewal. The agreement was beneficial to both countries "as a means of facilitating U.S. retention or acquisition of certain military rights in Canada, as a means of communication and consultation, and, in general, as a symbol of cooperation."

By the time the Goodby study was completed in the spring of 1967, Pearson's government was finding it difficult to meet even these diminished expectations. Throughout 1966 and early 1967, American excesses in Southeast Asia and the apparent thaw in Western relations with the Soviet Union reduced popular support for Canada's military alliance with the United States. Popular attitudes towards NORAD's nuclear weapons, which many feared made it more difficult to resolve East-West differences, shifted profoundly (table 1).[62]

A younger generation of scholars who did not share the wartime and postwar experiences that shaped the world view of most senior Canadian policymakers mounted a sustained attack on Canada's role in

Table 1   Acceptance of Nuclear Weapons by the Canadian Public

	November 1962	March 1963	June 1966
Yes	54.4	48.6	34.4
No	31.6	31.0	43.8
No opinion	8.2	14.0	17.5
Qualified	5.6	3.5	4.1
Rejects		2.5	
Total	99.8	99.1	99.8

both NORAD and NATO. In 1966 two of the earliest critics, Lloyd Axworthy and John Warnock, urged the government to scrap NORAD because it was "useless" in light of the declining bomber threat. More important, it symbolically linked Canada to Washington's military adventurism in Southeast Asia.[63] They were joined in their attack by the New Democratic Party (NDP), which moved from moderate support for NORAD in 1963 to strong opposition by 1966. The party's defence critic, Andrew Brewin, described the agreement as "obsolete" and urged the government to direct more of the country's efforts towards United Nations peacekeeping.[64]

At the same time, public doubts about NATO were expressed with increasing frequency. In the wake of France's withdrawal from the alliance, the influential University of Toronto political scientist Stephen Clarkson demanded that Ottawa reexamine its commitment to NATO. In the House of Commons, Brewin left no doubt about where the NDP stood: "We should withdraw our brigade and air divisions from Europe ... [and] concentrate on a tri-service, unified, slightly armed, highly mobile force available for peace keeping and other intervention roles."[65] Within a year a small but important group of Progressive Conservatives had also begun to question Canada's attachment to NATO. The party's president, Dalton Camp, gave voice to this view when he observed that the "psychological, political and military reasons for Canada's military presence in Europe may have already disappeared."[66]

By the spring of 1967 criticism of NORAD and NATO was heard more and more often at the cabinet table. Ministers like Pierre Trudeau, Gerard Pelletier, and Jean Marchand, who had never agreed with Pearson's decision in 1963 to accept nuclear warheads for Canadian forces, found a champion for their views in Walter Gordon. Gordon, who had rejoined the Cabinet in January 1967 and had became president of the privy council in April, was increasingly anxious to press upon the government a more "independent" foreign policy.

The prime minister, who continued to entertain his own doubts about the nature of Canada's commitment to NATO and NORAD, was certainly aware of the shifting balance of opinion in Cabinet. Following a British and American decision in April 1967 to reduce their force levels in continental Europe, he wrote Martin to express concern over "the developing inflexibility of our position re: Canadian forces with NATO." He added, "I think that we should give consideration to our own position; especially the maintenance overseas of RCAF squadrons in a nuclear attack role."[67] Martin responded vigorously and challenged the prime minister's premise regarding the "inflexibility" of Canada's NATO contribution, pointing out that in 1967 alone the government had reduced from eight to six the number of air squadrons in Europe. He also noted that further cuts to Canada's forces in Europe were anticipated. Greater reductions than those now being considered, the minister warned, "would open us to USA pressure to help carry the 'Western burden' elsewhere, perhaps in South-East Asia where the British are withdrawing. Rapid withdrawal from Europe would also expose us to a scale of commitment for a Vietnam peacekeeping operation which would be costly to maintain in both financial and manpower terms."[68]

Pearson acquiesced and let the issue drop for the time being; other members of Cabinet did not. On 12 and 13 May 1967, Gordon delivered two speeches on Canadian foreign policy to audiences in southern Ontario. In one he criticized Ottawa's support for American policy in Vietnam. In the other he questioned Canadian participation in NATO and NORAD, two alliances that he clearly felt symbolized American domination. Gordon wondered whether Canada should maintain air squadrons in Europe. The answer was obvious: "The French don't want us; the countries of Western Europe are now quite prosperous enough to maintain their own defence establishments if they wish to; both the U.S. and Britain have stated their intention to withdraw some of their troops from Europe. In these circumstances what is the sensible thing and the right thing to do?"[69]

Referring to the continuing uncertainty in the United States over the possibility of deploying an expensive ABM system, Gordon speculated that the "alternative for a country of our size may be to opt out of the contest altogether on the grounds that if there should ever be a nuclear war between the U.S. and the Soviet Union, there would be nothing effective we could do about it anyway. In circumstances such as these, Canada, instead of stepping up her defence budget considerably, might decide to concentrate her efforts on the maintenance of mobile peacekeeping or peace-restoring units to be available to the United Nations."[70]

Martin and Hellyer were furious. So too was Pearson, although he was increasingly sympathetic to Gordon's views, especially on the conflict in Vietnam. In a public statement rebuking his Cabinet colleague, the prime minister declared that Gordon's speeches went beyond "anything we have discussed – let alone decided – in the Cabinet as to what we should do about NORAD, NATO, and U.S. policy in Vietnam."[71]

Both NATO and NORAD, however, were on the Cabinet's agenda before the end of the month. On the basis of discussions between the State Department and the Department of Defense during the first stages of the Goodby study, the United States had decided in September 1966 to ask Canada to begin talks on renewing NORAD with suitable provisions for incorporating an ABM system if the two countries decided to deploy one. Canada's cautious response to the American overture reflected the country's growing unease with the alliance. Martin, who thought that the United States had approached the question of NORAD's renewal in a very circumspect manner, was anxious to cooperate. Potential domestic criticism might be muted, he thought, if Ottawa went no further at this stage than informing the State Department that Canada had commissioned interdepartmental studies on the future of air defence that assumed "continued Canadian participation in the integrated air defence of the continent ... after 1968." The prime minister concurred but warned the Canadian delegation to the PJBD meeting in October 1966 to avoid saying anything "at this stage which would prejudice our position in regard to the changes we might wish to make to the present form of air defence integration through NORAD."[72]

Pearson's doubts about NORAD continued to hinder the efforts of Martin and Hellyer to adopt a more forthcoming position for the next meeting of the PJBD in February 1967. The two ministers based their positions on recent studies by the Department of National Defence that concluded "that regardless of changes in the threat, or in the nature of the defences, there will be a continuing need for an automatic, integrated response system." They recommended to Pearson that Canada inform the Americans that, while Ottawa continued to study the future of NORAD, the government had concluded that "the principles of the present NORAD Agreement are as valid today as they were in 1958."[73] Pearson was not convinced. After reassuring Gordon that there would be a full debate in Cabinet on NORAD, he summoned Martin and officials from the Department of External Affairs and told them that he would not approve the renewal of NORAD until Ottawa was given more information on American plans to deploy an ABM system. In the meantime, he could not argue in Cabinet that the present principles remained valid, and he instructed the minister that Canada was "to express no views one way or the other with regard to any suggestion that might be made concerning the extension of the NORAD Agreement either in duration or in responsibilities and activities."[74]

The information that Pearson wanted on American plans for the proposed ABM system was obtained in early April when Hellyer met the American secretary of defense, Robert McNamara, in Washington. The American explained that current plans called for the deployment of an ABM system in the United States only. Naturally, Canada would be welcome to join the system at a later stage, but for the time being the question of an ABM system should not get tangled up in the discussions on NORAD's renewal.[75] The prime minister remained sceptical and thought that the ad hoc system for North American air defence in place before 1958 would do just fine. Nevertheless, he agreed to let Martin and Hellyer put the question of NORAD's renewal to Cabinet in preparation for the June meeting of the PJBD.

Well aware that Gordon's May speech reflected the mounting opposition in Cabinet to NORAD, Martin proceeded with considerable caution. His submission to Cabinet was modest. He reassured his colleagues that there were no plans to have NORAD include ABM defences. He informed them that the bomber threat would continue simply because the Soviet Union would not put all its eggs in the missile basket. To counter that threat and mobilize quickly and effectively, the defences of Canada and the United States required the kind of integrated command that NORAD currently provided. The alliance placed no specific demands on Canada, although there was an "implicit obligation ... to contribute in some fashion to North American air defence be it equipment, air space, bases, etc."

Allowing NORAD to lapse would only make bilateral relations more difficult for Canada, since it would continue to be confronted with American demands for help in defending the continent. Instead of having to deal with one overarching agreement, the government would be faced with the prospect of negotiating several individual agreements on such questions as overflights, nuclear authorization and consultation, and American bases. Each agreement exposed the government to potential domestic political pressure and placed additional strain on the country's relations with the United States. Moreover, added Martin, allowing NORAD to lapse might well provoke Washington into cancelling the joint defence production agreements of 1959 and 1963. While there was little scope for amending what was a very basic agreement, he tried to mollify the opponents of the treaty by suggesting that Canada could shorten the term of the agreement and add a termination clause. Setting aside the future of NORAD for the moment, Martin urged Cabinet at least to allow him to inform Washington that Canada "intends to cooperate with the United States in continental air defence."[76]

In addition to this memorandum on the future of NORAD, the Cabinet had before it instructions for the forthcoming NATO ministerial meeting. Martin, with the blessing of the prime minister, was anxious to weigh Cabinet support for Gordon's view of the alliance. In the relatively routine document that asked Cabinet to approve the delegation's instructions, Martin outlined his current thinking on the force levels for Canada's contribution to NATO for the next five years. The reductions in Canada's commitment to NATO were small. While the brigade group would remain in West Germany, the number of RCAF squadrons stationed in Europe would decline from six to four. Even this minor change would be subject to consultation and negotiation among the allies.[77]

For those responsible for Canada's relations with the United States, the results of the meeting were deeply disturbing. The Cabinet deliberations took place against the backdrop of the war in Vietnam. The French Canadian ministers, especially Marchand and Trudeau, questioned the five-year commitment. Other ministers suggested using the newly created Mobile Command Force to fulfil the Canadian commitment to NATO from bases in Canada. The reaction was so hostile that Martin decided not to seek approval for the five-year commitment.[78] NORAD fared slightly better. Cabinet authorized Martin to inform the United States that Canada would cooperate in an unspecified manner in the defence of North America. However, as Arnold Heeney, who succeeded Wilgress as the chairman of the Canadian section of the PJBD in early 1967, observed, this decision "did little more than gain us further time for dealing with the U.S. authorities."[79]

Neither Pearson nor Martin had any trouble grasping the significance of this temporary setback. The prime minister was particularly concerned with the division between Martin and Gordon and suggested that they attend the forthcoming meeting of NATO foreign ministers in Luxembourg together.[80] The trip did little to reduce Gordon's hostility toward the alliance. On the way back to Canada, he asked Robinson to meet with him, Trudeau, and Marchand to discuss NATO and NORAD. These unorthodox consultations, which were carried on throughout the summer, relieved some of Gordon's concerns, and by August "Gordon and company" were ready to accept "the idea of an evolutionary approach to the contribution of forces in Europe." Moreover, "they would not oppose a renewal of NORAD provided there was a reservation about ABMS and a suitable termination clause."[81]

Still, Martin and Hellyer were taking no chances. In early September, they presented Cabinet with four detailed and lengthy memoranda on NATO and NORAD. The first submission, on which no decision was required, placed NATO and NORAD in their larger context as part of Canada's postwar effort to erect an effective system of collective security and sought to illustrate how they contributed to Canada's foreign policy objectives:

For Canada, collective defence arrangements not only contribute to our own security but also represent one of the ways in which we have sought to play an international role recognized as being responsible. At the same time, in relation to the United States, these commitments have enabled Canada to maintain its sovereignty and have obtained for us a measure of influence with the United States Government. By accepting commitments in Europe, Canada has been able to develop its links with the area in which its principle overseas interests lie. A drastic unilateral reduction in the Canadian contribution to collective defence either in Europe or North America would mean that we could no longer contribute to our own security and would reduce the general effectiveness of Canadian foreign policy.[82]

The second and third memoranda focused directly on NATO and the immediate question of Canada's submission of a five-year plan to the NATO forces review. Although they acknowledged that the military threat that NATO was formed to counter was less immediate than it had been in 1949, they contended that "the improved climate of East-West relations depended on the maintenance of sufficient force in the West to balance the Soviet Union." The desire to improve East-West relations had to be weighed against the fact that "major force reductions or withdrawals can only be safely undertaken in the West if they are in some way balanced by corresponding action by the Soviet Union." This balance, cautioned the memoranda, must not be upset by unilateral troop reductions, lest "we ... give up our bargaining power, and at the same time tip the local power balance in the Soviet favour."

These two memoranda also presented specific arguments against Canadian withdrawal. Membership in NATO fostered relations with Europe that "offset the preponderant United States influence on Canada." It also provided a forum where smaller powers could influence the policies of larger ones and where Canada could "secure a voice in an eventual European settlement." Moreover, because Canada did not have the same resources as France to direct towards its own deterrent, the alliance represented a relatively inexpensive solution to the problem of Canadian security. "In sum," concluded the memoranda, "while

Canada might continue to be accepted as a member of NATO if it limited its defence activity to contributing to North American defence, we should lose those important political advantages which flow from our contributions to the defence of Europe."[83]

There was little debate. Martin argued that Canada's small contribution to Europe "carried with it very considerable influence" and warned that Canada's withdrawal might well cause the alliance to disintegrate. With a nod of support from Mitchell Sharp, the minister of finance, he underlined how low Canadian defence expenditures actually were. The only opposition came from Walter Gordon, who repeated yet again his view that altered international circumstances demanded a change in Canadian policy. At this point the prime minister intervened quickly and decisively. Canada's present contribution represented, he said, "the minimum price for club membership." Canada's withdrawal from Europe would leave an alliance dominated by "the United States and Germany, with the United Kingdom acting as a junior partner and France withdrawing completely." This, he insisted, would destroy NATO. Cabinet approved continued membership in NATO and the level of contributions requested.

The fourth and final memorandum under consideration asked Cabinet to authorize negotiations with the United States for the renewal of NORAD on the basis of the existing agreement.[84] While there was little opposition, several members of the Cabinet took the opportunity to remind Martin and Hellyer that they would only approve an agreement that was limited to a five-year term with a termination clause allowing either party to abrogate the agreement with one year's notice. Gordon unrealistically insisted that this decision did not commit the government to concluding an agreement with the United States.

The actual negotiations for the new NORAD agreement were easy and straightforward. The Canadian position was presented to the Americans at the PJBD meeting in late September, where it quickly removed much of the tension that had begun to cloud bilateral defence relations. Although American defence planners worried that the five-year term proposed by Ottawa was too short to allow for effective bilateral planning, the United States agreed not to counter-offer. By early February 1968, a draft agreement was ready for Cabinet. With the addition of clauses that terminated the pact in five years and specifically excluded ABM systems from its purview, the agreement was "substantially" the same as the treaty of 1958.[85]

However, as Martin prepared to present the new text to Cabinet, Gordon retreated from his September position of reluctantly supporting NORAD's renewal. In a letter to Pearson, he advanced several reasons for now opposing renewal. He reiterated his concern about the cost of air defence and the prospect of updating the nuclear-armed BOMARC missiles and Canadian interceptors. He continued to wonder whether NORAD was still useful in the missile age. He was inclined to think that it was not and that NORAD's renewal would eventually lead to a North American ABM system. However, the real reason for his opposition was the continuing war in Vietnam. Citing rumours that the United States was thinking of using tactical nuclear weapons in Southeast Asia and that the Pentagon would like to provoke a nuclear war with China, Gordon implied that renewing a military alliance with the United States might drag Canada into a nuclear war in Asia.[86]

Gordon was alone in his opposition to renewing NORAD. When Cabinet met in late February to discuss the issue, only Pearson agreed with Gordon's suggestion that the decision be left over for the new government. When Gordon insisted that there be a full discussion on NORAD's renewal, debate was inconclusively adjourned. Gordon was tired, and when he saw Pearson later that evening, he explained that he would continue to oppose NORAD in view of the Vietnam conflict, even though the Cabinet, the caucus, and the public seemed to support it. However, he did not wish to upset the government as the prime minister prepared to retire, and he asked Pearson to delay its final approval until his resignation, submitted two weeks earlier, had taken effect.[87] Pearson agreed. He accepted Gordon's resignation on 11 March 1968, delaying formal approval for NORAD's extension until 14 March 1968.

Not all Canadians were convinced that Pearson's government had gone far enough in adjusting Canadian defence and foreign policies to take into account the declining Soviet threat, Europe's recovery, and domestic pressures for a distinctly Canadian approach to the world. In April 1968 Trudeau, newly elected leader of the Liberal Party, expressed his desire for real and far-reaching change: "Most of our foreign policy today is based on ... pre-war premises or immediate postwar premises ... complete re-assessment is needed."[88] Some American observers were similarly unhappy with the Pearson government's altered approach to defence and foreign policy questions. Butterworth's assessment was blunt:

Canada's progressive withdrawal toward neutralism and its greater willingness to let the U.S. and others bear the burdens of security should make us take a new, clear look at our northern neighbour, good and grey as he used to be remembered. We have to keep in mind that an attack from our two most likely mortal enemies would no doubt include flights over the pole and Canada. Our trade and investment ties with Canada and its economy are so many and bulk so large that we should think what kind of place it is and what dependence we can or dare place on it.[89]

Clearly, bilateral disagreements over Canada's proper role in the Western alliance would continue. However, the 1960s made it equally clear that there was scope for Canada to pursue its own foreign and defence policies without jeopardizing bilateral relations. Under Pearson and Johnson, Ottawa and Washington began the difficult process of adjusting the close postwar military and political alliance in ways that made sense to both partners. This was never easy, but a willingness to accommodate each others' legitimate interests made it possible for the two countries to reconcile most of their foreign and defence policy differences.

CHAPTER FIVE

The Asian Conundrum

Throughout the mid-1960s the bilateral effort to reapportion Canada's contribution to Western defence and to shape a new North American defence relationship was complicated by Washington's growing preoccupation with the war in Southeast Asia. President Johnson's decision in July 1965 to escalate the war in Vietnam placed that conflict and Western relations with the People's Republic of China at the centre of domestic politics in both the United States and Canada. Canadian anxiety about Washington's seemingly irrational determination to continue excluding Peking from the international community reached new levels during the decade. More important, the growing public opposition to the Vietnam War raised questions about the very nature of American society and Canada's relationship with it.

Pearson's government was caught between domestic demands for a distinctive response to the Asian crisis (one that reflected Canada's evolving self-image as a peacemaker) and Washington's expectations about the behaviour of a close and loyal ally. As the war intensified, there was clearly little chance that sharply divergent Canadian and American views on the Far East could be reconciled. Instead, differences over Asia needed to be managed constantly and carefully contained. More and more preoccupied with the search for peace in Vietnam, the secretary of state for external affairs, Paul Martin, was inclined to overlook this important bilateral truth. Pearson was not, though his room to manoeuver was constrained by his complicated relationship with Martin. Friends and rivals for many years, the two men respected one another's abilities. Yet Pearson did not completely trust Martin's political instincts; in turn, the prime minister's successes were sometimes resented by his foreign minister. The reserve that characterized their uncertain partnership and a reluctance to undermine his minister's authority obliged Pearson to tread cautiously when he entered Martin's domain. Nevertheless, the prime minister increasingly seized control of Canada's Asian policy, deflecting his foreign minister's efforts to pursue a course in the Pacific independent of American interests in the region. Pearson resisted popular pressure to adopt extreme positions, and in so doing, by the end of 1966, he had largely disarmed the threat posed by the war to relations between the two North American governments.

By the time that Pearson's government assumed office in the spring of 1963, the continuing crisis in Southeast Asia had already become a fixture on the Canada–United States bilateral agenda. For almost a decade the two countries had worked together in the uneasy peace that followed the signing of the Geneva Accords in 1954. As the Western representative on the three ineffectual international commissions established to oversee the provisions of the cease-fire agreements in Laos, Cambodia, and Vietnam, Canada had watched with mounting frustration as communist insurgents worked with effective impunity to undermine the Geneva settlements in Indochina.[1] For just as long, the United States had sought, through an array of military assistance programs and an ever-growing number of military advisors, to create a stable, independent, and anticommunist South Vietnam. Exposed to the same influences and exchanging information regularly, Canada and the United States shared the view that the Viet Cong insurgency in South Vietnam was inspired and supported by communist Hanoi.

Washington's failure to secure the kind of stability in South Vietnam in the early 1960s that was a prerequisite for an effective anticommunist campaign worried the new prime minister. Pearson harboured doubts about the nature and legitimacy of the American role in Asia, reflecting his experiences during the Korean War. During his meeting with Kennedy at Hyannisport, he reportedly encouraged the American president to abandon South Vietnam.[2] Paul Martin and his officials in the Department of External Affairs, on the other hand, were much more sanguine about American policy in Vietnam. Despite the collapse of the corrupt and ineffective regime of Ngo Dinh Diem in an American-sponsored coup in November 1963 and despite the rapid succession of military coups that followed, Martin and his principal advisors retained their confidence in Washington's ability to handle the crisis in South Vietnam. "The U.S.A attitude on Vietnam at present," the Canadian Embassy in Washington reported in early 1964, "appears to be characterized by a mixture of caution, patience and determination."[3]

Washington's desire to show Hanoi how determined it was not to allow communist insurgents to take over South Vietnam precipitated Ottawa's increasingly direct involvement in Southeast Asia in the spring of 1964. In a late-April meeting with Pearson and Martin, the American secretary of state, Dean Rusk, asked for Canada's help in ensuring that Hanoi understood the United States position. Rusk, whose approach was designed to soothe any possible Canadian concerns, stressed that Washington was determined to work within the existing Geneva framework. The United States was not anxious to widen the war but wished simply to tell Hanoi "that it would be wrong for the Viet Minh to expect that the United States were getting discouraged and were thinking of pulling out. It was important for them to realize that if they didn't put a stop to their operations they would be in deep trouble." Rusk asked the Canadians to send Blair Seaborn, who was soon to replace Gordon Cox as Canada's representative to the ICSC, to Vietnam as quickly as possible and to authorize him to act as an intermediary between Washington and Hanoi. The two Canadians readily concurred.[4]

Despite the forthcoming position adopted by Pearson and Martin, Rusk suspected that Ottawa would place clearly defined limits on its cooperation. He was right. In late May, Pearson met secretly with President Johnson in New York to review the general lines of the Seaborn mission. The prime minister agreed with the president's determination to avoid withdrawing from Vietnam and carefully endorsed the use of conventional bombing "if [the] action could be carefully limited and directed [to] the interdiction of supply lines from North to South." He cautioned Johnson against the use of tactical nuclear weapons, an idea then being touted by Republican presidential candidate Senator Barry Goldwater, and warned "that any drastic escalation would give great problems both in Canada and internationally."[5] The boundaries of Canadian cooperation were clearly laid out.

Simultaneously, Martin and his officials met in Ottawa with William Sullivan, Rusk's special advisor on Vietnam and head of the interagency Vietnamese Coordinating Committee. Officials quickly established the ground rules that would govern Seaborn's employment; not unexpectedly, the Canadians insisted that all communication with Seaborn pass through Ottawa, while Sullivan stressed the importance of transmitting American messages as faithfully as possible, whatever the Canadian government might think of them.[6] Martin was irritated and suspicious at the lapse in time between Rusk's initial approach in April and the present exercise in briefing Seaborn. The foreign minister wondered whether the mission had already been left too late. Twice during the meeting, he emphasized the domestic problems that would be created by an American decision to intensify the war. "The Opposition tended to be suspicious of United States policy in Indochina," Martin explained, warning that "he would find it difficult to condone ... direct [United States] intervention."[7] Like Pearson, Martin used the Seaborn mission as an opportunity to establish the limits of Canadian support.

The results of Seaborn's first visit to North Vietnam seemed likely to assuage Canadian fears. In a meeting with the North Vietnamese prime minister, Pham Van Dong, Seaborn delivered the American message, which underscored the administration's determination to defend South Vietnam, the consequences that would follow continued aggression, and the material benefits that would flow to Hanoi from a peaceful accommodation. Although the encounter resulted in no change to Hanoi's position, Ottawa was pleased that Pham Van Dong was ready to meet Seaborn again and that a channel had been successfully established between Washington and Hanoi.[8]

For different reasons, Washington was also grimly satisfied. By midsummer the administration had forged a "scenario" according to which the president, after securing a congressional resolution authorizing him to act, would launch a series of graduated air strikes against targets in North Vietnam. Seaborn's report confirmed the American view of an intransigent North Vietnam and the need to carry the war northward.[9] In August 1964 the United States was given cause for action when the administration concluded that North Vietnamese torpedo boats had attacked the USS *Maddox* in international waters off the coast of North Vietnam.

From the Canadian perspective, the American reaction to the Gulf of Tonkin crisis was measured and reassuring. Rusk, on Johnson's instructions, informed Pearson personally of the attack. The United States intended to respond, "but would ensure that the retaliation was relevant to the provocation and to the attack."[10] Charles Ritchie found the same considered tones echoed in discussions with members of the administration. "My impression ... is that the USA is fully aware of the gravity of the steps it has felt forced to take."[11] Well within the limits established by Pearson and Martin in the spring, United States bombing strikes in the fall of 1964 had little immediate impact on Canadian policy. If anything, by signalling the American intention to respond militarily to North Vietnamese aggression, the crisis reinforced Ottawa's inclination to lend Washington a helping hand. Nowhere, perhaps, was this more apparent than on the ground in Vietnam, where the Canadian representative to the ICSC redoubled his efforts to have the commission "take account of communist infringements of [the] Geneva Agreement, and build up a record of meaningful findings."[12] At the same time, Ottawa announced that it would substantially increase its nonmilitary aid to South Vietnam.[13]

Even as it brought Canada's public posture more closely into line with Washington's more aggressive attitude toward North Vietnam, Ottawa was becoming worried about the course of American policy. In the aftermath of the Gulf of Tonkin crisis, Canadian observers had watched Washington's interest in using the Seaborn channel evaporate but had remained hopeful that the United States might become more accommodating after the November presidential election.[14] However, by early December it was clear that the election had produced no desire among American officials for serious talks with Hanoi. Only after repeated Canadian prompting did the United States agree in mid-December to send another message to Hanoi through Seaborn.[15] Washington added nothing new to this message and even diminished its significance by insisting that Seaborn deliver it as his own personal estimate of American determination.[16] Canadian officials were disappointed at Washington's obvious lack of sincerity and resented its patronizing attitude towards the Canadian channel. These sentiments were accompanied by a growing sense that American officials were less than frank in discussing the evolving nature of United States policy in Vietnam.[17]

Pearson was even more uneasy than Martin and his officials in the East Block. His January 1965 meeting with Johnson at the LBJ Ranch in Texas stripped away the veneer of correctness that had defined their first two meetings and exposed their profound differences in outlook and temperament. Dressed in a formal black suit and diplomat's homburg, Pearson was discomfited on arriving at the ranch to discover the president in a cowboy suit. A barrage of television cameras awaited the two men, whose meeting began poorly when Johnson introduced Pearson as "Prime Minister Wilson." There was no time during the two-day meeting for the kind of leisurely, wide-ranging discussion of international developments that Pearson enjoyed. Instead, loaded into three cars, Johnson and Pearson, the "press," and the "ladies" embarked on a whirlwind tour of the ranch. The president dispensed drinks liberally and swore loudly. Dinner was a hurried and informal affair; steak and catfish on the same plate. Throughout, aides and valets bustled about and telephones rang. "General MacArthur would not have approved, nor, I suspect," Pearson observed, "John Kennedy."[18] The visit left him feeling deeply disturbed.

In early February 1965, the war in South Vietnam entered a new and more dangerous phase when Washington responded to a Viet Cong raid on the American base at Pleiku with a limited campaign of air strikes against North Vietnam. Within days, this series of raids was replaced by the gradually intensifying bombing campaign that signalled the start of Operation Rolling Thunder. Pearson tried to discuss the situation with Johnson over the telephone but was rebuffed. The prime minister feared "escalation" and thought that the South Vietnamese "were the first to want to get rid of the Americans, and that a compromise would have to be reached."[19]

The prime minister was given an opportunity to voice some of his apprehensions in early February, when India appealed for an unconditional halt in hostilities and a Geneva-style conference. In drafting a statement for the prime minister's use which endorsed Indian prime minister Lal Bahadur Shastri's call for a negotiated settlement, R.L. Rogers, the head of the Far Eastern Division, and Marcel Cadieux, the under-secretary of state for external affairs, were aware of a small but distinct shift in Canadian policy.[20] Though hedged with conditions designed to secure the United States position in Indochina, the conference proposal clearly represented a retreat from the steadfast support accorded American policy thus far in Vietnam.

Pearson went even further than Martin or his officials expected when he spoke to the Canadian Club in Ottawa on 10 February 1965. Already sensitive to the growing number of domestic critics of the bombing, he hinted at Canada's growing disagreement with the United States over the militarization of American policy. Pearson's oblique criticism of American policy was neatly presented in the context of defending "quiet diplomacy." Acknowledging that Canada's security depended on American support, Pearson warned his audience that "official doubts about certain United States foreign policies often should be expressed in private, through the channels of diplomacy." The prime minister dutifully acknowledged the role of North Vietnamese aggression in expanding the war but went on to observe that "we cannot overlook the fact that U.S. policies in Vietnam seem to have found no solid basis of support through a South Vietnam government of strength and popularity."[21]

The difference in view between Pearson and Martin grew wider as the bombing intensified and rumours concerning the use of napalm and nerve gas made the rounds in early March. It was widely assumed that Pearson had Washington's ear, and the international pressure on him to do something to stop the bombing mounted. U Thant, the United Nations secretary general, begged Pearson to use his influence as the United States' closest ally "to convince [the] Americans that no lasting settlement in Vietnam could be achieved by [the] use of force alone."[22] Canadian missions in the Soviet Union and Eastern Europe, where the bombing seemed likely to complicate Sino-Soviet relations further by driving North Vietnam into closer alignment with Peking, reported that their interlocutors hoped that Canada would help reduce Washington's enthusiasm for bombing.[23]

The bombing helped the various elements of the increasingly vocal Canadian antiwar movement to coalesce. Disproportionate among their numbers were the intellectuals and younger members of Canadian society whom Pearson wished to attract to the Liberal Party. Pearson was also influenced by the views of his wife, Maryon, and his son, Geoffrey, who both thought that American policy was dangerous.[24] Escott Reid, an old friend and colleague who had served under Pearson in the Department of External Affairs, joined in urging the prime minister to speak out.[25] Gradually, Pearson moved toward the idea of making public his concerns about American bombing.

Still very much undecided on his next step, the prime minister asked Cadieux to incorporate the idea of using a bombing pause to test Hanoi's willingness to talk into a speech he was scheduled to deliver at Temple University in Philadelphia. When told of Pearson's plans, Martin tried to dissuade the prime minister from making his suggestion and cautioned "that a proposal of this kind would be more effective if it were put forward, in the first instance, privately to President Johnson."[26] Ritchie suggested that Pearson give the White House an advance copy of his speech.[27] Pearson agreed, and a meeting with Johnson at the White House was immediately arranged.

On 30 March 1965 Pearson met with Marquis Childs, the chief Washington correspondent of the St Louis Post-Dispatch, whom he had known since his first posting to the American capital in the early 1940s. Drawing upon information picked up in Washington, Childs warned Pearson "that President Johnson was embarked upon on a course which, in the next three or four weeks, would bring the United States perilously close to war with Communist China and the U.S.S.R."[28] Isolated and encircled by a small group of like-minded advisors, Johnson needed to hear a different point of view. Childs reassured Pearson that the general line of his speech "'would not be resented' in Washington." The prime minister decided to go ahead. Worried that Johnson might persuade him to abandon his call for a bombing pause, Pearson cancelled his meeting with the president and informed Martin that he planned to suggest a brief halt in the bombing.[29]

Martin threatened to resign, but quickly withdrew his threat when he saw that it would have no impact on the prime minister. On 2 April, Pearson addressed Temple's graduating class. Firmly located within the context of continued Canadian support for American objectives in Vietnam, Pearson's suggestion for a bombing pause was decidedly understated:

After about two months of air strikes, the message should now have been received loud and clear. The authorities in Hanoi must know that the United States with its massive military power can mete out even greater punishment. They must also know that, for this reason, the cost of their continued aggression against South Vietnam could be incalculable ... There are many factors which I am not in a position to weigh or even know. But there does appear to be at least the possibility that a suspension of such air strikes against North Vietnam, at the right time, might provide the Hanoi authorities with an opportunity, if they wish to take it, to inject some flexibility into their policy without appearing to do so as the direct result of military pressure.[30]

The president's reaction was immediate. Pearson had violated one of Johnson's rudimentary but sacrosanct political precepts: "you don't piss on your neighbour's rug."[31] Moreover, the prime minister's timing could not have been worse. Johnson had just helped Pearson secure an exemption from American balance of payments measures and was struggling to get the Autopact through Congress, a battle he had reluctantly undertaken at the prime minister's behest. The Canadian's transgression occurred in the midst of an internal debate over the direction of American policy, a discussion in which Johnson perceived himself as the moderate, resisting hardline demands for a greater American role in Vietnam. The president was worried that Pearson had undercut his own position and invited the prime minster for lunch at his Camp David retreat. After a tense meal, during which he spent most of the time on the phone, Johnson led Pearson into the garden for a frank exposition of his position. From a distance, Ritchie watched the pantomime as the two men talked. The president "strode the terrace, he sawed the air with his arms, with upraised fist he drove home the verbal hammer blows ... From time to time Mike [Pearson] attempted a sentence – only to have it swept away on the tide."[32] "We are confident," the United States under secretary of state, George Ball, observed later with deliberate understatement, that "Pearson sensed [the] President's displeasure over import of speech at April 3 meeting."[33]

Once back in Ottawa, Pearson tried to undo some of the damage. He explained why he had made the speech in a lengthy and detailed letter to Johnson. Canada was anxious to give "all possible support, difficult and thankless ... [of] aiding South Vietnam to resist aggression." But, there was "a quite genuine feeling [in Canada] that current u.s. policy in Vietnam is wrong and heading for trouble ... [which] a minority Government cannot merely brush off ... as unimportant." It was against this background that he felt compelled to suggest that the United States might at some point suspend the bombing. Pearson explained exactly how circumscribed his suggestion really was:

In my proposal for a 'suspension' or 'pause' in the series of 'increasingly powerful retaliatory strikes,' I did not argue it should be done now but might be considered 'at the right time'; that it would be 'for a limited time' ...

My point is that, once the destructive effects of air strikes are really being felt by the Hanoi Government, they might wish to 'cry quits' but without being accused of doing so in the face of continued air action. In other words, this 'pause' would give them an opportunity to stop the fighting in the South – if they wished to use it for that purpose. If they didn't, then their aggressive intransigence would have been exposed and it would be made very clear who was preventing a negotiated solution. I should have thought that this would have strengthened your position diplomatically, without weakening it militarily, because the suspension would only be for a short time; long enough for Northern Communist intentions to be made clear.[34]

In Washington, Pearson's letter was grudgingly acknowledged as suitably repentant. Nevertheless the relationship between Pearson and Johnson, never close, was seriously strained.

Despite the unpleasant American reaction to the Temple speech, *both* Pearson and Martin remained anxious to find some means of helping the United States escape from Southeast Asia. This was especially true following Johnson's decision in July 1965 to send large numbers of American troops to Vietnam. This step, which fundamentally changed the nature of the conflict, meant that the war could no longer be treated as just a struggle for the freedom of South Vietnam. It had become part of the American effort to contain Communist China and, therefore, heightened the risk of a confrontation with China or the Soviet Union, or both.[35] Indeed, in private Pearson had already "said he was afraid of possible escalation of the conflict, particularly as a result of entry by the Chinese ... [and] expressed concern over the possible use in Viet Nam of Chinese nuclear weapons, which seemed to him to be a real possibility."[36]

Pearson and Martin differed – and this difference would grow over the course of the following year – on the right approach to take toward helping the United States extricate itself from Vietnam. The prime minister was much more inclined to wait and take his cue from Washington. In August 1965 he let the White House know informally that he was ready to help the United States whenever he was needed: "It is the hope and desire of the Prime Minister that he can be useful to the President in behind-the-scenes talks, probings, and searchings which have as their objective unconditional discussions ... as a winner of the Nobel Peace Prize, the Prime Minister has contacts throughout the world which would allow him, if the President determined it wise, to quietly seek out ways to bring the matter off the battlefield and into a meeting hall."[37]

Pearson was given his opportunity to help in late December, when the United States unilaterally extended a Christmas bombing pause. The American gesture seemed genuinely designed to test North Vietnam's willingness to negotiate, to uncover any competing concerns among the interested Communist states and to garner public support for the administration's efforts in Vietnam. Pearson was delighted with the president's conciliatory gesture and the news that Johnson was prepared to negotiate without conditions. When asked to guarantee the genuineness of the American offer in New Delhi, Pearson was happy to oblige. He asked the Canadian high commissioner to India, Roland Michener, to "impress on Shastri that I am convinced this is a genuine and sincere attempt by President Johnson and not just an attempt to score propaganda points. This attempt may not be successful but the Americans should be given full points for trying."[38] Canada's action in underwriting the extension of the bombing halt was appreciated in Washington; after all, this was the kind of intimate sharing of information and diplomatic effort that had been the hallmark of Canadian-American relations during the mid-1950s.[39]

However, Pearson's "quiet diplomacy" was no longer enough for Martin, who was convinced that the seriousness of the international situation demanded extraordinary efforts to get talks underway.[40] Martin was in part responding to the hostile public reception that greeted the publication in July 1965 of the Merchant-Heeney study on the principles of partnership. Its sensible conclusion that it "is in the abiding interest of both countries that ... divergent views between two governments should be expressed and if possible resolved in private" was widely denounced in Canada as a "diplomatic sell-out."[41] The foreign minister wondered whether "we could stick with the United States in defence of its basic purpose, if we did not show that we were taking extraordinary steps towards getting negotiations started." Moreover, and quite legitimately, he sought the kind of personal diplomatic triumph that would secure his position as the front-runner in the undeclared race to succeed Pearson.

After considering several possible initiatives using the ICSC, Martin approached Pearson in mid-January with a proposal to send Chester Ronning, a retired Canadian diplomat, to Peking and Hanoi. Martin had toyed before with the idea of using Ronning to break the United Nations deadlock on Chinese representation and to duplicate the minister's 1955 success in solving the problem of the admission of new members. Now Ronning was being asked to resolve the question of Chinese representation while seeking to determine whether North Vietnamese views had shifted under the brunt of the American bombing campaign. The son of American missionaries in China, Ronning spoke fluent Mandarin and was acquainted with leading members of both the Chinese and North Vietnamese governments. He was a seasoned diplomat who had accompanied Pearson to the 1954 Geneva Conference and had served as high commissioner to India and head of the Canadian delegation to the 1962 Laos conference.[42]

Martin was clearly motivated by a number of considerations in proposing this particular enterprise. He was naturally attracted to the domestic political benefits that would follow a successful mission. "Public opinion in Canada would welcome an initiative," he assured his prime minister, "which could be presented as a contribution to the search for peace in Vietnam."[43] The secretary of state for external affairs was also convinced that Johnson's willingness to undertake unconditional negotiations was genuine and that his declarations to this effect were an invitation to act. Recalling Washington's earlier request for Seaborn's help, the minister argued that Ronning would fulfil an American need for a mediator and add to Canada's standing in Washington. "It seems to me that, however things may shape up in Vietnam in the months to come, such influence as we may have in Washington in relation to this problem could be enhanced if we respond to the invitation in a way that is regarded as useful from the United States point of view." Pearson was sceptical but allowed Martin his head.

As the prime minister suspected, American officials greeted the projected mission with undisguised hostility. Insofar as Martin's scheme was presented in the context of the president's peace offensive, American policymakers felt that they had no option but to agree to the Ronning mission. But most American officials viewed Ronning, who was widely known to be critical of American policy in Asia, with unfriendly suspicion.[44] Martin's sponsorship of the mission was a further problem. American officials were uncomfortable with his tendency to "politicize everything" and were inclined to discount him and his diplomacy.[45] The American assistant secretary of state for Far Eastern affairs, William Bundy, dismissed him as "pas sérieux."[46] Rusk tended to treat Martin, a little indulgently perhaps, as a "nuisance."[47] Any chance that the scheme had of achieving some sort of standing in Washington disappeared in late January when Pearson (perhaps to protect his own fragile standing among American policymakers) pulled away the ground on which his minister stood. "Pearson confirmed," Butterworth reported to Washington, that the "Ronning mission was Martin's idea, that it entailed greater dangers than Martin had perhaps appreciated and that he had 'scared the hell out of Paul last night' ... if anything went wrong, his government would disavow any involvement in the Ronning mission."[48] Not surprisingly, Rusk dismissed the Canadian initiative. "Quite frankly," he assured the American ambassador to Saigon, "I attach no importance to his [Ronning's] trip and expect nothing out of it."[49]

Ronning's initial meetings with the North Vietnamese authorities were unrewarding. In the first two days of his visit, the Canadian emissary met with a number of senior officials, including the foreign minister, Nguyen Duy Trinh, without discerning any movement in the DRVN position. The DRVN's representatives politely but staunchly insisted that the possibility of negotiations rested entirely on Washington's willingness to accept Hanoi's Four Points. Only in the final stages of a two-hour meeting with the prime minister, Pham Van Dong, did Ronning unearth an apparent shift in DRVN policy. Under persistent questioning, Pham admitted that North Vietnam would be prepared to undertake preliminary talks in exchange for "an official declaration that it [the United States] will unconditionally stop for good all military operations against [the] territory of NVN."[50] Ronning was delighted, although Pham's meaning was not entirely clear because he added that North Vietnam "had already suggested a similar offer in the January 4th [1966] foreign ministry statement."[51] In this response to the Christmas bombing halt, Hanoi dismissed the exercise as propaganda and insisted that "a political settlement of the Vietnam problem can be envisaged only when the US ... has accepted the 4-point stand of the DRV, has proved this by actual deeds, has stopped unconditionally and for good its air raids and all other acts of war against the DRV."[52] In linking his offer to Ronning with the foreign ministry's statement, Pham introduced a dangerous element of ambiguity.

Ronning was nevertheless inclined to think that he had achieved a small break-through. Although he realised that such terms as "official declaration" would need to be defined before progress could be made, he was quite sure that Pham had offered a "condition which if accepted by [the] USA, could result in negotiations."[53] Seaborn's successor on the ICSC, Victor Moore, accompanied Ronning and sent a report to Ottawa that also overlooked the ambiguous nature of Pham's offer. He contended that Pham's offer "lifted from its context in January 4th foreign ministry statement bombing issue and made it [the] sole condition for negotiations."[54] This was the only explicit attempt made by any Canadian official to locate Pham's offer within the context of Hanoi's January declaration. Martin accepted without question Moore's contention that it represented an unequivocally new offer. In early March he called Rusk to say that Ronning had brought back a proposition and that "we attached importance to it as possible evidence of an unblocking of channels."[55]

In Washington, where Ronning arrived on 20 March 1966 to brief State Department officials, the discussion turned on the question of the relationship between Pham's offer and the January declaration. Neither Ottawa nor Ronning had anticipated this. During the talks that followed his presentation, Ronning admitted that Pham had "started to hedge ... [and] had implied that his statement was nothing more than had already been said in the DRVN foreign ministry statement of 4 January."[56] William Bundy seized on this remark and pointed out "that the link between the DRVN's 4 points and the declaration on cessation of bombing was ambiguous in the January 4th statement ... it could conceivably be argued, if certain punctuation was accepted, that there was a hint that issuance of declaration on bombing would imply an acceptance of the 4 points." Ronning's certainty wilted: "He might be entirely wrong in concluding that DRVN was separating bombing from the Four Points but this was undoubtedly the impression that Pham Van Dong wished to create."[57] Not surprisingly, Washington interpreted this to mean that "on balance, [Ronning] frankly did not himself think anything significant had emerged from his visit."[58] The question was closed as far as Bundy and his American colleagues were concerned.

Martin was disappointed at Bundy's lack of enthusiasm. Despite Bundy's legitimate concerns about Pham's offer to Ronning, Martin waited hopefully for a more considered and positive reaction. None was forthcoming. In early April, Bundy brushed off the first of several informal Canadian requests for a response. After repeated prompting the American official replied that the United States did not wish to respond to Hanoi through the Canadian channel at the present time.[59] The unyielding American behaviour troubled Canadian officials. Moore seemed particularly concerned and reminded Ottawa that now was the time to act: Hanoi's patience was not inexhaustible. He warned that, since the United States had already begun to consider bombing Hanoi and Haiphong, the risks associated with employing Ronning were beginning to mount.[60]

Cadieux discounted the dangers connected with a renewed Canadian mediatory effort on the basis of reports from Washington. In order to get a second Ronning mission started, he wanted to send the State

Department a list of Moore's scheduled ICSC visits to remind it of
Ottawa's desire to see the momentum maintained.[61] Martin was
inclined to go even further. He "impulsively picked up the telephone"
and called Bundy directly, upbraiding the American for Washington's
failure to provide Hanoi with a more positive response and pointing
out that the Canadian government attached the "greatest importance
to [the] channel which had been opened up by Ronning. In [the] current situation it appeared to us to be one of the very few channels
which held any promise of opening up possibilities of moving towards
some kind of peaceful settlement of Vietnam conflict."[62] Bundy
promised a reaction soon.

The official American response – presented as a memorandum to
the Canadian government – was prepared largely in an effort to patch
up relations with Martin. The State Department acknowledged the
potential worth of the Canadian channel, which it wished to keep
open, but pointedly reminded Ottawa that the United States had been
in direct contact with Hanoi throughout the bombing pause without
success. Since then, North Vietnam had continued to insist that the
United States accept its Four Points before any negotiations. If
Pham's offer to Ronning suggested that North Vietnam's position was
beginning to moderate, its exact meaning remained open to interpretation. "It seems most probable," concluded the memorandum, "that
this was still intended to be linked with acceptance of the 'four
points.'"[63]

Despite this pessimistic conclusion, the United States was ready to
make another effort to determine precisely what Pham's suggestion
meant and to pursue the matter through either a Canadian intermediary or "the established direct channels." Included in the American
memorandum was the text of an oral message that Washington wished
to convey to Hanoi. This categorically rejected the North Vietnamese
proposal. The United States simply reiterated its willingness either to
talk unconditionally or to agree to a reciprocal reduction in military
activity to de-escalate the conflict.

Canadian officials were uncertain how to react. The draft American
message, which seemed too pessimistic, was a particular concern. Some
of this worry was alleviated when the message was redrafted, making
it clear that Canada was not acting simply as an American spokesman
but as a state whose position on the ICSC gave it an independent and
unique interest in the conflict in Vietnam. The new emphasis that the
revised message placed on Washington's interest in maintaining the
Canadian channel was also reassuring, if not entirely accurate.[64]

As momentum gathered around the second Ronning mission, an
unrealistic sense of optimism replaced the initial apprehension experi-

enced by Canadian officials. Despite continued evidence of Hanoi's intransigence, the North Vietnamese decision to receive Ronning a second time was encouraging. In early May, Ronning and Klaus Goldschlag, head of the Far Eastern Division, met Bundy and Paul Kreisberg, the officer-in-charge of Mainland China Affairs, to discuss the amended message. The attitude adopted by the two State Department officials, who were satisfied that the Canadian revision accurately reflected their original intentions, was comforting. Goldschlag reported that the "Americans regard this exchange as serious. Because it involves issues which are of the greatest importance from their point of view, they are anxious to re-open a direct channel of communication with the North Vietnamese ... Meanwhile, they appreciate the availability of the Canadian channel and would wish to see it kept open."[65]

These positive indications were misleading. By the end of May the mission was fraught with tension. In a further effort to emphasize the Canadian nature of the initiative and to preserve Ottawa's local standing in Vietnam, Martin insisted on briefing South Vietnam about Ronning. American officials in both Washington and Saigon were "disturbed" by this Canadian effort to insert themselves into a relationship that they regarded with proprietary interest.[66]

For their part Canadian officials were distressed to learn from published reports in early June that the United States had conveyed the sense of the second Ronning message to Chinese officials at the regular monthly Sino-American meetings held in Poland. Indeed, the Americans had gone much further and had explained that they would suspend the bombing in exchange for a halt in the infiltration of North Vietnamese troops and equipment.[67] Canadian officials were surprised at the American effort to sabotage the mission. "While this is not something you will wish to say to Rusk, we find it difficult to comprehend why a message on these lines should be conveyed to Hanoi through the intermediary [Peking] which is known to be most vehemently opposed to any form of accommodation in Vietnam."[68] They urged Martin, then in Paris for a NATO ministerial meeting, to explore the relationship between the Canadian and Chinese messages with Rusk. The American declined to answer the minister's questions directly and explained that there could be no bombing suspension without a stop to the infiltration. This, Martin remarked plaintively, was not the message that Ronning was carrying.[69]

Moore observed that Ronning's message lacked any new elements and argued that the mission was destined to fail. Washington, he asserted perceptively, had already reached this conclusion and had adjusted its strategy accordingly. "The Americans appear to be putting

Hanoi behind the eight-ball again and to be escalating what was allegedly a serious and practical cease-fire overture into a peace offensive reminiscent of their campaign last January."[70] Pearson was distraught. "It would be a sad ending to our initiative in this matter," he telegraphed Martin, "if we became merely an instrument of USA propaganda or for putting the DRVN on the spot."[71]

Officials in Ottawa did not share the prime minister's concern. They insisted that the United States remained interested in receiving the DRVN's confidential response and that this represented the most important element of the Canadian mission. Moreover, if these Canadian concerns were raised in Washington, the United States might simply suggest that Ronning not visit Hanoi. The prime purpose of the Ronning exercise was increasingly limited "to making sure that [the] channel we have been able to open up to Hanoi is not closed."[72] Encouraged to believe that Canada's role as an intermediary might be preserved, Martin decided to proceed but cautioned his officials against having any "illusions as to possible success."[73]

The new set of instructions prepared for Moore made a virtue of necessity. The general nature of the original Canadian message made it possible for Ronning to range widely in seeking a positive response from Hanoi. Ronning's role was effectively transformed from channel to mediator, and he was instructed to "make the point that if the cause of peaceful settlement of [the] Vietnam problem is to be advanced ... there will have to be willingness on both sides to move beyond their present positions."[74] Canada was ready to help advance this process. In the event that such probing failed, Ronning was to explore in detail Pham's interpretation of the third of Hanoi's Four Points. This point – that South Vietnam's problems must be settled by the people of South Vietnam without any outside interference – had been the subject of earlier discussions between the United States and North Vietnam in Burma, and there was a distant possibility that something might emerge upon which a subsequent exchange could be based. "It is important that in any event," the instructions concluded, "Ronning should do everything to keep open the contact, regardless of the result."

Even as Canada moved towards an increasingly exposed position as a mediator running an independent operation, there were further indications that American motives had changed. After a long debate, Robert MacNamara, the secretary of defense, had agreed in early June to authorize bombing strikes against petroleum facilities in Hanoi and Haiphong. He pressed Rusk for support. Rusk counselled delay and suggested that the United States wait for the results of Ronning's second message. These would almost certainly reveal Hanoi's continued intransigence and justify the bombing in the eyes of those allies, like British prime minister Harold Wilson and Pearson, who questioned American policy. In the meantime Rusk promised his colleague that he would ask to receive an early report on the Ronning mission.[75] Bundy made no effort to hide the American intention to link the scale of hostilities in Vietnam with the results of the Ronning mission. The request was made "so that USA authorities could receive info on situation as soon as possible in case some prompt USA response, such as a change in the scale of USA activities, appeared desirable."[76] Martin and his officials were concerned at this latest development but agreed that Ronning would reveal the "general flavour" of the exchange if he considered that this might have an "immediate" bearing on American deliberations.[77]

Ronning was treated "courteously and hospitably" on his arrival in Hanoi on 14 June, and he transmitted the oft-revised American message to Nguyen Co Thach, the vice-minister of foreign affairs. Four days later he was received by the deputy prime minister, Nguyen Duy Trinh, who accurately dismissed the American message as nothing "that had not already been published in the western press."[78] He accused the United States of insincerity and denounced the Canadian effort. Ronning failed to discover any flexibility in the North Vietnamese position. After persistent challenges, however, Trinh qualified his remarks and acknowledged that the Canadian channel remained open. Ronning and Moore were delighted and moved quickly to protect the Canadian investment, fearful that the United States might "take the position that the Canadian initiative has failed due to DRVN intransigence ... and thus repeat the Seaborn episode (exploiting publicly the results of Canadian exploration as 'confirming a negative')."[79] The two Canadians thought that in the circumstances no information should be passed to the United States until Canadian officials had developed "a carefully qualified interpretation" of the North Vietnamese response.[80]

Ottawa did its best to preserve the Canadian channel. Martin asked Rusk to ensure that the United States did not step up its bombing operations in the immediate aftermath of Ronning's visit. He did not divulge Hanoi's response. The minister called in officials from the American embassy on 20 June and repeated his request that the United States not jeopardize the Canadian channel by increased bombing right after Ronning's return from Hanoi. Again, he refused to reveal the results of Ronning's visit.[81] This tight-lipped approach was resented in Washington as an effort "to keep us hemmed in on the grounds that the channel is still open."[82] When the results of the mission were at last given to Bundy on the afternoon of 21 June, Martin interpreted the North Vietnamese rejection in the best light possible, underlining Hanoi's declared interest in using the Canadian channel again. He drew Washington's "attention to the adverse effects which an early escalation of U.S. activities against North Vietnam is likely to have both retroactively on the Ronning mission and potentially on the future use of the Canadian channel."[83] The Canadian presentation was so convincing that Bundy himself was initially uncertain exactly how Martin saw the results. However, he was not long distracted by the Canadian interpretation: "Basically, Hanoi turned Ronning down cold on their paying any price whatever for the cessation of bombing."[84]

That evening Martin and his officials briefed Bundy more fully over dinner. Martin was obviously upset with the failure of the mission and complained bitterly that the American position "had not been forthcoming enough."[85] Within a week, there were grounds for further recriminations. In late June news of the Ronning mission was leaked. On the respected television program *Meet the Press* the American under secretary of state explained that "there was nothing in what Ambassador Ronning brought back which gives any encouragement that Hanoi was prepared to come to a conference table. In fact, the line that they have been taking seems to us to be quite as hard as it has been at any time." Martin quickly called the American ambassador and expressed his outrage.[86] A few days later, Martin was dismayed to learn that the United States had begun to bomb petroleum facilities near Hanoi and Haiphong. Butterworth was quickly told of the minister's displeasure.[87]

The Ronning missions and the unseemly bickering between Bundy and Martin that accompanied them had two important consequences. In Ottawa they undermined Pearson's confidence in Martin's judgment. The prime minister's unhappiness with Martin had been growing since Ronning's first mission in early 1966, and he did not try to hide his distress. In the fall he told Walter Gordon that Martin's views on foreign policy no longer mattered.[88] A few months later he remarked to Paul Hellyer, the minister of national defence, that he "wanted to get Paul Martin out of External Affairs ... [he] is getting too involved in the Vietnam thing to the exclusion of our overall relations with the U.S."[89]

In Washington the Ronning experience fuelled concerns in the White House and the State Department about the drop in support in Canada for American policy in Vietnam and the effect that this might have on bilateral relations. In early 1966 Butterworth had warned Washington how difficult it was becoming to maintain Canadian support for American policies in Asia: "We wrung from Pearson and

Martin fulsome official statements of support for U.S. policy in Vietnam, but the Prime Minister in particular and the Government in general continued to have grave misgivings about the conflict's escalation, were prone to be oversensitive to criticism from Canadian Vietniks, and still had difficulty relating Vietminh/Vietcong aggression to their own and Western security. If and as the war worsens, we can expect to find that whatever lip-service they give to our effort will be extracted from them in future, as in the past, against their emotional predilection. A by-product will be their restraint from doing what they are fully inclined to do, such as recognizing Red China and voting for its admission to the UN."[90]

Polling conducted in April and May showed that Canadian support for Washington's "handling" of the war had declined sharply; although 35 percent still approved of the American effort in southeast Asia, a startling 34 percent disapproved.[91] Johnson demanded to know if there is "anything constructive we can do in relation to Canada at the present time."[92] Rusk recommended a presidential visit to dispel the widespread doubt in Canada about Washington's Asian policies. "The political and psychological climate in Canada suggests that a visit by you," Rusk told the president, "could have a tremendous impact in focusing the attention of Canadians upon the 'enduring common interests between our countries and in redirecting their fixation away from such problem issues between us as Vietnam and China, which they persistently view so astigmatically.'"[93] Throughout the summer Rusk and his department continued to press Johnson to visit Canada. After all, as the veteran American diplomat Robert McClintock reported to Ball in May 1966, Pearson, "despite his harsh criticism, particularly over Vietnam ... is still one of the best friends the United States has."[94]

Reluctant to leave Washington and the business of running the war in Vietnam, Johnson hesitated before deciding impetuously in early August to pay a brief visit to New Brunswick, where Canada and the United States were transforming Franklin D. Roosevelt's summer home into an international park. Vietnam – "our military restraint, our non-military efforts and our continued hope for some sign of reason from Hanoi" – topped the president's agenda.[95] Isolated in the White House by domestic opposition to the war, Johnson was encouraged by the popular reception accorded the presidential cavalcade as it swung north through the New England states to Campobello Island. He arrived in New Brunswick in a good mood, and his private talks with Pearson "took place in the most friendly atmosphere throughout."[96] American officials were gratified by the results of the meeting.[97] When Pearson hinted that his government might drop its opposition to

Communist Chinese representation at the United Nations, Johnson made clear his disagreement and insisted that the two allies approach this problem together: "He thought that the two governments should keep in close touch on the issue and that the relationship [being] what it is between our two countries we could always work out any differences between us."[98] Canadian officials quickly understood that Johnson's interest "seemed to presage at least the possibility of pressure on us to support the United States position as the vote draws near. It would, therefore, appear that, if the Canadian Government wishes to change its vote, the timing and tactics to use vis-à-vis the United States will be important and delicate."[99]

The president's views, expressed in the midst of a debate in Ottawa over how far Canada should go toward seeking a resolution to the problem of Peking's exclusion from the United Nations, reinforced Pearson's natural inclination to proceed cautiously in this matter. Martin, however, remained anxious to press on with the second part of his two-pronged policy for resolving the conflict in Vietnam and admitting Peking to the United Nations. Ronning, whom the Chinese had refused to see on his way to Hanoi in March, had failed to advance this project. Martin was inclined to try a more direct approach. He endorsed a proposal that Canada abandon its opposition to the habitual Albanian resolution, which called on the United Nations to expel Taiwan from the international organization and assign the Chinese seat to Peking. Instead, Canada would abstain and support a simple resolution that gave Peking a seat in the United Nations without explicitly mentioning Taiwan.[100]

Pearson was doubtful. He rejected his minister's assertion that an abstention would have a minimal impact on Canada's relations with the United States. Washington, he noted, would consider an abstention a "radical departure" from Canada's established position and no less irritating than a decision to take an active role in the expulsion of Taiwan. He objected to Martin's reluctance to pursue a "two-Chinas" resolution, arguing that "we are too emphatic *against* delaying tactics – they may turn out to be the best of evils." To bolster his case, he enlisted the support of Norman Robertson, the venerable former under-secretary of state for external affairs, who shared Pearson's view that recent developments in Vietnam made it "unwise ... for Canada to contemplate a shift [in policy] this year." The prime minister decided to defer his decision until the probable American reaction could be explored more fully.[101]

During the course of the following few weeks, Martin had ample opportunity to learn how the United States would respond to a Canadian initiative on the Chinese question. Rusk made it perfectly clear in late September that he considered any move to legitimize Peking's international status to be inimical to Western interests in Southeast Asia.[102] The Washington embassy reported an equally rigid attitude among American officials in the State Department.[103] This confirmation of the Liberal leader's fears made it difficult for Martin to sell Pearson on a China initiative. The foreign minister was therefore obliged to adopt Pearson's view that Canada should promote a "'one-China, one-Taiwan' resolution that would have representatives of both governments seated in the Assembly as an interim solution."[104] While this resolution would please neither Peking nor Taiwan, "the principles it enunciates are entirely in accord with the Canadian position and will appeal to a small but respectable group of middle powers who like ourselves do not like extreme positions." It would allow Canada to oppose an Albanian-type resolution, using this opposition to secure from Washington "passive acquiescence" for the Canadian initiative. Pearson approved this proposed plan; indeed, he was instrumental in pushing it through Cabinet over the objections of "some ministers" who thought that Canada should immediately recognize Peking.[105]

Significantly, the final position that Pearson forced on Martin was not all that different from the policy Washington was preparing to adopt. In late October, Martin informed Rusk of the Canadian decision to explore some form of "two-Chinas" resolution at the twenty-first General Assembly. The American response was "glum but restrained."[106] Rusk and the State Department did not minimize the importance of the Canadian decision to the American strategy of containing Peking: "The Canadian shift makes a critical difference. If we lose the support of these friends, it is probable that the Albanian resolution will obtain a simple majority for the first time [and] ... we will have suffered an important defeat." Canada, the State Department estimated on the basis of its recent contacts with Canadian officials, could not be dissuaded, and might even attract the support of Belgium and Italy, whose governments were under strong left-wing pressure to accommodate Peking. The United States could not simply "stand pat," since passage of the Canadian resolution, with its suggestion that Peking assume China's seat on the Security Council, was not a position Washington could allow the General Assembly to endorse.

In early November, Rusk urged Johnson to compromise and to support a resolution that would establish a "study committee" to examine the issue before the next General Assembly. As the United States would neither control the membership of this committee nor its terms of reference, Rusk was not sanguine in anticipating the results of the exercise: "At a minimum, I would expect that this Committee would recommend some form of 'two-Chinas' solution."[107] In effect, Canada and the United States differed, and only marginally, over a question of timing.

After discussing the problem with Johnson, the secretary of state wrote Pearson, reiterating the familiar American position. A move forward would simply encourage Peking's belligerent policies in Southeast Asia and Vietnam. In addition, Rusk outlined a number of problems with the specific wording of the Canadian resolution. There was only one possible American response to the Canadian initiative as it now stood: "We would have to oppose your resolution in its present form, if it were introduced, and indeed, would have to exert every ounce of our influence to defeat it by the heaviest possible margin. I need not underscore the seriousness of such a split between our two nations." As an alternative course, Rusk proposed, Canada might join with one or two other countries in sponsoring a resolution to establish a study committee that would examine the question of Chinese representation at the United Nations.[108]

The negative American reaction was echoed in the capitals of some of Canada's closest allies, who learned of the Canadian demarche on 7 November 1966. The Canadian resolution, thought Australia, was "regrettable, untimely and possibly leading to disaster."[109] The Japanese reaction was equally blunt. The level of support from Belgium and Italy, with whom Canada had frequently consulted on this question, was also limited. Belgium would only support the Canadian resolution subject to a number of presentational amendments, while Italy wished to redraft the entire resolution to take into account U.S. objections.[110]

Pearson was disturbed by the American and international reaction, but Martin was determined. He indicated that, subject to the prime minister's views, the Canadian Permanent Mission in New York should continue its consultations with the Italians, the Belgians, and the Americans. The delegation should be prepared to discuss the American suggestion for a study committee but without any implicit or explicit commitment, using the possibility of a Canadian abstention on the Albanian resolution as a threat "to induce the USA and Italians to move to [a] position which is in closer accord with our own resolution."[111]

The following day, 12 November 1966, George Ignatieff, Canada's permanent representative to the United Nations, reached an agreed text with his Belgian counterpart. If the Italians were brought round to the Belgian-Canadian position, the American delegation hinted to Ignatieff, Washington might be convinced to abandon its study committee proposal.[112] Late in the evening of 16 November the Italian, Belgian, and Canadian representatives in New York agreed upon a final text *ad referendum*.[113] The tripartite draft called for a study committee that would take into account "the conflicting territorial claims of the two governments [of China] and the need to seek an appropriate solution taking into account ... the political realities of the area." Unfortunately, the Italians retreated the next day and with Chile's backing began to solicit support for a resolution establishing a more neutral study committee.

With debate on the Chinese question scheduled to begin shortly in the General Assembly, Martin turned to the Cabinet for advice. The government had to decide whether the Italian-Canadian-Belgian draft represented the minimum Canada could accept and if so, whether Canada should disassociate itself publicly from the Italian initiative. In addition, the government needed to consider how Canada would vote on the Italian and the Albanian resolutions. Martin hoped that "the Canadian delegation [would] be left free to vote in the negative or to abstain from voting" on an Albanian-type resolution.[114] Cabinet endorsed most of Martin's recommendations: it agreed that Canada could go no further than the tripartite compromise resolution and that it should make a full statement explaining its position and its unsuccessful efforts to advance Chinese representation. Pearson refused to allow Martin to abstain on an Albanian-style resolution without prior consultation, effectively retaining control over Canadian policy.

The prime minister's reluctance forced Martin to return to New York in search of a compromise. On arrival he was met by the United States ambassador to the United Nations, Arthur Goldberg. Martin explained to him that the government could not support a neutral study committee without appearing to retreat from its stated policy. The Canadian suggested that Ottawa's position might be met if the Italian resolution could be amended to include a brief reference to the competing claims of Peking and Taiwan. While Goldberg undertook to consult Rusk and Johnson, Martin telephoned Pearson, who agreed that Canada would co-sponsor an amended resolution.[115] Washington, however, rejected the amendment, and the following day, in a meeting of interested delegations, Italy announced its determination to proceed with its own resolution.

During the following week, Martin was faced with conflicting advice from the members of the Canadian delegation to the General Assembly. Officials from the Department of External Affairs, convinced that Canada had gone as far as it could with its forceful advocacy of its resolution, pressed the minister to oppose the Albanian resolution. Other members of the delegation, including Pierre Trudeau, the prime minister's parliamentary secretary, vigorously pressed Martin to abstain. Pearson hoped that Canada would support the Italian resolution for a study committee.[116] On 23 November 1966 Martin intervened in the General Assembly debate on the question of Chinese representation and carefully explained why the Canadian government found both the Italian and the Albanian resolutions unsatisfactory. While indicating that Canada would reluctantly support the proposal for a study committee, he did not reveal how Canada would vote on the Albanian resolution.

During a meeting with Rusk two days before the vote, the question was not addressed. Instead, the Americans simply asked the minister to reassure U.S. allies in Asia that Canada had been pursuing its own policy during the preceding months and was not acting as an American stalking horse.[117] On the morning of 29 November 1966 Martin telephoned the prime minister and discussed how Canada might cast its vote. The minister contended that an abstention would disarm the government's domestic critics. It would also lend weight to the idea of an independent Canadian policy. Martin reassured the prime minister that an abstention would not greatly anger the Americans.

There was something in these assertions. Directed by Pearson, Martin had come so close to reaching a compromise with the United States that the differences between the two countries could be safely disregarded. When Pearson agreed that Canada would abstain, the Americans said little. Indeed, after discussing the question with leading members of the United States delegation, J.G. Hadwen, the minister's special assistant, concluded that the "general tenor of our exchanges ... was satisfactory. I would take it as the kind of exchange which Canadian and U.S. officials have on points on which their governments disagree ... I don't see, to judge from this conversation, that we will likely get any serious Washington fallout."[118] He was right.

In contrast to the differences that divided Washington and Ottawa over NATO, NORAD, and defence policy, the divisions over Asia were not easily or successfully reconciled. Canadian and American approaches to the Vietnam War and Communist China reflected their fundamental disagreement over the proper Western role in the Far East. As a global power with a historic stake in the Pacific, the United States naturally accorded Asia considerable significance. Canada, a small power whose interests were still dominated by its traditional European and North Atlantic connections, did not. As the Johnson administration became engaged in the crisis in Vietnam, Canada offered only limited assistance. Ottawa's few small gestures of support for its great power ally were still too much for some Canadians, and by early 1965, Pearson was under pressure to take steps to distinguish Canadian and American policy.

This was increasingly difficult to do. The hostile reception that greeted the prime minister's Temple University speech and Martin's unhappy efforts to find grounds for negotiations underlined clearly the risks associated with meddling in "Johnson's war." Pearson consequently assumed more control over Canadian policy, forcing Martin to moderate his approach to China. This did not reconcile Canadian and American differences over Asia, but it did minimize and contain them, largely removing the Far East as a source of bilateral tension. The struggle to sustain this moderate posture, which won few friends on either side of the border, would become the central feature of Pearson's Far Eastern policy in the final year of his mandate.

CHAPTER SIX

Containing the New Nationalists

The differences in view over Western strategy in Asia that emerged during 1966 left policymakers in Ottawa and Washington shaken and uneasy. This divergence could not have come at a worse time. Though temporarily checked by the hostile reaction accorded the federal budget of June 1963, the nationalist impulse that was reflected in the Liberal Party's progressive wing refused to subside and was beginning to flower on the eve of the country's centennial celebrations. The lengthy struggle by cultural nationalists to secure government protection found expression in 1964 and 1965 in legislation to preserve Canada's mass media from American competition. Careful Canadian diplomacy in Washington and a sharp eye for legitimate American economic interests muted the impact of these measures on Canada's relations with the United States.

For a while it seemed that Ottawa's efforts to address the other major item on the nationalist agenda – the 'Canadianization' of the small American-owned Mercantile Bank – might also be dealt with in a pragmatic fashion. Unfortunately for relations between the two governments, both Walt Butterworth, the American ambassador to Canada, and Walter Gordon were determined to use this issue as a platform from which to force their respective governments to resolve the questions associated with the role and status of American investment in Canada. In transforming the Mercantile Bank's status into a symbol, the two men sparked a nasty and very public brawl that threatened to poison relations between the two countries.

The affair fed the anti-Americanism from which Canadian national-ists drew much of their inspiration. As they sought to distinguish Cana-dians from Americans and Canada from the United States, nationalists focused with increasing vehemence on the single most obvious differ-ence between the two governments – the war in Vietnam. Opposition to the war reinforced cultural and economic nationalism and created a new, radical critique of Canada's relations with the United States. Nei-ther Pearson nor Martin could ignore the antiwar movement forever, and over the course of 1967 Ottawa slowly distanced itself from Unit-ed States policy in Southeast Asia. Observers in Washington were dis-tressed, and for a brief moment in the fall of 1967 the two countries seemed headed for the kind of collision that had marred relations dur-ing Diefenbaker's final year in office.

Canadian magazines, held sacred by several generations of national-ists as outlets for the expression of Canadian attitudes and opinions, had been under threat since the early 1920s. The problem had become acute by the mid-1950s. American periodicals, which enjoyed much cheaper unit-production costs than their Canadian competitors, held 80 percent of the Canadian market by 1954. Moreover, Canadian edi-tions of American magazines like *Time* and *Reader's Digest* attracted almost 40 percent of the money spent on periodical advertising in Canada and threatened to bankrupt magazines like *Maclean's* or *Sat-urday Night*.[1] In 1956, the Liberal minister of finance, Walter Harris, had tried to protect Canadian magazines by imposing a 20 percent tax on advertising in non-Canadian periodicals. This tax was withdrawn in 1958, and in its stead a royal commission on publications, chaired by Grattan O'Leary, publisher and editor of the *Ottawa Journal*, was appointed. It reported in May 1961 and recommended that expenses incurred for advertising directed at the Canadian market in foreign periodicals (including Canadian editions of American magazines) should not qualify for an income tax deduction. O'Leary also urged that the customs act be amended to prevent the entry into Canada of foreign periodicals containing Canadian domestic advertising.[2] In Jan-uary 1963 Diefenbaker announced that he would carry out O'Leary's recommendations, exempting the Canadian editions of *Time* and *Reader's Digest* on the grounds that they were already established in Canada.[3]

Diefenbaker's legislation never appeared, and when the new Liberal government took office in April 1963, it immediately came under intense pressure to act. Two days after the election, C.J. Laurin, vice-president of Maclean-Hunter Publishing and president of the Canadi-an Periodical Association met with Walter Gordon, the minister of finance, and urged him "most strongly to deal with the matter in the

June budget."4 Gordon, however, was inclined to delay, a decision that reflected the sound advice offered by his experienced assistant deputy minister of finance, A.F.W. Plumptre: "In this field, as in others, it is undesirable, indeed dangerous, for the Government to announce that it is going to do something until it has a fairly clear idea of what it intends to do. The dangers in this field are in fact greater than in most because of the complexity of the subject, the wide variety of views that are held, and the strong feelings that are aroused."5 Pearson agreed that nothing would be done before the parliamentary summer recess.6

During August and September, Plumptre and Robert Bryce, the deputy minister of finance, tried to find some means of protecting Canadian magazines from their American competition. They focused their efforts on three possible solutions. First, the government could revert to some version of the Harris tax, though this step "would be loudly opposed by the whole advertising fraternity, and ... by many daily newspapers." Second, the government could adopt O'Leary's recommendation to disallow income tax deductions on advertising costs incurred in foreign periodicals, modifying it to exempt *Time* and *Reader's Digest*. Third, the government could erect a punitive tariff on imported editorial content in order to deal with American magazines tailored for the Canadian market. Bryce noted that the Canadian Periodical Association wanted the government to increase the postal rates charged *Time* and *Reader's Digest* by denying them the discount enjoyed by other Canadian publishers.

Bryce, who thought an amendment to the postal rates was too radical, was sceptical of the value of all three courses of action. The time for action had long since past. "The magazine publishing industry in Canada is now dominated by *Time* and *Reader's Digest*," he stated bluntly, and "the cost, in terms of relations with the U.S.A, of forcing these two publications out of Canada will be very high and yet action short of forcing out *Time* and *Reader's Digest* may be nothing more than a temporary stimulant. The United States Government will find it very difficult to condone such measures as are under consideration, even if *Time* and *Reader's Digest* are made exempt." The deputy minister of finance reminded the prime minister that amending the customs act would involve complicated international negotiations under the General Agreements on Tariffs and Trade (GATT) and that any move in this field was likely to disrupt the Canadian advertising community. In short, the "proposed omelette cannot be made without breaking a number of eggs."7

Unwilling to antagonize either the Canadian press or the United States, Pearson asked officials in early September to continue their search for a solution. The views of E.P. Zimmerman, publisher of the

Canadian edition of *Reader's Digest*, were canvassed. He suggested that additional revenue for Canadian magazines could be generated by placing a levy on all magazines sold in Canada, the funds to be distributed to publications that incurred a certain proportion of their editorial and production costs in Canada.[8] Tom Kent, the prime minister's principal assistant, joined the discussion at this point and strongly endorsed the idea that *Time* and *Reader's Digest* pay first-class postage rates rather than the subsidized rate enjoyed by other Canadian periodicals. Kent calculated that this would cost the two magazines over $5.5 million and effectively exclude them from the Canadian market. A tariff barrier against special editions completed Kent's prescription. Although he argued that removing the postal subsidy could be more readily explained and easily defended than adjustments in the income tax act, he recognized that any effective action ultimately involved defying Washington. Kent cautioned that "if we did this we would be blasted by *Time* and *Digest*, and their powerful friends in the u.s., with fury beyond bounds." However, as he pointed out, "this is true for anything effective we do. Anything effective means destroying *Time* and *Digest* in Canada. The only alternative is the death, sooner or later, of *Maclean's* and the continued absence of any other significant Canadian magazines. We have to decide whether we're prepared to pay the price. If not, we must sooner or later expect more foreign control of the Canadian printed word. It will be a bit late to wring our hands, or try to lock the stable door, then."[9] Zimmerman and Kent failed to sway the Department of Finance. The first advocated a solution that was too novel and radical for a government anxious to avoid controversy, and the second, a course of action that was simply foolhardy. Gordon suggested the Cabinet do nothing.[10]

Kent redoubled his efforts to convince the prime minister to strengthen the Canadian magazine industry, which he described as the country's "only national voice." He agreed that the government could not take on Washington in the wake of Gordon's first budget and proposed giving *Time* and *Reader's Digest* "squatter's rights." The risk of a major confrontation with Washington over action to eliminate the threat of future "Canadian editions" was much smaller and one the government ought to run "for an important national purpose." After all, as Kent pointed out wryly, "we have hitherto annoyed the Americans for less purpose." He recommended that the government proceed on the basis of the two O'Leary recommendations, exempting *Time* and *Reader's Digest*.[11]

Kent's intervention was decisive, and Gordon's recommendation to do nothing was turned back by the cabinet committee on economic policy, trade, and employment in early October. At the end of the month, after Kent's proposals were reviewed by both the Cabinet committee and an ad hoc interdepartmental committee of officials, the full Cabinet provisionally agreed to adopt the modified O'Leary proposal. In order to overcome the opposition of those who feared a hostile reaction from Washington, the government would consult the United States administration before taking a final decision.[12]

The prime minister himself handled much of the diplomacy involved with stick-handling the compromise through Washington. He wisely delayed consultations with the Americans until the furore over the government's expanded automotive incentive scheme had subsided. By then, rumours of the impending action had already reached the State Department, and when Charles Ritchie, Canada's ambassador to Washington, called on United States officials, he found them more or less reconciled to Canadian policy. Philip Trezise, the deputy assistant secretary of state for economic affairs, explained that the United States could live with Canada's policy if the reaction from the American media was not "too passionate." Nevertheless, he warned that the restrictions would be criticized as interfering with the free flow of ideas and "aimed at a particularly sensitive area of Canada-USA relations." On the whole, Ritchie characterized the American reaction as "quite mild."[13] When Pearson raised the issue with President Lyndon Johnson during his visit to Washington in January 1964, he received an equally reassuring response from George Ball, the under secretary of state.[14] Six weeks later, Pearson unveiled the new policy in the House of Commons.

In contrast to the subdued response in Washington, the reaction in Canada to the government's proposed legislation was hostile. Although a Maclean-Hunter representative called it "the best practical solution," most commentators were quick to denounce the government's decision to exempt *Time* and *Reader's Digest*. J.A. Daly, president of Southam Business Publications, accused the government of "locking the door after the horse was stolen."[15] The *Toronto Star*, a paper close to Gordon, claimed that the legislation meant "a fatal weakening of the O'Leary Report ... the death-knell for Canadian national magazines."[16] Its publisher, Joseph Atkinson, worried that the legislation "may actually work to our disadvantage by according Canadian status to *Time* and *Reader's Digest*, thus removing the last psychological bar to Canadian business advertising in foreign publications."[17] The opposition was so virulent that Floyd Chalmers, president of Maclean-Hunter, reversed his company's position and withdrew its lukewarm support for the government's measures.[18]

The parliamentary support on which Pearson's minority government depended to pass its legislation quickly evaporated. Although the opposition Conservatives had favoured virtually identical legislation in 1962, they made it clear that their support was no longer certain.[19] More troubling still, a number of Liberal backbenchers and cabinet ministers, unhappy with the decision to exempt *Time* and *Reader's Digest*, were threatening to oppose the government.[20] Sensing defeat, Gordon refused to table the resolutions necessary to give effect to the government's policy when he introduced his second budget in late March 1964.[21] He urged Cabinet to either rescind the exemptions for the two magazines or abandon the legislation.[22]

Aware that the government might be tempted to strengthen its legislation in order to disarm its domestic critics, the American embassy warned Canadian officials "that any departure from the basis of the legislation outlined in the Prime Minister's statement to the House would provoke violent criticism in the United States."[23] To underline the importance it attached to this question, Washington asked that the proposed legislation be placed on the agenda of the forthcoming meeting of the Canada–United States Ministerial Committee on Trade and Economic Affairs. Officials hurriedly reminded the secretary of state for external affairs and the prime minister that with the automotive incentive program under attack in Washington, now was not the time to act.[24] Caught between the domestic opposition and the vigilant administration in Washington, the government scrambled to find "positive measures for Canadian magazines to add to the mix."[25]

In early May, Kent provided the prime minister with the solution. Acknowledging finally that it would be neither right nor wise to include *Time* and *Reader's Digest* in any measures that would force them to leave the country, Kent suggested that the government do something else to satisfy its critics. He noted that the most vociferous opponents of the exemption were also the most strident advocates of a general "Canadian ownership" policy for media and suggested that the measures to protect Canadian magazines should be extended to newspapers, radio, and television. The exemption for *Time* and *Reader's Digest*, as well as one or two small newspapers that had acquired similar "squatter's rights," would be qualified by giving these publications three years to achieve 55 percent Canadian content. Kent's proposals were obviously attractive: "Because we would be taking action over a broader field, there would be far more satisfaction to nationalism and therefore it would be easier to get away with not requiring Canadianization of *Time* and *Reader's Digest* in ownership and control."[26]

Pearson introduced Kent's suggestions to Cabinet, where Gordon immediately grasped their significance for his own, more economic, nationalist objectives. He withdrew his opposition to the exemption for *Time* and *Reader's Digest* in exchange for extending the measures to a broader field. "The protests of the periodical press seemed of less importance than the protection of Canadian ownership of media generally," he explained to his colleagues, "and the action taken on the latter score would be likely to satisfy, or at least mollify, those who were critical of the failure to protect Canadian magazines."[27] Gordon's shift was important, but while the Cabinet agreed that the legislation should be extended to other media, it remained divided over the question of imposing Canadian content requirements on *Time* and *Reader's Digest*, a move that some members felt was unfair to the two magazines and certain to antagonize the United States.[28]

During the summer, the government made some progress in resolving its differences over media policy. By early October 1964 the prime minister was ready to ask the cabinet committee on economic policy, trade, and employment for its views. Pearson's measures were a good deal stiffer than those unveiled in February. He wanted to amend the income tax act to disallow deductions for advertising costs in foreign-owned newspapers, radio, and television stations and to modify the existing exemption for *Time* and *Reader's Digest* to require them to achieve 25 percent Canadian content within one year. Moreover, the postmaster general was to explore the feasibility of reducing the postal subsidies given to *Time* and *Reader's Digest*.[29]

The Department of External Affairs was alarmed by these proposals and urged Martin to protest vigorously. Washington had never shown much sympathy on this issue, acquiescing only because the exemption to *Time* and *Reader's Digest* effectively protected its real interest. American media would protest loudly and effectively against any effort to dilute the exemption. The decision to include newspapers and other media would also provoke comment, since it was difficult to argue that a problem existed in these areas. Most important, the prime minister's timing was disastrous: "With the looming United States elections and the accompanying dangers of irritations in United States–Canada relations, it does not seem like a very good moment to bring this issue forward again. If we are to have any success with such important negotiations as for example those taking place with regard to the rationalization of the automobile industry, we will need a good deal of support and understanding from United States public opinion."[30] Though Martin accepted these arguments, they made little impression on Pearson, who was anxious to remove this tiresome item from the Cabinet's agenda. He dismissed Martin's worries and convinced Cabinet to begin drafting the necessary legislation.[31]

Work on the legislation proceeded slowly, hindered in part by dogged opposition from officials in the Department of External Affairs. The department was given another opportunity to advance its case in early February 1965 when the ad hoc interdepartmental drafting group turned to the Cabinet for more guidance. The group recommended scrapping the earlier suggestions for Canadian content regulations, which had proven too difficult to administer without tripping up the ethnic press in Canada. It asked Cabinet to decide whether it wished to limit *Time* and *Reader's Digest* to an intermediate preferential rate or ordinary second-class privileges. Whatever the decision, the government should expect an adverse reaction from the United States and charges of "nationalism" and "interference in the free flow of ideas." Clearly swayed by the arguments advanced by External Affairs, the interdepartmental panel warned that the "timing of the introduction of these new proposals ... should therefore be looked at against other current issues in U.S.A-Canada relations, including the Congressional debate on the automotive programme and on the interest equalization tax renewal."[32]

The warning had a sobering effect, and even Kent began to hesitate.[33] In Cabinet, Martin was joined by Mitchell Sharp, the minister of trade and commerce, and Jack Pickersgill, the minister of transport, in opposing any action. Martin pointed out that none of the advocates of protection had gone out of business since the 1963 election. Sharp worried about the possible adverse impact on bilateral arrangements with the United States for marketing Canadian oil and wheat.

Gordon challenged the three ministers. "The present proposals were justifiable and considerably more realistic than those that had been made earlier," he argued. "He saw no reason to subsidize *Time* and *Reader's Digest*, which in his view constituted dumped material in Canada."[34] The time had come to stop the United States from taking over Canada's newspapers.

Gordon's intervention swung the momentum of the debate clearly in favour of the nationalist contingent. The following week Pearson returned to Cabinet with three clear recommendations. The income tax act would be amended along the lines set out in his statement to Parliament of February 1964, with the provisions for magazines extended to cover newspaper, radio, and television advertising. *Time* and *Reader's Digest* were to be given their promised exemption but would have to use ordinary second-class mail in the future. The customs act would be amended to prohibit the importation of special Canadian editions. Pearson's strong commitment to the measures guaranteed Cabinet's approval.[35]

In keeping with its commitment to inform Washington of developments in this field, Ottawa instructed Ritchie to give copies of the proposed legislation to the State Department in mid-March. The reaction was "surprisingly strong." Tresize reiterated Washington's familiar objections, denouncing in particular those clauses that discriminated between Canadian and non-Canadian publications on postal rates. This would materially diminish the value of the exemption provided *Time* and *Reader's Digest*. Tresize was sorry that Ottawa had decided to proceed with these measures just when the two countries had begun to improve their bilateral economic relations. "The proposed measures in publications," he pointed out, "would clearly be out of keeping with the recent trend and would be regarded as a retrograde step in USA-Canada relations."[36]

The phlegmatic Ritchie was clearly impressed by the vehemence with which Trezise insisted that United States subsidiaries in Canada should be given the same treatment as domestic companies. He warned Ottawa that Washington would not "be satisfied with a mere re-statement of our position." Indeed, he was deeply concerned about the effect a "negative response to [the] USA approach might have on general climate of our relations. I would therefore hope ... that we are willing to reexamine postal rate question in light of their objections."[37] The next day, Joe Scott, the minister at the United States Embassy, and Francis Linville, the economic counsellor, called on Ed Ritchie, the assistant under-secretary of state for external affairs, to underline Washington's concern.[38]

The impact of the American representations was immediate. The idea that Canada might try to convince the Americans to accept the revised postal rates was dropped. Instead, within a week, Cabinet decided that Gordon would announce only the proposed changes to the income tax and customs act and simply refer to the government's intention to review the postal rates paid by *Time* and *Reader's Digest* as part of a general review of rates.[39] Gordon's supporters were devastated. Peter Newman, one of his most ardent champions and a former editor at *Maclean's*, denounced the minister of finance to a friend: "You are reading the letter of an *ex*-Walter Gordon disciple. His militant sponsorship of legislation forever garotting Canadian periodicals and awarding *Time* and *Digest* a monopoly over the Canadian magazine industry, is a step that has disillusioned me ... Gordon has now handed over to two American magazine empires the monopoly over the printed word for national distribution in Canada. I think he's inconsistent and stupid."[40] Washington, however, was gratified by Cabinet's decision and was reassured to discover that the more extreme manifestations of Canadian nationalism might still be kept safely at bay.[41]

But American observers did not expect the nationalist problem to disappear completely. The issue, as Butterworth well knew, was deep-rooted and reflected Canada's historical ambiguity about the attractions and dangers of a close relationship with the United States.

"Canada's economic relations with the United States," he commented in January 1966, "are still beset by the dichotomy between belief that economic growth depends on close ties with the United States and the fear that economic interdependence with the United States would eventually lead to political absorption." Butterworth believed that Pearson's reelection in November 1965 as head of the country's third consecutive minority government "was symptomatic of [Canada's] uncertainty ... and immaturity." Among the many fundamental questions that Canadians still had to resolve was the choice between closer economic ties with the United States or economic nationalism and multilateralism. As a result, he warned the State Department, Canadian nationalism was likely to continue to plague the relationship "in odd ways."[42]

Still, he thought, there were hopeful indicators that in the next little while there might be less trouble for Washington than in the past few years. The uncertain election results were a chastening experience for both the government and the opposition and would encourage them to adopt "a more cautious approach to u.s.–Canadian problems which should augur well for United States interests in the economic area." The humiliation of Gordon, who accepted responsibility for the government's poor showing and resigned from the Cabinet after the election, was counted "a great gain for us." Butterworth was also encouraged by the addition of Robert Winters as minister of trade and commerce and Sharp's promotion to minister of finance. These changes, he thought, "will have a definite strengthening, and perhaps conservative, effect [on the government]."

Butterworth's optimism was not entirely misplaced. During the first few months of 1966 it was clear that Sharp and the revamped government seemed inclined to adopt a more flexible approach to the question of foreign investment in Canada. This was evident in how they proposed to deal with the problems created for the Mercantile Bank by the revision of the bank act. The dispute first arose in the summer of 1963, when representatives of the First National City Bank of New York (Citibank) met with Gordon and explained to him that they had just concluded an agreement in principle to purchase the small, Dutch-owned Mercantile Bank. Gordon, who was convinced that it was "most important that Canadian control be maintained of our principal financial institutions ... [for] these institutions form the very core of our financial and business system," warned his American interlocutors on 18 July 1963 that the government would probably amend the bank act to limit foreign ownership of banks and near-banks. Despite this warning, Citibank proceeded with its purchase.[43]

The new bank act was introduced only in the spring of 1965. It included clauses limiting foreign ownership to 25 percent and restricting individual holdings to 10 percent. The bill was not retroactive, and Citibank was spared these provisions. Section 75(2)(g), however, specifically targeted the Mercantile Bank. It prohibited any bank from having liabilities of more than twenty times its authorized capital stock if more than 25 percent of its shares were owned by any one individual owner or group of owners. This clause effectively meant that Citibank would need to reduce its holdings in the Mercantile Bank to 25 percent before the bank could expand.

Though Gordon's bill died on the order paper when the 1965 election was called, Sharp was expected to reintroduce a bill to revise the bank act early in the new session. Not unexpectedly, the United States, which had remained silent on this issue during the election campaign, protested against the provisions in Gordon's original legislation at the meeting of the Canada–United States Ministerial Committee on Trade and Economic Affairs in March 1966. The American delegation pointed out that the legislation was both discriminatory and retroactive and rejected as unfounded Canadian fears that the Mercantile Bank would ever be in a position to dominate banking in Canada.[44]

The exchange was not especially bitter. Off the record, T.C. Mann, the United States under secretary of the treasury, volunteered to help Sharp work out a compromise with Citibank that would limit Mercantile's growth and remove the need for offensive provisions in the legislation.[45] Later that month, Sharp met with Butterworth to pursue this possibility. Well aware of Gordon's looming presence on the government's backbench, Sharp refused to amend the bill to eliminate section 75(2)(g). However, he was ready to risk a public dispute with Gordon in order to permit the Mercantile Bank to increase its capitalization under the present legislation. The American ambassador immediately understood the significance of this concession. It would effectively "finesse Mercantile's problem" by allowing the bank to expand *before* the restrictive legislation was in place.[46]

The United States kept up a gentle pressure on the Canadian government, registering a formal objection with the Department of External Affairs in mid-April. The protest note, which hinted broadly at the possibility that Canadian banks in the United States might suffer if Ottawa discriminated against American banks in Canada, was a clever piece of diplomatic drafting. Although it was not intended for publication, the note was unclassified and could therefore be made public without Canada's permission if Washington later wished to escalate the disagreement into a confrontation. The note itself addressed only the principle of discrimination against American banks in Canada and did not mention the Mercantile Bank by name, allowing both governments considerable room to manoeuvre. When he delivered it, Charles Wootton, the United States embassy counsellor for economic affairs, made it clear that it was designed essentially to encourage a settlement. While the United States complaint may have been about banking in general, the problem really was "a de facto one and related to Mercantile." Washington wanted primarily "a solution ... which would be satisfactory to Mercantile ... a compromise of some sort which would avoid a head-on collision."[47]

By early May a solution along the lines that Sharp had outlined to Butterworth in March was within reach. The minister of finance approached Robèrt MacFadden, the Canadian president of the Mercantile Bank, early that month to discuss how the bank might circumvent the coming legislation. They discussed in detail Mercantile's expansion plans and agreed that they could be met by allowing it to increase its capitalization before the new bank act came into effect. The timing was left open, though Sharp proposed "to say when he moves the legislation that this is the Government's view — that it is the Government's intent — to allow an increase in the capitalization of Mercantile." All that remained was to seek Cabinet's approval for the arrangement. Bryce conveyed the news to Butterworth. "Amid their mutual laughter at the reference to the July 18 misunderstandings," the ambassador was ready to accept the deal "with reservations."[48]

While the two United States principals involved – the State Department and the Mercantile Bank – considered Sharp's suggestion, the finance minister's operating environment changed for the worse. In early May, Gordon published *A Choice for Canada: Independence or Colonial Status* and ignited a public debate over the Mercantile Bank. In his polemic Gordon reviewed his meeting of July 1963 with representatives from Citibank and claimed that they had been fairly warned not to proceed. Mercantile responded with its own press release.[49] Drawing on his nationalist allies in caucus, Gordon launched an active campaign against any adjustment in the provisions relating to the Mercantile Bank. Increasingly suspicious of Sharp, whom he accused of stealing his ideas for a national development fund, he floated the idea of moving an amendment to the bank act from the floor of the House of Commons to give Parliament, rather than Cabinet, the power to increase bank capitalization. At the same time, Gordon attacked the central feature of Sharp's version of the revised bank act, the provision for removing the six percent ceiling on bank loans.[50]

In this context Cabinet met repeatedly throughout May and June to review the bank act. Sharp's version of the legislation included the same provisions limiting the growth of the Mercantile Bank as Gordon's, but Sharp proposed to amend the clause in a manner that would delay its coming into effect until 31 December 1967.[51] He also planned

to inform Parliament that "any reasonable request for an increase in
the authorized capital of the Mercantile Bank ... would be given sympathetic consideration."[52] Sharp argued that the bank could be
allowed to double its size without it having any appreciable impact on
the Canadian banking system. There was considerable support for this
position. Martin, Winters, and John Turner, minister without portfolio, were united in warning that the legislation as drafted by Gordon
was "discriminatory and would complicate relations with the United
States."[53] However, with Gordon's threatened amendment gathering
support in caucus, Pearson and other ministers urged Sharp to maintain the government's original, unyielding position.[54]

As he sought to negotiate a suitable compromise with Gordon and
his supporters over the decision to lift the 6 percent ceiling on interest
rates, Sharp was in no position to force the government to give the
Mercantile Bank more generous treatment. In the end he secured Cabinet's support only for his technical amendment, which would allow
the Mercantile Bank to grow until the end of December 1967 if authorized by Cabinet.[55] It was a hollow victory, since Cabinet was under no
circumstances going to permit the bank to increase its capitalization.

Officials at the United States embassy reacted with anger when they
learned that the compromise sketched out by Sharp and the Mercantile
Bank had collapsed. Wootton urged Washington to "express its
extreme displeasure" at the Canadian action. Although this would be
unlikely to lead to any changes in the legislation, the economic counsellor thought that it might help the Mercantile Bank to secure an
increase in its authorized capital. He also pressed the administration to
eliminate the preferential treatment enjoyed by Canadian banks in the
United States to "bring home to the G[overnment] O[f] C[anada] our
determination to protect U.S. economic interests in Canada and to
resist further inroads such as might be directed against other types of
U.S. firms on another occasion."[56]

In early July, Sharp introduced his bill to amend the bank act, unde-
terred by the threat of retaliation. The Canadian banking community
in the United States was thought to be too small to merit much sustained attention from the administration. Moreover, Sharp and his officials were well aware that the United States government lacked the
constitutional authority to retaliate, since banking was a state responsibility. Nevertheless, when his bill came up for second reading in the
House of Commons in early October, Sharp hinted that he would be
prepared to authorize United States banks to open agencies in Canada
if Washington muted its opposition to the bank act.[57]

Mercantile was not interested in this meagre offer, which did little to
address the immediate threat to its interests. Instead, Walter Wriston,

the executive vice-president of Citibank, and Harry Harfield, the bank's counsel, arranged to meet the acting secretary of state, Nicholas Katzenbach, in Washington. The two bank executives explained that they had heard from "unnamed friendly sources" in the Liberal Party that Sharp would withdraw the offending clauses in his bank act if ordered to do so by the prime minister. A message from Johnson to Pearson, they continued, would have the desired effect. Katzenbach was noncommittal, but after further discussions with Citibank, State Department officials concluded that a stern note to the Canadian government was in order. They turned to Butterworth for advice.[58]

The American ambassador relished the prospect of a fight. He insisted that the proposed note and the verbal message that would accompany it must be strong – strong enough to convince Ottawa that the United States was determined to see the Mercantile Bank treated fairly. More important, the note must convince the Canadian government once and for all of Washington's fundamental opposition to "retroactive discrimination." This principle remained vitally important to all United States companies in Canada, for they could all be "adversely affected by retroactive changes in the rules of the game." Indeed, the affair had global implications, since "not a few underdeveloped countries are looking over Canada's shoulder to see how she makes out in bilking Uncle Sam's investment." The ambassador recalled the discriminatory dividend tax in Gordon's first budget, explaining that this "is test number 2. The stakes are the same and we must mean what we say for should they disregard our formal warning and we act accordingly, we will nevertheless by retaliation ensure that retroactive discrimination will never be tried again."[59]

Butterworth's views were influential in shaping both the note to be delivered to Canada and the tactics to be followed in handing it over. On 11 November 1966, Ed Ritchie, who succeeded Charles Ritchie as Canadian ambassador to the United States in July 1966, was called into the State Department to receive the formal American protest from Katzenbach. The under secretary of state emphasized the degree of concern felt by the United States and explained that this was "not limited to [the] specifics of Mercantile case but arose in great part because of [the] precedent which [the] legislation would set with regard [to] other US interests both [in] Canada and abroad."[60] The written protest that accompanied Katzenbach's oral presentation was described by Ritchie as "a very rough note." It asked Ottawa to remove the offending clauses in the bank act and threatened retaliation not only against Canadian banks but also against any Canadian economic interest in the United States, since the legislation undermined "the ground rules on which all American-owned firms operating in Canada must rely."[61]

Officials and politicians in Ottawa alike were appalled. The threat
of retaliation was particularly disturbing, since it was only a matter of
time before the existence of the note would become public in leak-
prone Ottawa, painting the government into an uncomfortable corner.
Sharp, who was scheduled to visit New York on 15 November,
arranged to travel on to Washington to meet with Henry Fowler, the
United States secretary of the treasury. The visit was intended both to
determine how united the administration was behind their hard line
and to let the United States know how little room Sharp had to
manoeuvre.

On meeting his American counterpart, it was soon apparent to
Sharp that the administration was not completely united. Fowler
agreed with the United States position, but he did not like the note. He
explained that "he had not come down on the points raised in the
note," and he quickly offered his "good offices in discussing [the]
issue with State Department." In his view there were two possible
solutions: Ottawa could agree to increase Mercantile's authorized capital, or it could amend the legislation to allow foreign-owned banks to
maintain a ratio of total liabilities to authorized capital that was the
same as national average. Either approach would allow the Mercantile Bank to grow without permitting it to dominate the banking
industry in Canada.[62]

The State Department was also entertaining some second thoughts
about its tactics following Sharp's visit to Washington. Rufus Smith, the
department's officer responsible for Canadian affairs, suggested to Butterworth that the United States had accomplished its primary objective
when it registered its opposition to discriminatory legislation in the
November note. This question could be pursued later in order to drive
the point home. Meanwhile, Smith thought he had found a device to
defuse the crisis "which is consistent with our basic position, but which
might still avoid taking us very far down the path of retaliation."
Ottawa might ask all banks to inform or consult the Treasury Board or
the Bank of Canada before they increased their ratio of liabilities to
authorized capital. In effect, Canada would adopt the kind of "voluntary guidelines approach" that the United States used to address its balance of payments problem. This would allow the Canadian government
to claim that it had preserved the essential purpose of the legislation –
monitoring the activities of foreign banks in Canada – while at same
time "maintain[ing] 'free enterprise' in the banking system." The United States could also claim that the discriminatory features of the legislation had been removed and no precedent had been set.[63]

Butterworth rejected the suggestions advanced by Fowler and Smith.
Having expressed the American viewpoint so strongly in the Novem-

ber note, the ambassador believed that a decision to withdraw now would mean retreat and defeat. Intensifying the crisis represented the most effective American option: "I do not believe our interest will be served by back-tracking. After all, if Canadians push through legislation and U.S. follows through with its promised retaliation, we gain broader advantage of demonstrating to Canadians, as well as to other countries peering over their shoulders, high cost of retroactive discrimination against U.S. interests. In my view, therefore, it is not up to us but rather to Canadians to suggest compromise."[64] The ambassador's judgment was again decisive, and the administration remained committed to its November note.

Developments in Canada were further eroding the government's ability to seek a negotiated solution. As Sharp and his officials had anticipated, news of the American note become public in an article by Peter Newman, writing in the *Toronto Star*.[65] Sharp was immediately faced with a host of hostile questions in the House of Commons. Anxious to dampen the controversy, the minister of finance approached MacFadden, who was scheduled to appear before the House of Commons Committee on Finance, Trade and Economic Affairs to testify on the bill early the following week. Sharp asked the bank president to postpone his appearance until January. At the same time, he called Ritchie, asking him to let Katzenbach know what he was trying to accomplish, with the implication that Washington might do the same.[66]

Katzenbach was noncommittal; Butterworth was not. Learning of Sharp's growing concern over the crisis, the ambassador insisted that MacFadden should testify as scheduled and advised the administration in Washington not to give way: "It seems to me all the more important that our own course must now be steady. We must not allow ourselves to be deterred by G[overnment] O[f] C[anada] ploys from defending [the] principle of non-retroactive discriminatory treatment of our interests."[67] The State Department concurred, and though MacFadden agreed to delay his testimony, Smith told Citibank representatives that the administration was not interested in settling. Asked for his advice on learning that Ottawa might try again to change the legislation to meet Citibank's needs, Smith told the Mercantile representative that "any response Citibank makes ... should carry [a] clear caveat that what might be satisfactory to Citibank would not necessarily be acceptable to US G[overnment] ... US would [not] back away from principle. Such stance, he thought, was essential to broad interests of Citibank and other US interests both [in] Canada and elsewhere even though in short run it may not solve Mercantile problem."[68] Citibank, which surely never anticipated that its interests would diverge quite so sharply from Washington's, had little choice but to stay the course.

There was now every indication that Ottawa too would not retreat. In early January the prime minister invited Walter Gordon to re-enter his Cabinet, in an effort to appease the party's progressive and nationalist wing. Pearson, Sharp, and Gordon met at the prime minister's residence the night before the decision was made public to settle their differences over economic policy. Gordon was "bitter and uncompromising," and the three men agreed "that there would be no compromising on the subject of the Mercantile Bank."[69] Cabinet later approved a defiant note in response to Washington's November protest, but Sharp continued to hint that a compromise might eventually be possible. At the same time, the Department of Finance stepped up its propaganda efforts, releasing additional material on the two meetings of July 1963, when Citibank was warned of the government's plans.[70]

The press revelled in the controversy, but more responsible observers in Ottawa and Washington were worried that the public posturing might spin out of control. Ritchie reported "serious and widespread" concern in Washington and urged the government to compromise.[71] Fowler, whose efforts to deal with Washington's continuing balance of payments difficulties required Canadian help, disassociated himself from the November protest.[72] Bryce Mackasey, a Liberal member of parliament and a member of the House of Commons Committee on Finance, Trade and Economic Affairs, shared this concern and decided to negotiate on his own. After clearing his idea with Sharp and Pearson, he headed for New York on 28 January. During a series of meetings with MacFadden, senior Mercantile Bank executives, and Rockefeller over the next two days, the Canadian convinced Citibank not to "rule out the sale of some Mercantile shares to the Canadian public at some future date."[73]

The minister of finance was told of the bank's small, yet important, concession. A meeting was quickly scheduled between Sharp and the bank's representatives. It was clear, however, that he would not easily get Cabinet's approval for a compromise. When he broached the question of a meeting with Citibank on 30 January, Gordon insisted that "no major concession should be made." Indeed, the new minister without portfolio insisted that Mercantile not be allowed to increase its authorized capital until it had sold 90 percent of its shares. Sharp pressed ahead and suggested that the bill be amended to include a provision specifying that "during a certain period of time, [Citibank] would sell their stock to Canadians while at the same time obtaining approval of an increase in authorized capital." Gordon restated his opposition, and Cabinet refused to let Sharp begin negotiating on this basis with the First National City Bank.[74] Replying to Ritchie, the prime minister could offer little that was "hopeful or helpful at this stage."[75]

The next day, as scheduled, Sharp met with Stewart Clifford, a Mercantile Bank executive. Sharp was asked about his willingness to give the bank more time to sell its shares, but without Cabinet's support no firm answer was possible. The minister testified before the Committee on Finance, Trade and Economic Affairs a few days later, using the occasion to explore in public the possibility of a compromise. He reported that he had been told indirectly that the Mercantile Bank was ready to sell its shares, that he was aware of the difficulties this posed for the bank, and that he was willing to listen to any suggestions. He thought two possibilities existed: allow an increase in Mercantile's authorized capital with the new shares issued to Canadians or extend the deadline.

Sharp declined to pursue either course until 22 February, when Citibank agreed in writing "to seek share participation by Canadian residents when it is appropriate to make an attractive offering." Appearing before the House of Commons committee, the minister of finance was led by Mackasey's gentle questioning to reiterate his own preference for a compromise and to invite the committee to come up with a solution. Mercantile's new readiness to divest itself of shares, Sharp informed the committee, was "such a step forward in this controversy that I believe that this committee should not in any way discourage the bank from doing that. I do not believe that an extension of the date is contrary to the spirit of the act, and it is possible that it would advance the cause of converting the Mercantile Bank into a predominantly Canadian-owned institution ... I am inclined to believe that there is likely to be a more constructive outcome if some time is given to the bank to get its affairs in order before they are required to sell shares."[76] On cue, Mackasey quickly moved to amend the bill. The amendment, a draft of which was conveniently found in the briefcase of the inspector general of banks, gave Citibank five years to expand before it had to sell 75 percent of its stake in the Mercantile Bank. Seconded by Colin Cameron, the New Democratic Party's financial critic (thereby securing Sharp's left flank), it was adopted that afternoon.

Travelling in Western Canada, Gordon was justifiably livid when he learned of these developments. Only days before, he had asked Pearson what was going to happen with the bank act and was told "that Sharp had decided not to do anything at all ... He might bring the matter up again later on but there will be no changes proposed in the present Bank Act revision."[77] Gordon immediately returned to Ottawa determined to scuttle the deal. Like Butterworth, he had come to see the entire issue as having "symbolic significance insofar as the whole foreign control issue is concerned."[78] He insisted that there be no concessions. If there was to be some sort of a compromise, Citibank should be forced to reduce its holding in the Mercantile Bank to 10 percent. "Sharp was completely adamant that he would make no concessions to me whatever," Gordon recorded, adding "that in these circumstances he or I would have to go."[79]

The Cabinet turned the problem over to the prime minister and a group of ministers, who eventually reached a compromise in early March. The government would make two amendments to the legislation. Shareholders who held more than 10 percent of a bank's shares were prohibited from acquiring additional shares. In addition, Citibank's five-year extension was made conditional on Cabinet's periodic approval. Both Gordon and Sharp agreed to these amendments. The ministers also agreed that Cabinet would adopt two additional resolutions. Citibank's extension would not be forthcoming unless it gave Cabinet compelling evidence of its intention to sell 75 percent of its shares to Canadians, and the Mercantile Bank's authorized capital would not be allowed to grow until Citibank's holding was reduced to 10 percent. Consideration of these two resolutions was deferred until an actual request for an increase in authorized capital was received from the Mercantile Bank, avoiding a Cabinet split over the issue.

Gordon's success in transforming the Mercantile Bank into a nationalist symbol signalled the arrival in late 1966 and 1967 of a more sustained and integrated critique of the United States and its influence on Canada. By the spring of 1967, the tenets of economic and cultural nationalism were fused with the growing opposition to United States foreign policy, particularly the war in Vietnam, and recast into a potent and popular brand of anti-Americanism. Against the backdrop of the war in Southeast Asia, the export of American popular culture and United States foreign investment took on a more sinister colouration. Partly inspired by the work of radical social and political theorists from the former European colonies of Africa and Asia, who were exploring in critical terms the nature of colonialism, a growing number of Canadians were inclined to depict Canada–United States relations in neocolonial terms. In April 1967, for instance, the political scientist Gad Horowitz described Canada's "relationship with the United States ... [as] analogous to the relationship of Finland with the Soviet Union."[80] Mel Watkins, a professor of political economy at the University of Toronto, recalled that the "anti-war movement in Canada developed into anti-imperialism and ... that translated into nationalism."[81]

Canada's artistic and literary communities quickly adopted the neo-colonial rhetoric as their own. Nourished on a diet of Canada Council grants, a new generation of writers and critics forcefully signalled their coming of age in 1967 with the creation of the House of Anansi Press in Toronto. Its early authors included Dennis Lee, Dave Godfrey, Margaret Atwood, and Al Purdy. A disparate group, recalled Douglas Fetherling, Anansi's first employee, "they were all, at some fundamental level, against more or less the same thing: Americanism, with its republican brutality and hatred of culture."[82] Their profound distrust of modern America and its values was reflected in the work of George Grant, the McMaster University professor of philosophy, whose influential critique in 1965 of Ottawa's failure to respond to the depredations of American corporations, *Lament for a Nation*, set the shrill tone that infused the "new nationalism."[83] Like Grant, the poet Lee attacked Canada's "Liberal" elite for producing a "nation of losers and quislings":

> In a bad time, people, from an outpost of empire I write
> bewildered, though on about living. It is to set down a nation's
> failure of nerve; I mean complicity, which is signified by the
> gaseous stain above us ...
> And the consenting citizens of a minor and docile colony
> are cogs in a useful tool, though in no way
> necessary and scarcely
> criminal at all, and their leaders are
> honourable men, as for example Paul Martin.[84]

Others launched their assaults directly against the United States, whose foreign policy and urban race riots seemed an accurate and disturbing reflection of the country's raw and violent character. A verse from Atwood's poem "Backdrop Addresses Cowboy" succinctly combined the poet's observations on United States popular and political culture into a sudden, savage attack on the bombing in Vietnam:

> Your righteous eyes, your laconic
> trigger-fingers
> people the streets with villains:
> as you move, the air in front of you
> blossoms with targets.[85]

Artists like Joyce Wieland and Greg Curnoe reflected this anti-American sentiment visually. The text on a 1965 graphic by Wieland left no room for misunderstanding: "Patriotism / Big Cash Savings / Canada Si Yankee No! / Human Missiles / Marrow Death / Pesticides / Orbital Spies / Genocide / Pepsi / C.I.A."[86]

The celebrations to mark Canada's centennial in 1967 helped stoke the nationalist fervour. Pearson's government poured money into the festivities. New arenas, libraries, and statues were erected across Canada. Centennial projects resulted in hundreds of subsidized works on Canada and its accomplishments. To the unforgettable strains of Bobby Gimby's catchy tune "CA-NA-DA" the government sent the Centennial Train, a travelling museum of Canadiana, across the country, while tens of thousands of Canadians made the pilgrimage to Montreal to visit the 1967 World's Fair.

The nationalist mood was also fortified by the first wave of postwar baby-boomers coming of age in the mid-1960s. Largely freed from want by the postwar economic boom that provided their parents with safe, clean, and prosperous suburbs, these young people pressed uneasily against the established order. The *Globe and Mail* noted in 1966 that they shared "a curious mood of rebellion, of resentment, not perhaps clearly recognized but nevertheless expressed."[87] Rock 'n' roll, drugs, and collapsing sexual mores helped create and sustain an atmosphere of experimentation and innovation.[88] The anti-American and nationalist critique of United States domestic and foreign policy advanced by Grant and his disciples reverberated among campus audiences. The large number of American academics who taught in the country's rapidly expanding universities and the increasing number of draft-dodgers who made their way north into Canada added their own brand of anti-Americanism to the volatile mixture.[89] Early in 1967, the cries for the United States to get out of Vietnam – and Canada – began to spill into the streets.

The government's failure during 1966 to advance materially the cause of peace in Vietnam, either directly through Canadian "good offices" or indirectly by securing a United Nations seat for Peking, left it exposed to this growing domestic criticism. In mid-January 1967, a delegation from the Faculty Committee on Vietnam from the University of Toronto's Victoria College met with Martin and Pearson to express their concern with the war. Specifically, the faculty members asserted that the government's support for a negotiated settlement in Vietnam conflicted with its policy of selling arms to the United States under the terms of the Defence Production Agreement. The protesters had a point; the war in Vietnam had been good to the Canadian defence industry. In the four-year period before 1965, Canadian military exports to the United States averaged approximately $150 million per year. These exports ballooned to $260 million dollars in 1965 and increased again in 1966 to $300 million, easing Canada's balance of payments position and reducing the country's continuing need for American capital.[90] When the problem was first recognized in 1965, the United States had made it clear that it would not accept any limits on its use of military equipment purchased from foreign suppliers.

Pearson's government was caught. As Cadieux pointed out to Martin, "our participation in arrangements leading to the integration of Canadian and U.S. defence industry, with the result that Canada has become the sole source in North America of certain lines of military equipment, clearly implies a long-term commitment not to place restrictions on the export of arms to the U.S. The consequences of attempting to reverse this policy would thus have far-reaching effects, not only in the economic sphere, but also on our political relations with the U.S."[91] The prime minister and foreign minister vigorously defended the program against the Faculty Committee's charges, pointing out that the agreement was designed to meet the country's overall North American and NATO defence commitments as well as contributing to a positive balance of trade with the United States.[92]

In late January 1967 a Canadian Press story reignited the controversy.[93] In the House of Commons, Martin reiterated the government's opposition to the war in Vietnam and reviewed his efforts to use Canada's connections in Washington and Hanoi to get talks started. While the government's position might be illogical, he admitted, it was only fair to consider the circumstances under which the program had originally been developed in 1959.[94] The issue was further complicated when the government refused free transportation of medical supplies to North and South Vietnam for Quaker relief groups, on the grounds that this would be inconsistent with government aid policy, which called for recipient countries to pay shipping charges.[95]

In late May the government was faced with a new set of charges when Gerald Clark, associate editor of the *Montreal Star*, accused Canadian members of the International Commission for Supervision and Control (ICSC) of "betraying their trust by acting as informants for U.S. intelligence agencies ... functioning as spies when they are supposed to be serving as International Civil Servants."[96] Martin vehemently denied the accusations. While there was no doubt that Canadian diplomatic and military representatives on the ICSC provided American intelligence authorities with information on conditions in North Vietnam, it was equally clear that they did not break the rules that governed diplomatic behaviour. In the heated domestic debate, however, this distinction was lost on the government's critics.

The domestic criticism during the first few months of 1967 worried Martin, who was anxious to score a diplomatic success as he pressed his bid to become Pearson's successor. At the same time, however, his capacity for independent action was considerably reduced. While rumours of Pearson's unhappiness with Martin did not quash the minister's interest in pursuing a settlement in Vietnam, they did encourage him to confine his efforts largely to more modest initiatives that derived their legitimacy from Canada's status as a member of the ICSC and that were unlikely to embarrass the United States. This probing for an opening, which the United States encouraged by its constant efforts to reassure Martin that Canada's role as a member of the ICSC had a place in American considerations, may have provided the minister with some consolation that he was not entirely inactive. But it did little to help him quiet his domestic critics.[97]

Consequently, Martin turned his own hand to peace-making in April 1967. In a statement before the House of Commons Standing Committee on External Affairs, he proposed a "stage-by-stage return to the Geneva cease-fire arrangements." This would be accomplished in four distinct steps. First, it would be necessary to restore the demilitarized zone and reactivate those provisions of the Geneva Accords that prohibited the use by either side of bases in North or South Vietnam for carrying out acts of hostility against the other. Second, there would be an undertaking "to freeze the course of military events at its current level," a step that implied a prohibition on the import of military material and reinforcements. Third, all hostilities would stop. The fourth step envisioned a return to the complete Geneva Accords with the repatriation of prisoners of war and the withdrawal of all outside forces.[98]

Hanoi flatly rejected the minister's effort. In Washington, where Martin's domestic difficulties were understood, the Canadian plan was given a sympathetic, if sceptical, reception. Both Secretary of State Dean Rusk and William Bundy, assistant secretary of state for Far Eastern affairs, told Ritchie that the forthcoming American and South Vietnamese responses were intended to permit the minister to show his domestic critics that the United States was not the problem in Vietnam.[99] Unfortunately, the available evidence suggested otherwise. In a frank and distressing conversation with Arthur Goldberg, the U.S. ambassador to the United Nations, Martin learned in late April that rumours of a possible escalation in the American commitment were true. Johnson was determined to persist in his present course, even at the risk of his presidential nomination. Goldberg, claiming that moderates like himself and McNamara no longer had any influence, warned Martin against any public appeals against the bombing but urged the Canadian to get together with other powers "at the highest ministerial level to throw out ideas for negotiation in the hope that they might be taken up in direct dialogue between Washington and Hanoi."[100]

It was becoming more difficult for Martin to resist demands that he act. A growing number of officials and Cabinet members wanted him to bring more pressure to bear directly on the United States. In early May the acting Canadian High Commissioner in London, Geoff Murray, suggested that Ottawa seek to persuade the United States to halt the bombing in conjunction with a proposed truce marking Buddha's birthday.[101] Similarly, the Canadian embassy in Paris suggested that the heads of government from several countries friendly to the United States jointly urge Johnson to suspend the bombing in Vietnam. Cadieux quickly scotched these suggestions.[102] He could do nothing, however, to control the public musings of critical Cabinet ministers. In a speech in Toronto, Gordon maintained that the United States had become bogged down in a civil war "which cannot be justified on either moral or strategic grounds." He called on Martin and Pearson "to continue to do everything in their power to press the Americans to stop the bombing."[103] They, in their turn, were outraged. The prime minister publicly repudiated Gordon's remarks but allowed him to remain in Cabinet, thus according his speech a certain legitimacy.[104]

The United States was not unaware of the pressure mounting on Pearson and Martin. As it prepared for the president's visit to Expo '67, the White House was anxious to counter "the criticism [the u.s.] has gotten recently from some top-level Canadians" and urged Johnson to remind the prime minister of his repeated efforts to have Hanoi begin negotiations.[105]

The president's peace efforts, however, were not the subject of the talks between Johnson and Pearson during their brief meeting at Harrington Lake in late May. When the two met privately after lunch, the president was "calm and relaxed" when discussing Vietnam, emboldening Pearson to suggest that the United States should stop the bombing without any conditions. Johnson promised to consider this suggestion, but when they were joined by Martin and their various advisors, he "was more vigorous in his defense of the present policy of bombing and more reluctant to consider proposals of any kind for a change which was not associated with a concession of some kind on the part of the north." He spoke with great feeling about the loss of American lives, emphasizing that whenever he called a pause, the "blood of Americans and their friends who were killed was 'on my hands ... if our casualties go up from 337 a week to 1037 I am the one who will be responsible.'"[106]

Neither Pearson nor Martin knew precisely what to make of their talk with the president. To Pearson, Johnson was "more of an enigma than ever, only he is now an older and more impatient and irascible enigma; feverish in his insistence on activity, verbal and physical; moving so much and so fast in the hope, perhaps, that movement is progress." Martin was equally puzzled by Johnson. "As a result of the President's visit," he explained to the British prime minister, "we did not seem to know a great deal more than before as to how the U.S. intended, in practical terms, to approach a settlement."[107]

Martin continued to press the United States in private to adopt a more flexible policy. Accompanied by Gordon, to whom he wished to demonstrate the alliance's usefulness, Martin attended the NATO ministerial meeting in June 1967, hopeful that some progress might be made. In a secret session on the international situation, the secretary of state for external affairs criticized Washington's refusal to stop the bombing and blamed the United States for placing its allies in an awkward position with their domestic audiences. Gordon recorded the scene: "It was an excellent presentation and took courage. Dean Rusk replied somewhat superciliously and proceeded to slap Paul [Martin] down. In doing so, he made it clear that, when it comes to foreign policy, the U.S. sees things in blacks and whites; there is nothing between, certainly no place for grey ... No one else said anything."[108]

In Martin's subsequent private discussion with Rusk, who this time made an effort to take the Canadian's preoccupations seriously, the results were initially more hopeful. Martin found the secretary of state preoccupied by the outbreak of the Six Day War in the Middle East and "receptive to suggestions that the bombing [in North Vietnam] be stopped." Rusk indicated that he was prepared "to stop the bombing permanently in exchange for an undertaking from Hanoi that they would accept an international force in the [demilitarized zone]." Martin offered to have the new Canadian commissioner, Orme Dier, deliver the message. Officials in Ottawa reacted optimistically and even suggested that Cadieux, who was in Paris with Martin, could stay behind to discuss the idea with DRVN representatives. But in Washington, Bundy quickly put an end to the notion of an international force.

Throughout the summer, domestic opposition to the war continued to mount. Escott Reid, Douglas LePan, and A.F.W. Plumptre, respected figures from the "golden age of Canadian diplomacy" and now prominent Canadian academics, made public a letter to the prime minister urging him to call a bombing halt.[109] By August, 41 percent of Canadians wanted the United States to withdraw from Vietnam; only 18 percent thought that it should stay.[110] Given the government's efforts to resist these pressures to disassociate Canada from United States policy in Vietnam, Martin was dismayed to learn in early September that the United States wished to have its friends on the UN Security Council, where Canada was serving a two-year term, confront the Vietnam problem. A nicely balanced resolution, urging both Hanoi and Washington to de-escalate the war would help the administration meet its critics at home without weakening American support for the government in Saigon. Martin was doubtful. He warned Rusk that such a resolution was likely to be amended by the Soviet Union so that it called on the United States to stop its bombing unilaterally. In view of the growing domestic opposition to the war, the Liberal government would not be able to vote against an amended motion.[111]

Washington's interest in using the United Nations to protect the administration's domestic flank undoubtedly made it much easier for Martin to adopt a public position that reflected Canadian domestic opinion more closely. When the Danish foreign minister urged the United States to stop the bombing unconditionally in a speech at the UNGA, Martin concluded that "it might be necessary for Canada to say something of the same sort."[112] His speech to the General Assembly, though, was a study in ambiguity. He urged Washington to halt the bombing, but linked it to the first step in his April 1967 program for disengagement and implied that any halt in the bombing must be accompanied by a reciprocal gesture from Hanoi. "As a first step toward disengagement," he proclaimed, "the bombing of the North might be terminated and the demilitarized zone restored to its intended status subject to effective international supervision."[113]

The speech could not have been delivered at a more inopportune moment. In the fall of 1967 the bilateral agenda was suddenly crowded with a host of irritants, both minor and major. The Mercantile Bank affair, which had been dormant for several months, resurfaced in August when the United States delivered a final protest against the new bank act.[114] The review of the post office act promised in 1965 was now also complete, and Ottawa informed Washington in late September that it would proceed with its plans to increase the postal rates charged *Time* and *Reader's Digest*.[115] These irritants, combined with Martin's failure to consult Washington over his speech to the United Nations, stirred the redoubtable Butterworth into action. In late October he dispatched a particularly "flamboyant" telegram to Washington, denouncing the "anti-American tone of recent Canadian Government actions" and warning that "there were both quantitative and qualitative strains on our relations [with Canada] at the present time." While the very number of issues dividing the two countries created "stresses and strains," the differences between Canada and the United States over Vietnam weighed most heavily.[116]

Ritchie, who quite possibly picked up echoes of Butterworth's analysis in Washington, adopted a remarkably similar diagnosis of the state of bilateral relations. Like Butterworth he argued that the very number of issues at play in the fall of 1967 created a unique strain on the relationship. Any one of these subjects could easily be blown out of proportion and ignite a bilateral confrontation.

At the present time there appears to be a noticeable atmosphere in Washington, particularly in some important quarters of the State Department, of a growing dissatisfaction and impatience with Canada and that this coupled with the Administration's preoccupation over Vietnam (bordering on a sort of neurosis) and with the forthcoming election campaign, provides an environment where even minor differences can quickly get distorted and be treated as major disagreements. In such an atmosphere perspectives in Washington are becoming badly warped; an issue which in other circumstances might pass quietly or go almost unnoticed may come to be regarded as a test of almost our whole relationship with the United States.[117]

The ambassador warned the government (as he had in the spring of 1963) that Canada needed to choose carefully which issues it wished to pursue with the United States. With this consideration in mind, he suggested that Ottawa try to defuse tensions by postponing its efforts to increase the postal rates applied to *Time* and *Reader's Digest*.

Rusk, like Ritchie and Butterworth (whose telegram he almost certainly read), initially reacted with alarm at the mounting number of bilateral differences between the two countries. At a reception at the Nepalese Embassy in early November, he cornered the Canadian ambassador and "vigorously" announced that "we were headed for trouble." Ritchie could hardly have been surprised, and he quickly arranged to meet Rusk for a private discussion. The talk provided an opportunity for a balanced examination of the relationship and proved immensely reassuring. Armed with a lengthy brief from his officials on the state of bilateral relations across the full spectrum of issues, Rusk was "considerably more relaxed" and the "whole conversation was low-keyed and ... friendly throughout."[118]

The secretary of state began "with a tone of humor," asking Ritchie if "anti-Americanism was good politics in Canada." He went on to acknowledge Canada's help with the Kennedy Round in GATT and with United States balance of payments problems, noting Canada's increased foreign aid and its peacekeeping commitments. Rusk remained concerned, however, with Ottawa's attitude toward the war in Vietnam, accusing Ottawa of adopting a policy of neutrality on the international control commission. When pressed, he retreated from this absurd claim, admitting that he had been shocked to learn that Canada would have been forced to vote for a unilateral bombing halt if such a resolution had been presented to the United Nations. He was disappointed that Ottawa had not solidly endorsed Johnson's most recent peace plan.[119]

All in all, Rusk's appreciation of the relationship was not unduly disturbing. The White House too arrived at a fairly balanced analysis.

Increasingly hardened to criticism of its Vietnam policy, it largely ignored Martin's speech to the United Nations, which National Security Council officials characterized as simply "marking a further edging away from the United States position."[120] Similarly, the national security advisor, Walt Rostow, dismissed Butterworth's views as unnecessarily alarmist. "The developments Butterworth describes are not new," he assured the president. "Nor do they require immediate u.s. action. In part they reflect the present unsteady condition of Canadian politics. The Liberal Party is divided and dispirited. The Quebec issue is cutting deep. Martin is trying to establish a reputation for himself, in part at Pearson's expense ... In such a climate, the nationalist drum is a good one to beat."[121] By the end of the year, the flurry of concern had completely passed. Not once during "several good talks" that Martin and Rusk enjoyed during the December NATO ministerial meetings did the two foreign ministers feel compelled to discuss bilateral questions.[122]

This was hardly surprising. Ottawa and Washington were both aware of the constraints that Canadian nationalism placed on the Pearson government. Bilateral pragmatic compromises permitted some measure of control over these volatile forces. This point had been underlined in 1966 when bilateral mechanisms collapsed during the Mercantile Bank affair and the dispute assumed mythic proportions – threatening to rage out of control. Consequently, it became all the more imperative in 1967 for both countries to acknowledge their differences. In some ways Washington's moderate response to Canadian efforts to distance Ottawa from American policy in Vietnam was a first step in admitting that the two countries would have to live together despite sometimes profound differences.

Conclusion

Pearson's government came to power as the postwar economic and political order fragmented, confronting Ottawa with the kind of choices and opportunities that it had not dealt with since the 1940s. The booming 1950s, which allowed the United States and Canada to submerge bilateral economic differences in the general prosperity, had collapsed. The European Economic Community, with its protective trade policy, and Washington's balance of payments problems threatened the liberal trading regime on which North American postwar prosperity depended.

At the same time, Cold War tensions eased, holding out the prospect of more stable relations with the Soviet Union and the People's Republic of China. Western Europe's political and economic recovery left NATO unsettled, as France and West Germany sought new roles in the alliance, raising questions about the nature of the Canadian contribution to Western security. As the prospect of war in the North Atlantic receded, Ottawa redirected its resources to domestic social programs. The United States, however, was sceptical of détente and worried about Western fortunes in the emerging nations of Africa and Asia, where communism mixed easily with indigenous nationalism. Pearson responded to this shifting economic and political landscape in ways that changed the character of Canadian-American relations in significant ways.

The most important developments during the Pearson era were economic. The Liberal Party came to office in April 1963 uncertain about its approach to economic relations with the United States. Nationalists like Finance Minister Walter Gordon, who wished to reduce Canada's dependency on American markets and capital, vied for influence with members of the party who held a more traditional, liberal perspective. The conflict between these two views was brought to a head in early 1964, when Washington challenged the finance minister's unilateral scheme to improve Canada's balance of trade with the United States by encouraging automotive exports through duty rebates.

Washington worked hard to convince Ottawa that its objectives, a larger domestic automotive industry and increased exports, could be achieved through a negotiated agreement that emphasized the two countries' shared economic interests. At the same time, Canada was offered an opportunity to secure its access to the American market by negotiating far-reaching bilateral tariff reductions under the GATT. The automotive dispute and the prospective tariff negotiations faced Ottawa with a fundamental choice: Canada could either seek an integrated and more structured economic partnership with the United States, or it could pursue its future alone, without the security provided by the large and lucrative American market.

The debate in Cabinet raged quietly, but fiercely, throughout 1964. Gordon stood out against both the Autopact and the Kennedy Round, certain that they would reduce Canada's freedom to shape its economic future. The effort was futile. Gordon's opponents, led by Mitchell Sharp, the minister of trade and commerce, convinced Cabinet to endorse measures that integrated the North American automotive industry and to offer significant tariff reductions at the GATT. These two steps created a more structured and formal economic relationship with the United States, strengthening Canada's continental orientation.

This was a lesson that was reinforced during the 1960s by Ottawa's efforts to deal with Washington's increasingly elaborate proposals to strengthen its balance of payments. Securing an exemption from Treasury regulations that restricted U.S. capital exports, a complicated diplomatic and political exercise, was no sure thing. In the short term, the process emphasized a shared North American interest in the dollar's future and the importance of a continental common market for capital. Its long-term impact was even more profound. The government's uncertain experience with its exemption from the interest equalization tax – which it lost in 1971 – helped convince many policymakers in Ottawa of one important lesson: to deal effectively with American policies that might adversely harm its interests, Canada needed to pursue still closer and more formal economic relations with the United States.

While Pearson's government thus took the first few steps towards a new form of North American economic partnership, it also demonstrated that this kind of close economic relationship need not impair Canada's ability to pursue a distinctive foreign and defence policy. Between 1963 and 1968, the Liberal government adopted diplomatic and military postures that acknowledged the diminished Soviet threat, European recovery, and growing domestic demands for a Canadian approach to the world. It undertook this task carefully, with due regard for Washington's strategic interests in North Atlantic solidarity and continuing bilateral arrangements for continental defence. The United States generally accepted Ottawa's evolutionary approach and realistically amended its expectations for Canadian policy. As a result, by the time Pearson left office in the spring of 1968, the process of adjusting the close Cold War alliance to accommodate the altered international climate and the evolving needs of both countries was well under way in Washington and Ottawa.

The Pearson government's pursuit of closer economic relations with the United States and its contradictory desire to adopt an increasingly distinct approach to the world reflects the ambiguity that has traditionally characterized continental relations. Perhaps, therefore, it is not surprising that Pearson simultaneously pursued two courses so divergent; that he accomplished this without seriously damaging his government's relations with Washington is impressive. This substantial achievement reflected his government's capacity to devise the kinds of pragmatic compromises that allowed Canada to straddle the gap between dependence and independence.

This was especially true of Canadian policy in Asia, where the conflict in Vietnam exposed Canadian ambiguity to attack and made it difficult for Ottawa to reconcile domestic pressures for a distinct Canadian response to the crisis with American demands for diplomatic and material support. Edging aside Paul Martin, the secretary of state for external affairs, Pearson dominated policymaking in this field. The prime minister resisted demands that his government adopt extreme positions, minimizing Canada's differences with the United States over Asia. He did not fully eliminate these distinctions but encouraged carefully hedged initiatives at the United Nations to seat Red China and to suspend bombing in Vietnam. These actions established the Canadian position without pushing Washington too hard and inviting retaliation.

Although Pearson's handling of the Vietnam war defused the conflict as a source of continuing bilateral controversy, rising nationalist sentiment made it difficult to preserve cooperative relations during the 1960s. Containing manifestations of Canadian nationalism was a joint enterprise that relied on policymakers in Ottawa and Washington adhering to a shared vision of the future course of bilateral relations and working together to shape practical compromises. The two governments found the common ground required to amend the legislation protecting Canada's magazines to take into account American interests. They were much less effective in solving the problem created by the sale of the Mercantile Bank to American investors. The initial effort to negotiate a settlement was upset when influential policymakers in each capital tried to define the issue in symbolic terms. Although the prime minister was eventually able to engineer a compromise, the affair underlined the growing strength of the "new nationalism."

Unwilling to accept the uncomfortable compromises that partnership sometimes demanded, the nationalist movement would plague Pearson's successor, driving him to experiment with options and policies that tried unsuccessfully to refute Canada's destiny as a North American nation.

Notes

INTRODUCTION

1 Charles Ritchie, *Storm Signals*, 79–80.
2 Figures cited in Bercuson, "Canada, NATO, and rearmament," 104–5.
3 Mackenzie, "Canada's International Economic Relations."
4 Irving Brecher and Simon S. Reisman, *Canada–United States Economic Relations*, 333.

5 Ibid., 88.
6 Cited in Granatstein, "When Push Came to Shove," 87.
7 Lacey, *Historical Statistics*, G415–28.
8 Bruce Hutchison, *Canada: Tomorrow's Giant*.
9 Levitt, *A Vision beyond Reach*, 152.
10 Figures derived from Lacey, *Historical Statistics*, A110–53. According to the 1951 census, 48 percent of the population was British (English, Irish, or Scottish) in origin. This figure declined to 43 percent by the time of the 1961 census.
11 Robinson, *Diefenbaker's World*, 17.
12 Granatstein, *Canada*, 44–5.
13 Hilliker and Barry, *Canada's Department of External Affairs*, 237–9.
14 Bothwell, *Canada and the United States*, 77–8.
15 See Patterson, "Kennedy's Quest."
16 Plumptre, *Three Decades of Decision*, 155–8.
17 Royal Commission on the Automotive Industry, *Report*, 58–60.
18 United States Department of Commerce, *Historical Statistics*, 864.
19 English, *The Worldly Years*, 208.
20 Bryden, "The Liberal Party of Canada," 35–40.
21 Cited in Azzi, *Walter Gordon*, 73.
22 Cited in Azzi, "The Limits of Affluence," 143–4.
23 Gordon, *A Political Memoir*, 81. Emphasis in the original.
24 English, *The Worldly Years*, 231.
25 Beck, *Pendulum of Power*, 370–1.
26 Bothwell, *Canada and the United States*, 70.
27 Ibid., 71.
28 Thompson and Randall, *Canada and the United States*, 238.
29 Ibid., 243.
30 Granatstein and Hillmer, *For Better or For Worse*, vii.
31 Ibid., 234.
32 Hart, "From Colonialism to Globalism," 327.

CHAPTER ONE

1 H.H. Carter, Memorandum to A.E. Ritchie, 17 April 1963, Department of External Affairs (DEA) File 1415–40, National Archives of Canada (NA). Canada's ambassador to Washington, Charles Ritchie, expressed similar fears. See Ritchie, *Storm Signals*, 47.
2 Ibid., 46.
3 A.E. Ritchie, Memorandum, 16 April 1963, DEA File 1415–40, NA.
4 William H. Brubeck, Memorandum for Mr McGeorge Bundy, 18 April 1963; William H. Brubeck, Memorandum for Mr McGeorge Bundy, 28 April 1963, National Security Files (NSF), Country Files: Canada, Box 19,

Kennedy Library. Prompted by his senior policy advisor, Tom Kent, Pearson also insisted that the meeting not be held in Washington, in an effort to protect his government's nationalist credentials. Kent suggested Ogdensberg, New York, but Pearson opted instead for the Kennedy retreat at Hyannisport. See Tom Kent, Memorandum for the Prime Minister, 15 April 1963, Kent Papers, Box 2, Queen's University Archives (QUA).

5 Willis Armstrong, Foreign Affairs Oral History Collection, Georgetown University Library, 24 February 1988.

6 McGeorge Bundy, Weekend Reading, 6-7 April 1963, Index of Weekend Papers 04/63–06/63, National Security Files (NSF), Box 317A, Kennedy Library.

7 Central Intelligence Agency (CIA), Office of Central Registry, Bio Register, "PEARSON, Lester Bowles (Mike) [April 1963], NSF, Country Files: Canada, Box 19, Kennedy Library.

8 McGeorge Bundy, National Security Council Action Memorandum No. 234, 18 April 1963, Department of State, *Foreign Relations of the United States (FRUS)*, 1961–63, Vol. *13: West Europe and Canada* (Washington, 1994), 1201.

9 Visit of Prime Minister Pearson: Briefing Memorandum for the President, 6 May 1963, NSF, Country Files: Canada, Box 9, Kennedy Library.

10 Washington to Ottawa, Tel. No. 1403, 9 May 1963, DEA File 1415–40, NA. For the more detailed report on which this telegram was based, see H.B. Robinson, Memorandum: George Bain's report on briefing by McGeorge Bundy, 9 May 1963, H.B. Robinson Papers, Vol. 12, File 1, NA.

11 Cabinet Conclusions, 9 May 1963, RG 2, Vol. 6253, NA.

12 English, *The Worldly Years*, 268–70. The Washington circle in which both Pearson and Kennedy moved is described in Blumenthal, "The Ruins of Georgetown," 221–37.

13 Cabinet Conclusions, 13 May 1963, RG 2, Vol. 6253, NA.

14 Record of a Meeting between the Prime Minister of Canada and the President of the United States, Hyannisport, MA, 10–11 May 1963, DEA File 1415–40, NA. Pearson claimed that he planned to address this problem by informally urging American industry to promote Canadian managers. He would also create a Canadian development corporation "to buy into industrial companies in such a way as not to invite legitimate U.S. criticism." Kennedy was sceptical. For the American record of the first day's conversations, see FRUS, 1961–63, Vol. *13: West Europe and Canada*, 1201–6.

15 Author interview with Charles Ritchie, 29 November 1992.

16 McGeorge Bundy, Weekend Reading 25–26 May 1963, Index of Weekend Papers, April–June 1963, NSC: Meetings and Memoranda, Boxes 317A–318, Kennedy Library.

17 McGeorge Bundy, National Security Action Memorandum No. 248, 3 June 1963, *Freedom of Information Act (FOIA)* Request 9202777.

18 Dana Wilgress to Paul Martin, 24 June 1963, DEA File 50218-A-40, NA.

19 William H. Brubeck, Memorandum for Mr McGeorge Bundy, 31 May 1963, NSF, Country Files: Canada, Box 19, Kennedy Library.

20 Walt Butterworth to Walter Lippmann, 20 May 1963, White House Confidential Files (WHCF), Country File: Canada, 16 May 1963 to 30 June 1963, Kennedy Library.

21 Louis Rasminsky, Notes on the Budget, 31 May 1963, Rasminsky Papers, Bank of Canada Archives (BCA).

22 Canada, House of Commons, *Debates*, 13 June 1963, 997–1001.

23 Saywell, *Canadian Annual Review for 1963*, 200.

24 Ibid.

25 Eric Kierans to Walter Gordon, 18 June 1963, printed as an appendix in Canada, House of Commons, *Debates*, 19 June 1963, 1366–9.

26 Author interview with Basil Robinson, 5 October 1993; see also H.B. Robinson, Memorandum for File: Canadian Budget, 21 June 1963, Robinson Papers, Vol. 12, File 2, NA; *FRUS*, 1961–63, Vol. *13: West Europe and Canada*, 1205–7; see also R.R. Carlson, Memorandum of Conversation: Discriminatory Tax Measures, 28 June 1963, NSF, Country File: Canada: General, Box 19, Kennedy Library; Washington to Ottawa, Tel. No. 2125, 29 June 1963, Bank of Canada Records, File 5C–100, BCA.

27 R.R. Carlson, Memorandum of Conversation, 28 June 1963, NSF, Country File: Canada, General, Box 19, Kennedy Library.

28 Louis Rasminsky to Walter Gordon, 12 June 1963, Rasminsky Papers, File 76-552-47, BCA. This point had also been made to American officials at an Organization for Economic Cooperation and Development (OECD) meeting in July. See Plumptre, *Three Decades of Decision*, 206.

29 Tom Kent, For the Prime Minister and the Minister of Finance: Budget Modifications [20 June 1963]; Tom Kent, For the Prime Minister: Revised Memorandum on Budget Modifications, 24 June 1963; Tom Kent, For the Prime Minister Only: Budget Changes, 3 July 1963, Kent Papers, Box 2, QUA.

30 Cabinet Conclusions, 2, 4, and 5 July 1963, RG 2, Vol. 6253. The conclusions for 8 July 1963, when the actual modifications were decided upon, remain closed. The brutal nature of the discussions is captured best by LaMarsh, *Memoirs*, 175–6. "We gathered on straight chairs, around the dining room table," she writes, "and there we destroyed Walter Gordon."

31 A.F.W. Plumptre to Claude Isbister, 4 July 1963, RG 19, Vol. 3930, File 5085-04-2, NA.

32 Canada, House of Commons, *Debates*, 8 July 1963, 1951.

33 Ottawa to Secretary of State, Tel. No. 7170, 9 July 1963; David Klein to McGeorge Bundy, 12 July 1963, NSF, Canada: General, Box 19, Kennedy Library.

34 Paul Martin, Memorandum for the Prime Minister, 19 July 1963, DEA File 171-B-40, NA.

35 Washington to Ottawa, Tel. No. 2308, 19 July 1963, DEA File 171-B-40, NA.

36 R.B. Bryce, Memorandum for the Minister, 19 July 1963, RG 19, Vol. 4452, File 8070/U58-4-1, NA.

37 Delmar R. Carlson, Memorandum of Conversation: Canadian Reaction to US BOP Measures," 19 July 1963, NSF, Canada: General, Box 19, Kennedy Library; and Washington to Ottawa, Tel. No. 2307, 19 July 1963, DEA File 171-B-40, NA.

38 [Alan Hockin], Memo[randum] to File [19 July 1963], RG 19, Vol. 4452, File 8070/U58-4-1, NA.

39 Plumptre, *Three Decades*, 207.

40 Cited in Muirhead, *Against the Odds*, 256.

41 Louis Rasminsky, Meeting of Canadian and U.S. Officials on the Proposed Interest Equalization Tax, Washington, DC, 24 July 1963, DEA File 171-B-40, NA.

42 Louis Rasminsky to L.B. Pearson, 27 August 1963, Rasminsky Papers, File LR76-365, Box 47, BCA.

43 Beigie, *Automotive Agreement*, 12–19.

44 Reisman, *Canadian Automotive Industry*, 15–16.

45 Royal Commission on the Automotive Industry, *Report*, 58–60.

46 Walter Gordon, Memorandum for Ministers, 28 August 1963, RG 19, Vol. 3947, File 8705-08-16, NA.

47 Walter Gordon to L.B. Pearson, 4 September 1964, Gordon Papers, Vol. 16, NA.

48 Memorandum to Cabinet, Document 238-63, and Cabinet Conclusions, 9 September 1963, RG 2, Vol. 6253, NA; see also The Canadian Balance of Payments and Related Problems, 10 September 1963, DEA File 8483-40, NA.

49 Ball, *The Discipline of Power*, 113.

50 Washington to Ottawa, Tel. No. 2916, 12 September 1963, and Washington to Ottawa, Tel. No. 2895, 12 September 1963, DEA File 50312-8-40.

51 Ben Read to McGeorge Bundy, 10 September 1963, and attached memorandum from Raymond Vernon to Secretary of State, n.d., NSF, Country Files: Canada, Box 19, Kennedy Library.

52 Raymond Vernon to Secretary of State, n.d., NSF, Country Files: Canada, General, Box 19, Kennedy Library.

53 Joint U.S.-Canada Committee on Trade and Economic Affairs: Scope Paper, 18 September 1963, RG 40, Acc. NNN 3-40-87-1, Box 1, United States National Archives (USNA).

54 J.D. Edmonds to Frank Stone, 16 August 1963, DEA File 50316-8-40, NA.

55 Paul Martin's marginalia on U.S. Draft of Agreed Statement of Principles [20 September 1963]; see also Summary Record of the Joint U.S.–Canada Committee on Trade and Economic Affairs, 20–21 September 1963, DEA File 35-4-5-1-1963, Department of Foreign Affairs and International Trade (DFAIT).

56 Ottawa to Washington, Tel. No. E-1625, 20 September 1963, DEA File 50136-8-40, NA.

57 Summary Record of the Joint U.S.–Canada Committee, 20–21 September 1964, DEA File 35-4-5-1-1963, DFAIT.

58 United States Aide-Mémoire, 24 October 1963, DEA File 37-7-1-USA-2, DFAIT.

59 C.M. Drury, Canada, House of Commons, *Debates*, 25 October 1963, 3999.

60 McGeorge Bundy, Memorandum for the Secretary of State, 11 November 1963, NSF, Country Files: Canada, General, Box 19, Kennedy Library. Staff at the Canadian embassy in Washington welcomed Brubeck's appointment. "[Brubeck] struck me as calm and sensible, and I think he should be a real asset to us," the minister-counsellor, Basil Robinson, recorded, "especially with problems involving relations between different United States Government departments." See his Memorandum for the Ambassador, 23 December 1963, Robinson Papers, Vol. 12, File 7, NA.

61 Walter Gordon to Bud Drury, 8 November 1963, DEA File 37-7-1-USA-2, DFAIT.

62 William H. Brubeck, Memorandum for the President, 19 November 1963, NSF, Canada: General, Box 19, Kennedy Library.

CHAPTER TWO

1 Memorandum to Ted Sorenson, 10 December 1963, White House Confidential Files (WHCF), Country Files: Canada, Box 18, Johnson Library.

2 Cited in Martin, *The Presidents and the Prime Ministers*, 212.

3 John Macy, Memorandum for the President, 24 August 1966, WHCF, Country File: Canada, Box 19, Johnson Library.

4 American Embassy to Department of State, Airgram A-581, 3 January 1964, National Security Files (NSF), Country File: Canada, Box 165, Johnson Library.

5 Brands, *The Wages of Globalism*, 6–10. In order to emphasize the continuity between the two administrations, Johnson retained many of Kennedy's most important domestic and foreign policy advisors. This group included Dean Rusk, who remained secretary of state, and Robert McNamara, who stayed on as secretary of defence. McGeorge Bundy and

George Ball continued to serve as national security advisor and under secretary of state, respectively.

6 Dean Rusk, Memorandum for the President, 12 December 1963, NSF, Country Files: Canada, Box 165, Johnson Library.

7 Bill Brubeck, Memorandum for Mr Bundy, 7 January 1964, NSF, Country Files: Canada, Box 165, Johnson Library.

8 George Ball to McGeorge Bundy and attached Memorandum for the President, 7 January 1964, RG 59, Box 1247, United States National Archives (USNA).

9 Ibid.; see also, National Security Files (NSF), Administrative Histories: Department of State, Chapter 3, Part D, 17 [1968], Records, Vol. 1, Johnson Library.

10 Bill Brubeck, Memorandum for Mr Bundy, 7 January 1964, NSF, Country Files: Canada, Box 165, Johnson Library.

11 Dean Rusk, Memorandum for the President [14 January 1964], NSF, Country Files: Canada, Pearson Visit Briefing Book, 1/21-22/64, Box 167, Johnson Library.

12 Washington to Ottawa, 4 November 1963, and Paul Martin, Memorandum for the Prime Minister and Pearson's marginalia, 6 November 1963, DEA File 37-7-1-USA-1, DFAIT.

13 H.H. Carter, Memorandum (and attachment) for European Division, 18 December 1963, Department of External Affairs (DEA) File 20-Cda-9-Pearson, National Archives of Canada (NA).

14 Jack Valenti, Memorandum for the President, 12 December 1963, Statements of LBJ: Visit of PM Pearson, Box 94, Johnson Library.

15 Memorandum of Conversation, 25 November 1963, Department of State, *Foreign Relations of the United States (FRUS)*, 1961–63, Vol. *13: Western Europe and Canada* (Washington, 1994), 1214–16.

16 H.B. Robinson to O.W. Dier, 12 December 1963, DEA File 20-Cda-9-Pearson, NA.

17 H.B. Robinson, Memorandum: Prime Minister's Visit to Washington, 19 December 1963, DEA File 20-Cda-9-Pearson, NA. On the discussions arranging the prime minister's visit, see Washington to Ottawa, Tel. No. 4010, 5 December 1963, ibid.; see also H.B. Robinson, Memorandum for File, 3 December 1963, and Memorandum for the Ambassador, 23 December 1963, Robinson Papers, Vol. 12, File 7, NA. The Americans explained their reluctance to invite Pearson to the ranch by noting that they were proceeding on the basis that "timeliness was more important than display."

18 N.A. Robertson, Memorandum for the Prime Minister, 12 December 1963; O.W. Dier, Memorandum for the Prime Minister, 26 December 1963; O.W. Dier, Memorandum for the Prime Minister, 27 December 1963, Pearson Papers, Vol. 284; See also Cabinet Conclusions, 27 December 1963, RG 2, Vol. 6253, NA.

19 *Public Papers of the Presidents of the United States: Lyndon B. Johnson,*
   1963–64, book 1, 103–4.
20 Ottawa to Washington, Tel. No. M-14, 23 January 1964, DEA File 20-
   Cda-9-Pearson, NA.
21 Author interview with H.B. Robinson, 5 October 1994.
22 Pearson, *Mike,* Vol. 3, 124. Paul Martin's judgment was less favourable.
   He thought that Johnson "appeared to be paying little attention to the
   responsibility of government and matters of state. For example, the President had, the previous day received fourteen different delegations which
   had nothing to do with the business of government. This was a luxury
   which a President of the United States could ill afford. However, the President had only acceded to his new position recently; this was an election
   year, and his attitude might become a more reassuring one in the longer
   term." See, Cabinet Conclusions, 23 January 1964, RG 2, Vol. 6264, NA.
23 H.B. Robinson, Memorandum for File, 2 February 1964, DEA File 20-
   Cda-9-Pearson, NA.
24 Meetings between President Johnson and Prime Minister Pearson in
   Washington, 21–22 January 1964, DEA File 20-Cda-9-Pearson, NA;
   Memorandum of Conversation: Statement of Principles of United
   States–Canadian Relations, 22 January 1964, NSF, Country File: Canada,
   Pearson Visit 1/22/64, Box 167, Johnson Library.
      In February 1964, Pearson and Johnson asked a Canadian, Arnold
   Heeney, and an American, Livingston Merchant, to constitute the study
   group. Each had served two terms as ambassador to the other's country.
   The process of drafting their report, which was overtaken by events
   before it was published, is discussed in Heeney's *Things That Are Caesar's,* 190–4.
25 Washington to Ottawa, Tel. No. 312, 27 January 1964, DEA File 37-7-1-
   USA-2, DFAIT.
26 Memorandum of Conversation, 22 January 1964, United States Department of State, *Foreign Relations of the United States (FRUS),* 1964–68,
   Vol. 12: *Western Europe* (Washington: 2001), 675–7.
27 H.B. Robinson, Memorandum for File, 2 February 1964, DEA File 20-
   Cda-9-Pearson, NA.
28 Summary Record of the Joint U.S.-Canada Committee on Trade and Economic Affairs, 29–30 April 1964, DEA File 35-4-5-1-1964, DFAIT. See
   also Memorandum by President Johnson, 28 April 1964 and Douglas
   Dillon, Memorandum for the President, 1 May 1964, in *FRUS,* 1964–68,
   Vol. 12: *Western Europe,* 679–81.
29 Cabinet Conclusions, 27 April 1964, RG 2, Vol. 6264, NA.
30 Philip Trezise to Ed Ritchie, 4 May 1965; Washington to Ottawa, Tel.
   No. 1607, 4 May 1964, DEA File 37-7-USA-2, DFAIT.
31 A.E. Ritchie to Phil Trezise, 14 May 1964, DEA File 37-7-1-USA-2, DFAIT.

32 Washington to Ottawa, Tel. No. 1929, 28 May 1964, DEA File 37-7-1-USA-2, DFAIT.

33 B.G. Barrow to O.G. Stoner, 29 May 1964, DEA File 37-7-1-USA-2, DFAIT.

34 Author interview with Philip Trezise, 25 October 1995.

35 W.L. Gordon, Memorandum for File: Automobile Policy, 1 June 1964, RG 19, Vol. 3947, File 8705-08-16, NA. A copy of this memorandum, together with an exchange of messages between Dillon and Gordon, was sent to the Department of External Affairs, where one official described the American message as "The iron hand in the velvet glove." In reply, another quipped, "Not much velvet, either." See, DEA File 37-7-1-USA-2, DFAIT.

36 Washington to Ottawa, Tel. No. 2027, 5 June 1964, DEA File 37-7-USA-2, DFAIT.

37 S.S. Reisman's marginalia on Washington to Ottawa, Tel. No. 2027, 5 June 1964, RG 19, Vol. 3947, File 8705-08-16, NA.

38 S.S. Reisman, Memorandum for the Cabinet Committee on Finance and Economic Policy, 9 June 1964, RG 19, Vol. 3946, File 8705-02, NA.

39 Gordon, *A Political Memoir*, 168–70.

40 J.F. Grandy, Memorandum for Cabinet, 11 June 1964, RG 19, Vol. 3947, File 8705-08-16, NA.

41 Cabinet Conclusions, 11 June 1964, RG 2, Vol. 6265, NA.

42 My account of the 7 July 1964 meeting is based on Memorandum of Conversation: Possible Free Trade Arrangement in Automotive Products, 7 July 1965; Ottawa to the State Department, Tel. No. 6148, 8 July 1964, RG 59, Box 1249, File IT 7-12-CAN, USNA; Memorandum to the Cabinet Committee on Finance and Economic Policy, 10 July 1964, RG 19, Vol. 3946, File 8705-02, NA.

43 Russ McKinney to O.G. Stoner, 26 July 1964, DEA File 37-7-1-USA-2, DFAIT.

44 Memorandum for the Cabinet, 12 August 1964, RG 19, Vol. 3946, File 8705-02, NA.

45 Cabinet Conclusions, 13 August 1964, RG 2, Vol. 6265, NA.

46 My account of the August meeting is based on M. Cadieux, Memorandum for the Minister, 24 August 1964, DEA File 37-7-1-USA-2; R.Y. Grey to R.B. Bryce, 19 August 1964 and R.Y. Grey, Memorandum for the Minister, 24 August 1864, RG 19, Vol. 3946, File 980-1, NA; Memorandum of Conversation: Free Trade Arrangements for Automobiles, 17 August 1964, and Ottawa to State, Tel. No. A-198, 31 August 1964, RG 59, Box 1249, File IT 7-12-CAN, USNA.

47 Ottawa to State, Tel. No. 306, 4 September 1965; See also, Ottawa to State, Airgram A-539, 21 January 1965, RG 59, Box 1248, File IT 7-12-CAN, USNA.

48 Washington to Ottawa, Tel. No. 3209, 8 September 1964, DEA File 37-7-1-USA-2, DFAIT.

49 Memorandum for the Cabinet, 16 September 1964, RG 19, Vol. 3946, File 8705-02, NA.

50 Luther Hodges to Dean Rusk, 25 August 1964, RG 59, Box 1249, File IT 7-12-CAN, USNA.

51 Luther Hodges to Douglas Dillon, 17 September 1964, RG 59, Box 1249, File IT 7-12-CAN, USNA.

52 Cabinet Conclusions, 17 September 1964, RG 2, Vol. 6265, NA. On Martin's talks with Rusk, see, Memorandum of Conversation, 14 September 1964, in FRUS, 1964–68, Vol. 12: *Western Europe*, 686–9. Johnson, ostensibly in British Columbia to conclude arrangements related to the development of the Columbia River system, exploited the visit to demonstrate to American voters his capacity to handle foreign policy, one of his acknowledged weaknesses. Canadian officials (and presumably their political masters) were aware of the dangers of allowing Canada to be used as a political prop in the American presidential elections. See also Martin, *The Presidents and the Prime Ministers*, 218.

53 Cabinet Conclusions, 17 September 1964, RG 2, Vol. 6265, NA.

54 NSF, Administrative Histories, Department of State, Chap. 3, Part D, [1968], Vol. 1, Johnson Library. See also Memorandum from Secretary of State Rusk to President Johnson, 18 September 1964 in FRUS, 1964–68, Vol. 12: *Western Europe*, 689–91, especially n4.

55 My account of the September meetings is based on the following sources: J.F. Grandy, Memorandum for the Minister of Finance, 25 September 1964, RG 19, Vol. 3946, File 8705-02, NA; Marcel Cadieux, Memorandum for the Minister, 29 September 1964, DEA File 37-7-USA-2-1, DFAIT; Memorandum of Conversation: Possible Free Trade Arrangement in Automotive Products, 24–25 September 1964, RG 59, Box 1249, File IT 7-12 CAN, USNA.

56 My account of the two meetings in October and November is based on the following sources: Marcel Cadieux, Memorandum for the Minister, 19 October 1964, DEA File 37-7-1-USA-2, DFAIT; Memorandum to the Cabinet Committee on Finance and Economic Policy, 16 November 1964 and Memorandum for the Cabinet, 18 November 1964, RG 19, Vol. 3946, File 8705-02, NA; Memorandum of Conversation: Possible US-Canadian Free Trade Arrangement in Automotive Products, 9 October 1964, and Memorandum of Conversation: Possible Free Trade Arrangement in Automotive Products (4th General Round of Discussions), 12–13 November 1964, RG 59, Box 1249, File IT 7-12 CAN, USNA.

57 Philip Trezise to Henry Wilson and attached Memorandum for the President, 25 November 1964, Frances Bator Papers, Box 1, Chron (NSC)

9/1/64-12/31/64; See also NSF, Administrative Histories, Department of State, Chap. 3, Part D, [1968], Vol. 1, Johnson Library.

58 M. Schwarzmann, Memorandum for the Ambassador, 15 April 1963, RG 25, Vol. 3175, File GATT 1954–63, NA.

59 Lacey, *Historical Statistics*), G415–28.

60 Memorandum, 23 April 1963, RG 20, Accession 85/86/665, Box 66, File Kennedy Round (Result), NA.

61 Cited in Granatstein, *A Man of Influence*, 365.

62 Maurice Schwarzmann, Memorandum for the Ambassador, RG 25, Vol. 3176, File GATT 1954–64, NA.

63 Washington to Ottawa, Tel. No. 1182, 24 April 1964, RG 25, Vol. 5649, File 14051-2-40, NA.

64 Washington to Ottawa, Tel. No. 1182, 24 April 1963, RG 25, Vol. 6549, File 14051-2-40, NA.

65 Carl Kaysen, Memorandum to McGeorge Bundy, 29 April 1963, and Christian Herter, Memorandum for the President, 29 April 1993, NSF, Country Files: Canada, Box 19, Kennedy Library.

66 Department of State to Geneva, Tel. No. 1067, 16 May 1963, NSF, Country Files: Canada, Box 19, Kennedy Library.

67 Memorandum for the Cabinet, 9 May 1963, DEA File 37-7-3, DFAIT.

68 Cabinet Conclusions, 24 May 1963, RG 2, Vol. 6253, NA.

69 Washington to Ottawa, Tel. No. 1850, 10 June 1963, RG 25, Vol. 5649, File 14052-1-40, NA.

70 Head, Office of Trade Relations and Trade Committee to Hector McKinnon, 1 April 1964, Privy Council Office (PCO) File U-3-11(a), PCO. See also Ottawa to Geneva, Tel. No. E-707, 17 April 1964 and Ottawa to Geneva, Tel. No. E-760, 23 April 1964, DEA File 37-7-3, DFAIT.

71 Summary Record of the Joint U.S.-Canada Committee on Trade and Economic Affairs, 29-30 April 1964, DEA File 35-4-5-1-1964, DFAIT.

72 Cited in Girard, *Canada in World Affairs*, 129.

73 Cited in Saywell, *Canadian Annual Review for 1965*, 289.

74 Canada, House of Commons, *Debates*, 14 April 1964, 2161–5.

75 [Jim Grandy], Kennedy Round: Alternative Approaches, 26 October 1964, PCO File U-3-11(a), PCO.

76 O.G. Stoner, Memorandum for Mr Robertson, 3 November 1964, PCO File U-3-11(a), PCO.

77 A.E. Ritchie, Memorandum for the Under-Secretary, 4 November 1964, DEA File 37-7-3, DFAIT.

78 Ottawa to Washington, Tel. No. G-167, 9 November 1964, PCO File U-3-11(a), PCO.

79 Granatstein, *A Man of Influence*, 369. The Canadian offer also included an offer of free entry for tropical and semitropical products on the condition that other developed countries made the same offer. In addition, the

offer as a whole was conditional on reaching an agreement on binding margins of preference.

80 Tarifdel to Ottawa, Tel. No. 23, 23 March 1965, DEA File 37-7-3, DFAIT; See also R.G. Robertson, Memorandum for the Prime Minister, 26 March 1965, PCO File U-3-11(a), PCO.

81 Tarifdel to Ottawa, Tel. No. 195, 27 July 1965, DEA File 37-7-3, DFAIT. These discussions covered lumber and wood products, paper and paper products, nonferrous metals, nonmetallic minerals, fisheries, and most manufactured goods, except textiles and chemicals.

82 Tarifdel to Ottawa, Tel. No. 224, 3 August 1966, DEA File 37-7-3, DFAIT.

83 Sydney Pierce to Hector McKinnon, 25 August 1966, DEA File 37-7-3, DFAIT.

84 Preeg, *Traders and Diplomats*, 188. See also Tarifdel to Ottawa, Tel. No. 272, 6 October 1966, DEA File 37-7-3, DFAIT.

85 Tarifdel to Ottawa, Tels. No. 349 and 351, 6 December 1966, DEA File 37-7-3, DFAIT. The United States threatened to withdraw concessions on whisky, alone worth U.S.$100 million. Groundwood printing paper and nonagricultural tractors were the other two major items threatened.

86 Tarifdel to Ottawa, Tel. No. 77, 7 March 1967, and Tarifdel to Ottawa, Tel. No. 130, 10 April 1967, DEA File 37-7-3, DFAIT.

87 Memorandum: Kennedy Round Cereals Negotiations, 21 October 1966, PCO File U-3-11(a), PCO.

88 Ibid.

89 Draft Memorandum: Kennedy Round Cereals Negotiations, 28 October 1966, and O.G. Stoner, Memorandum for Mr Robertson, 31 October 1966, and Gordon Robertson, Memorandum for the Prime Minister, 31 October 1966, PCO File U-3-11(a), PCO.

90 Note on U.S. Position as set out in Washington Message Telegram 3231 of 25 October, and Gordon Robertson, Memorandum for the Prime Minister, 2 November 1966, PCO Files U-3-11(a), PCO.

91 C.R. Nixon, Memorandum for Mr Stoner, 22 November 1966, and attached Memorandum: Kennedy Round Cereals Negotiations: Exporter Position, 16 November 1966, PCO File U-3-11(a), PCO.

92 Tarifdel to Ottawa, Tel. No. CE7, 19 February 1967, DEA File 37-7-3, DFAIT. On these discussions, see also Economic Division to J.C. Langley, 17 February 1967, and Tarifdel to Ottawa, Tel. No. CE13, 27 February 1967, ibid., and Memorandum to Ministers: Kennedy Round – Cereals negotiations, 9 February 1967, PCO File U-3-11(a), PCO.

93 Economic Division to Mr J.C. Langley, 22 February 1967 and Tarifdel to Ottawa, Tel. No. CE9, 21 February 1967, DEA File 37-7-3, DFAIT.

94 Tarifdel to Ottawa, Tel. No. CE19, 6 March 1967, DEA File 37-7-3, DFAIT.

95 Tarifdel to Ottawa, Tel. No. CE26, 16 March 1967, DEA File 37-7-3, DFAIT.

96 Tarifdel to Ottawa, Tel. No. CE31 [4 April 1967], DEA 37-7-3, DFAIT. The telegram is erroneously dated 4 March 1967.

97 Tarifdel Geneva to Ottawa, Tel. No. CE39, 29 April 1967, DEA File 37-73, DFAIT.

98 Tarifdel to Ottawa, Tel. No. 170, 29 April 1967, DEA File 37-7-3-, DFAIT.

99 Marcel Cadieux, Memorandum for the Minister, 8 May 1967, DEA File 37-7-3, DFAIT; See also Kennedy Round Briefing Material, 10 May 1967, RG 20, Acc. 85-86/665, Box 68, NA, and Memorandum: Kennedy Round – Present State of Play, PCO Files U-3-11(a), PCO.

100 Tarifdel to Ottawa, Tel. No. CE45, 12 May 1967, DEA File 37-7-3, DFAIT.

101 Preeg, *Traders and Diplomats*, 253–4.

102 For details see ibid., 189–95.

103 Kennedy Round Briefing Material, 10 May 1967, RG 20, Acc. 85-86/665, Box 68, NA.

104 Saywell, *Canadian Annual Review for 1967*, 336–8. See also Hart, "Twenty Years," 603–4. On the importance of Canada's offer to reduce its tariff on machinery, see Preeg, *Traders and Diplomats*, 188.

105 Cited in Michael Hart, "Twenty Years," 606.

106 Ibid., 604.

107 Granatstein, "Free Trade," 46. On the importance of the Kennedy Round, see also Muirhead, "Canada's Foreign Economic Policy," 174–75.

108 Reisman, *Canadian Automotive Industry*, appendix A-1. Figures are in Canadian dollars.

109 Lacey, *Historical Statistics of Canada*, G401–7. Figures are in Canadian dollars.

110 Ibid., G415–28. The United States absorbed almost 69 percent of Canadian exports in 1972, before settling in around 65 per cent for the rest of the decade.

111 Diebold, "Canada and the United States," 403–4.

112 American Embassy to Department of State, Airgram A-1620, 4 September 1968, NSF, Country Files: Canada, Box 166, Johnson Library.

CHAPTER THREE

1 A.F.W. Plumptre to R.B. Bryce, 23 November 1964, RG 19, Vol. 3852, File 8070/U58-4-1, National Archives of Canada (NA).

2 Attachment to A.F.W. Plumptre to R.B. Bryce, 23 November 1964, RG 19, Vol. 3852, File 8070/U58-4-1, NA.

3 Meeting in the U.S. Treasury on Friday, 4 December 1964, RG 19, Vol. 4814, File 6285-01, NA; See also Draft Memorandum of Conversation, 12 December 1964, Bank of Canada Records, File 4B-324, Bank of Canada Archives (BCA).

4 Douglas Dillon, Memorandum for the President, 8 February 1965, White House Confidential Files (WHCF), Country File: Canada, Box 19, Johnson Library.

5 Meeting in the U.S. Treasury, 3 February 1965, and Meeting in the U.S. Treasury, 4 February 1965, RG 19, Vol. 4814, File 6285-01, NA.

6 McGeorge Bundy, Memorandum to the President, 9 February 1965, WHCF, Country File: Canada, Box 19, Johnson Library. Emphasis in original. On Johnson's claim about the language, see Gist of Conversation between the Prime Minister and the President – 9 February 1965, approximately 4 P.M., Gordon Papers, Vol. 8, File: Finance, NA.

7 Pearson, *Mike*, 136.

8 For the president's message to Congress, see *Public Papers of the Presidents*, book 2, 170–7; for an assessment of their impact on Canada, see Economic Division, Memorandum for A.E. Ritchie, 10 February 1965, DEA File 36-11-4-1-USA, DFAIT.

9 A.F.W. Plumptre, Memorandum to the Minister and attachment, 11 February 1965, RG 19, Vol. 4492, 8092/U58-2, NA.

10 Meeting with Treasury and Federal Reserve Representatives – Washington – 3 March 1965, RG 19, Vol. 4492, File 8092/U58-1, NA.

11 Meeting with Treasury and Federal Reserve Representatives – Washington – 3 March 1965, RG 19, Vol. 4492, File 8092/U58-1, NA.

12 Paul Volcker to A.F.W. Plumptre, 6 March 1965, RG 19, Vol. 4492, File 8092/U58-2. See also Meeting with Treasury and Federal Reserve Representatives – Washington – 3 March 1965, RG 19, Vol. 4492, File 8092/U58-1, NA.

13 Paul Volcker to A.F.W. Plumptre, 6 March 1965, RG 19, Vol. 4492, File 8092/U58-2, NA.

14 Draft Report of the Working Party on Ways in Which Canadian Banks Might be Asked to Co-operate with U.S. Balance of Payments Measures, 10 March 1966, RG 19, Vol. 4492, File 8092/U58-2, NA.

15 W.L. Gordon to G.A.R. Hart, President, Bank of Montreal, 1 April 1964, RG 19, Vol. 4492, 8092/U58-1. Gordon specifically asked: "In more detail, I am asking that the total claims of Canadian offices on residents of the United States, including your own U.S. agencies and branches, less deposit liabilities due to residents of the United States, be not diminished if it is a net asset position and be not increased if it is a net liability position."

16 Francis Linville to A.E. Ritchie, 8 February 1965, Rasminsky Papers, Box 48, File 76-370, BCA.

17 J.R. McKinney, Memorandum for A.E. Ritchie, 12 March 1965, DEA File 36-11-4-USA. Arnold Heeney, then in the concluding stages of preparing his report on the bilateral relationship, also opposed the creation of any new machinery.

18 Francis Linville to A.E. Ritchie, 14 July 1965, and A.E. Ritchie to Francis Linville, 22 July 1965, DEA File 36-11-4-1-USA, DFAIT.

19 Briefing for [the] Meeting between the Hon. W.L. Gordon and the Hon. H.H. Fowler, 30 July 1965, RG 19, Vol. 4492, 8092/U58-2, NA.

20 A.B. Hockin, Memorandum for R.B. Bryce, 5 October 1965, RG 19, Vol. 5713, File 2070/U70-3, NA.

21 Washington to Ottawa, Tel. No. 3381, 22 October 1965, RG 19, Vol. 4492, File 8092/U58-1, NA.

22 R.B. Bryce, hand-written notes dated 25 October 1965, RG 19, Vol. 5713, File 2070/U70-3, NA.

23 Washington to Ottawa, Tel. No. 3450, 29 October 1965, RG 19, Vol. 4492, File 8092/U58-1, NA; See also A.B. Hockin, Memorandum for R.B. Bryce, 25 October 1965, ibid.

24 R.B. Bryce, Notes dated 25 October 1965, RG 19, File 2070/U70-3, NA; See also Deferral of New Canadian Securities, [November 1965], RG 19, Vol. 4492, File 8092/U58-2, NA.

25 For Diefenbaker's criticisms, see *Globe and Mail*, 2 November 1965. See also, R.B. Bryce, W.L. Gordon – Notes of Call with Fowler in Notes dated 25 October 1965; [R.B. Bryce] Notes for Conversation with Deming, 2 November 1965; R.B. Bryce, Memorandum for the Minister, 4 November 1965, RG 19, Vol. 5713, File 2070/U70-3, NA.

26 R.B. Bryce, Memorandum to the Minister, 4 November 1965, RG 19, Vol. 5713, File 2070/U70-3, NA.

27 R.B. Bryce, Memorandum for the Minister, 5 November 1965; R.B. Bryce to Walter Gordon, 6 November 1965, RG 19, Vol. 5713, File 2070/U58-3, NA.

28 Washington to Ottawa, Tel. No. 3629, 16 November 1965, RG 19, Vol. 4492, File 8092/U58-1, NA.

29 A.B. Hockin, Memorandum for Mr Sharp, 22 November 1965, RG 19, Vol. 4492, File 8092/U58-2, NA.

30 Ibid.

31 R.B. Bryce, Notes for Telephone Conversation with Mr Deming, Under Secretary of the Treasury, 20 November 1965, RG 19, Vol. 4492, File 8092/U58-2, NA.

32 A.E. Ritchie, Memorandum for the Minister, 20 November 1965, DEA File 36-11-4-1-USA, DFAIT.

33 R.B. Bryce, Memo of Points for Discussion re New U.S. Balance of Payments Measures, 20 November 1965, RG 19, Vol. 4492, File 8092/U58-2, NA; [R.B. Bryce], Notes for Discussion with U.S., 22 November 1965, and L. Rasminsky, My Talking Notes on Points 4 & 7 of R.B. Bryce's Memo of 22 November 1965, Rasminsky Papers, LR76-367, Box 48, BCA.

34 R.B. Bryce, Memorandum to Mr Sharp, 3 February 1966, Rasminsky Papers, LR76-369, Box 48, BCA; on this meeting, see also R.B. Bryce's

hand-written notes, For Deming et al., 22 November 1965, RG 19, Vol. 4492, File 8092/U58-2, NA.

35 [R.B. Bryce], Suggested Revision in U.S. Draft Statement, 30 November 1965 and marginalia on attached note to Mr. Sharp RG 19, Vol. 4492, File 8092/U58-2, NA.

36 Newman, *Distemper of Our Times*, 410–11; see also Saywell, *The Canadian Annual Review for 1965*, 350.

37 *Globe and Mail*, 24 December 1965.

38 Stursberg, *Lester Pearson*, 226.

39 Newman, *Distemper of Our Times*, 411. This episode played an important part in shaping Kierans' nationalism. See Swift, *Odd Man Out*, 136–8, 141–7.

40 Eric Kierans to J.T. Conner, 4 January 1966, RG 19, Vol. 4490, File 8070/U58-4-1, NA.

41 Saywell, *The Canadian Annual Review for 1966*, 209.

42 *Toronto Star*, 10 January 1965.

43 Saywell, *The Canadian Annual Review for 1965*, 312, 318.

44 Saywell, *The Canadian Annual Review for 1966*, 297.

45 A.B. Hockin, Memorandum for R.B. Bryce, 17 January 1966, RG 19, Vol. 4492, File 8092/U58-2, NA. See also Sharp's statement in the House of Commons, 2 February 1965.

46 Canada, House of Commons, *Debates*, 2 February 1966, 605–6 and 617–20.

47 Press Release attached to Minutes of Meeting with Heads of Canadian Subsidiaries of United States Companies Concerning the Impact of the United States Balance of Payments Programme, 7 February 1966, RG 19, Vol. 4901, File 8092/U58-2, NA.

48 Marcel Cadieux, Memorandum for the Minister, 17 February 1966, DEA File 26-11-4-1-USA, DFAIT.

49 Joint United States–Canadian Committee on Trade and Economic Affairs: Scope Paper, 25 February 1966, Freedom of Information Act (FOIA) Request 9202977.

50 U.S. Treasury Department, The Channelling of U.S. Capital to and through Canada, 18 November 1965, and Lawson, Note on the Pass-Through Question, Bank of Canada Records, File 297-2-1, BCA.

51 A.B. Hockin, Memorandum for R.B. Bryce, 17 January 1966, RG 19, Vol. 4492, File 8092/U58-2, NA.

52 Sharp's marginalia on ibid.

53 Merlyn Trued to Alan Hockin, 19 January 1966, RG 19, Vol. 4492, File 8092/U58-2, NA.

54 A.B. Hockin, Memorandum for Mr Bryce, 24 January 1966, RG 19, Vol. 4492, File 8092/U58-2, NA.

55 Sharp's marginalia on ibid.

56 Mitchell Sharp, Canada, House of Commons, *Debates*, 16 March 1966, 2755–6. On the background to this statement, see R.B. Bryce, Memorandum for Mr. Sharp, 28 February 1966, DEA File 36-11-4-1-USA, DFAIT, and R.B. Bryce, Memorandum for Mr Sharp, 3 March 1966, RG 19, Vol. 4901, File 8092/U58-2, NA.

57 Communiqué from the Joint United States-Canadian Committee on Trade and Economic Affairs, Washington, 4–5 March 1966. The exact process of negotiating the bilateral deal and the communiqué is unclear. There do not appear to have been any records kept on these discussions. The official record of the meeting makes it clear that the issue was discussed primarily outside the meeting. See Joint United States–Canadian Committee on Trade and Economic Affairs, 4–5 March 1966, Draft Summary Record, DEA File 35-4-5-1-1966, DFAIT. A routine follow-up telegram from Washington confirms that a deal along these lines was indeed arranged but provides no details. See Washington to Ottawa, Tel. No. 730, 9 March 1966, DEA File 35-4-5-1-1966, DFAIT.

58 Canada, House of Commons, *Debates*, 31 March 1966, 3643 and 3713–14. The fourteen individual guidelines urged subsidiaries to adopt a number of policies that would enhance their status as "Canadian" companies. For example, subsidiaries were urged to develop export opportunities, competing where necessary against parent corporations. They were also expected to build manufacturing centres in Canada when appropriate, to undertake local research and development, and to work toward a "Canadian outlook within management."

59 Cited in Saywell, *The Canadian Annual Review for 1966*, 301.

60 Kunz, "Cold War Dollar Diplomacy," 106.

61 *Public Papers of the Presidents of the United States: Lyndon B. Johnson 1968-69*, book 1, 1–13.

62 On 1 January 1968 West Germany introduced a new system of value-added taxation that had the effect of imposing an additional 2.4 percent tax on imports. The United States was particularly upset with this development, since West Germany was already a creditor nation and seemed bent on improving its competitive position. The West German VAT was permissible under the General Agreement on Trade and Tariffs (GATT), which allowed indirect taxes to be removed from exports and placed on imports. However, the United States did not use indirect taxes and was consequently unable to adjust its taxation policies in a manner consistent with its obligations under the GATT. It proposed instead that West Germany suspend its VAT or that the United States be permitted to introduce either a tax or an export subsidy equivalent to between 2 and 3 percent.

63 Ottawa to London, Tel. E136, 5 January 1968, DEA File 36-11-4-1-USA, DFAIT.

64 L.B. Johnson to Mitchell Sharp, 31 December 1967, DEA File 36-11-4-1-USA, DFAIT.

65 Mitchell Sharp to L.B. Johnson, 2 January 1968, DEA File 36-11-4-1-USA, DFAIT; See also Saywell), *Canadian Annual Review for 1968*, 310–11.

66 Marcel Cadieux to R.B. Bryce, 2 January 1968, DEA File 36-11-4-1-USA, DFAIT.

67 Ibid.; see also Marcel Cadieux, Memorandum for the Minister, 10 January 1968, DEA File 26-11-4-1-USA, DFAIT.

68 Economic Division, Memorandum to the Under-Secretary of State for External Affairs, 12 January 1968, DEA File 36-11-4-1-USA, DFAIT.

69 R.Y. Grey, Memorandum for Mr Langley, 15 January 1968, RG 19, Vol. 3955, File 8780/U58-2-3; NA.

70 Marcel Cadieux, Memorandum for the Minister, 17 January 1968, DEA File 36-11-4-1-USA, DFAIT.

71 Ibid.; See also Marcel Cadieux, Memorandum for the Prime Minister, 21 January 1968, DEA File 36-1-4-1-USA, DFAIT; R.Y. Grey, Memorandum for Mr Bryce, 17 January 1968; and M.A. Crowe, Memorandum to Mr Grey, and attached Memorandum for Ministers, RG 19, Vol. 3955, File 8780/U58-2-3, NA.

72 L.B. Pearson to L.B. Johnson, 22 January 1968, Pearson Papers, Vol. 281, file 852 Secret, NA.

73 Wright, *Cooperation and Independence*, 191–3; see also Saywell, *The Canadian Annual Review for 1968*, 311.

74 Saywell, *The Canadian Annual Review for 1968*, 311.

75 Marcel Cadieux, Memorandum for the Minister, 22 January 1968, DEA File 36-11-4-1-USA, DFAIT.

76 Saywell, *The Canadian Annual Review of 1968*, 311.

77 Ibid.

78 Canada, House of Commons, *Debates*, 22 January 1968, 5761–2.

79 Walter Gordon, Memorandum, 26 January 1968, Gordon Papers, Vol. 16, NA. This memorandum records a discussion with Edgar Benson.

80 Walter Gordon to L.B. Pearson, 4 February 1968, Gordon Papers, Vol. 14, NA.

81 L. Rasminsky, Meeting with Prime Minister and Ministers, 4 February 1968, Rasminsky Papers, Box 64, File LR-525, BCA. With the Liberal Party's leadership race now in full swing, Rasminsky made a point of remarking that the crisis was "worthy of the concentrated and continuous attention of most senior Ministers."

82 Walter Gordon, Memorandum, 9 February 1968, Gordon Papers, Vol. 14, NA.

83 L.R. Rasminsky to Mitchell Sharp, 27 February 1968, Rasminsky Papers, Box 64, File LR-552, BCA.

84 L.R. Rasminsky to Mitchell Sharp, 26 February 1968, Rasminsky Papers, Box 64, File LR-552, BCA.

85 Ibid.

86 Walter Gordon, Hand-Written Note, 3 March 1968, Gordon Papers, Vol. 14, NA.

87 Memorandum from the President's Special Assistant (Rostow) to President Johnson, 4 March 1964, in FRUS, 1964–68, Vol. 12: *Western Europe* (Washington, 2001), 733–5. The only Canadian source for Sharp's remarks is a note by Walter Gordon recording a conversation with Edgar Benson, Sharp's parliamentary secretary. See Walter Gordon, Hand-Written Note, 3 March 1968, Gordon Papers, Vol. 14, NA.

88 Again, Gordon was not present. Gordon was invited to a meeting the following day. Although this meeting travelled over much the same ground, the decision in favour of seeking an American exemption had already been made. See Walter Gordon, Memorandum, 4 March 1968, Gordon Papers, Vol. 14, NA.

89 L.R. Rasminsky, Memorandum for File, 17 March 1968, Rasminsky Papers, Box 64, File LR-502, BCA.

90 L.R. Rasminsky, Memorandum for File, 17 March 1968, Rasminsky Papers, Box 64, File LR-502, BCA. For a brief discussion of these negotiations by one of the American participants, see Solomon, *The International Monetary System*, 117–18.

91 The final, formal terms of the arrangement are continued in an exchange of letters between Sharp and Fowler that are reprinted in Canada, House of Commons, *Sessional Papers, 1967–68*, No. 32e. For his part, Rasminsky was livid with the publicity that Sharp arranged for this exchange. He wondered if Sharp understood the possible implications for a country's foreign exchange position of admitting that the central banker was negotiating for help at 3 A.M. Rasminsky also resented the minister's attempt to use his efforts in Washington to advance his bid for the Liberal Party's leadership. See L.R. Rasminsky, Memorandum for File, 17 March 1968, Rasminsky Papers, Box 64, File LR-502, BCA.

92 Wright and Molot, "Capital Movements," 90.

93 Embassy Ottawa to Secretary of State, 4 September 1968, NSF, Country Files: Canada, Box 166, Johnson Library.

CHAPTER FOUR

1 Record of a Committee of the Privy Council, PC 1305, 16 August 1963. A copy of this minute was given to the author by John Clearwater.

2 Secretary of State for External Affairs to the United States Ambassador, Note No. 162, 28 September 1963, Department of External Affairs (DEA) File 27-11-Cda/USA-1, Department of Foreign Affairs and International Trade (DFAIT). See also Clearwater, *Canadian Nuclear Weapons*, 241–5.

3 Axworthy, "Soldiers without Enemies," 382–65; see also Hellyer, *Damn the Torpedoes*, 2–4, 32–9.

4 R.L. Raymont, "Report on Integration and Unification, 1964–1968," Raymont Papers, File 759, Directorate of History and Heritage, Department of National Defence (DHist).

5 Canada, House of Commons, *Minutes of Proceedings and Evidence, No. 19, 5 November 1963*, 665–7.

6 Draft White Paper, 19 December 1963, DEA File 27-11-1, DFAIT.

7 G.W. Hunter to C.M. Drury, Raymont Papers, File 759, DHist.

8 Cited in Smith, *Gentle Patriot*, 194.

9 Donaghy, "Canadian Military Assistance," 75–84.

10 Paul Martin to Paul Hellyer, 21 December 1963, Raymont Papers, File 768; see also Ross Campbell to Air Chief Marshal F.R. Miller, 6 February 1964, with attached draft, Raymont Papers, File 759, DHist.

11 Kent, *A Public Purpose*, 312; see also Marcel Cadieux, Memorandum for the Minister, 12 February 1964, Minutes of a Committee of Officials, 15 February 1964, and Norman Robertson, Memorandum for the Minister, 20 February 1964, DEA File 27-11-1, DFAIT.

12 Hilliker and Barry, *Canada's Department of External Affairs*, 279.

13 Granatstein, *Canada 1957–1967*, 236. For a critical view, see Leonard Beaton, "The Canadian White Paper," 364–70. Beaton called it "a very thin meal handsomely presented."

14 Canada, Department of National Defence, *White Paper on Defence*, 11.

15 Embassy Ottawa to State Department, Airgram A-581, 3 January 1964, National Security Files (NSF), Country Files: Canada, Box 165, Johnson Library.

16 Visit of Canadian Prime Minister Pearson: Background Paper on Joint Defence, 17 January 1964, NSF, Country Files: Canada, Pearson Visit 1/22/64, Box 167, Johnson Library.

17 Ottawa to State Department, Tel. No. 937, 21 January 1964 and State Department to Ottawa, Tel. No. 614, 22 January 1964, RG 59, File Def 4 Canada-U.S., United States National Archives (USNA).

18 Ottawa to State Department, Tel. No. 1253, 26 March 1964, RG 59, Box 1612, File Def. 1 Can, USNA; On the influence of Butterworth's report, see H.B. Robinson, Memorandum for the Ambassador, 2 April 1964, Robinson Papers, File 12-11 April 1964, National Archives of Canada (NA).

19 Ottawa to State Department, Tel. No. 1253, 26 March 1964, RG 59, Box 1612, File Def 1. Can, USNA.

20 Cited in Saywell, *Canadian Annual Review for 1964*, 226.

21 Pearson, "A New Kind of Peace Force," 151–4; see also Hilliker and Barry, *Canada's Department of External Affairs*, 386–87.

22 Donaghy, "Canadian Military Assistance," 78.

23 Pearson, *Mike,* Vol. 3, 134–5.

24 State Department to Ottawa, Airgram CA-798, 21 July 1964, *Freedom of Information Act (FOIA)* Request 9202777.

25 Saywell, *Canadian Annual Review for 1964,* 218.

26 American Embassy, Ottawa to State Department, 6 January 1965, NSF, Country File: Canada, Box 165, Johnson Library.

27 McGeorge Bundy, National Security Action Memorandum (NSAM), No. 248, 3 June 1963, *FOIA* Request 9202777.

28 Dana Wilgress to the Prime Minister, 21 October 1963, DEA File 27-4-PJBD-1963, DFAIT; See also, State Department to Ottawa, Tel. No. 617, 22 January 1964, *FOIA* Request 9202777.

29 Dana Wilgress to the Prime Minister, 11 February 1964, DEA File 27-4-PJBD-1964-Winter, DFAIT; See also State Department to Ottawa, Tel. 617, 22 January 1964, *FOIA* Request 9202777.

30 Walter Stoessel to Acting Secretary of State, 30 June 1966. The actual decision is recorded in NSAM No. 302, 22 May 1964. *FOIA* Request 9202777.

31 Paul Hellyer to L.B. Pearson, 26 February 1964, Raymont Papers, File 1108, DHist.

32 The general lines of the discussion can be found in Cabinet Conclusions, 25 March 1964, RG 2, Vol. 6264, NA. For more specific observations about the meeting and its actual impact on the prime minister's thinking, see Memorandum of Conversation: Canadian Government Attitude toward Nuclear Weapons, 19 July 1964, RG 59, Box 1613, File Def. 12 Can, USNA.

33 William Tyler, Memorandum for the Secretary of State, 24 June 1964, NSF, Country Files: Canada, Box 165, Johnson Library.

34 Confidential Source; see also Clearwater, *Canadian Nuclear Weapons,* 246–5.

35 William Tyler to the Secretary of State, 24 June 1964, NSF, Country Files: Canada, Box 165, Johnson Library and attachment, Canada-U.S. Ministerial Meeting on Joint Defence: Nuclear Weapons Authorization and Consultation Procedures, *FOIA* Request 9202777.

36 J. Harold Shullaw to Mr Tyler, 9 July 1964; Draft Memorandum for McGeorge Bundy: Canadian Proposal Regarding Use of NORAD Nuclear Weapons [October 1964]; J. Harold Shullaw to Mr Tyler, 2 November 1964; Scott George to Acting Secretary of State, 16 November 1964, and attached letter from Llewellyn E. Thompson to John McNaughton, 16 November 1964, *FOIA* Request 9202777.

37 Marcel Cadieux, Memorandum for the Prime Minister, 29 September 1964, DEA File 27-4-PJBD-1964-Fall, DFAIT; Dana Wilgress to the Prime Minister, 15 February 1965, DEA File 27-4-PJBD-1965-Winter, DFAIT.

38 William Tyler to John T. McNaughton, Assistant Secretary of Defence, 23 April 1965, *FOIA* Request 9202777; Dana Wilgress to the Prime Minister, 21 June 1965, DEA File 27-4-PJBD-1965-Summer, DFAIT.

39 Memorandum of Conversation: Interceptor Dispersal to Canada, 26 May 1964, RG 59, Box 1613, Def. 12 Can, USNA; Dana Wilgress to the Prime Minister, 30 September 1965, DEA File 27-4-PJBD-1965-Fall, DFAIT.

40 Wilgress to the Prime Minister, 30 September 1965, DEA File 27-4-PJBD-1965-Fall, DFAIT.

41 H.B. Robinson to Defence Liaison (1), 7 October 1965, DEA File 27-16-2-USA-2, DFAIT.

42 Marcel Cadieux, Memorandum for the Minister and attachment, 20 January 1966, DEA File 27-16-2-USA-2, DFAIT.

43 Dana Wilgress to the Prime Minister, 28 February 1966, DEA File 27-4-PJBD-1966-Winter, DFAIT.

44 Pearson's marginalia on Dana Wilgress to the Prime Minister, 10 June 1966, DEA File 27-4-PJBD-1966-Spring, DFAIT.

45 Author interview with Paul Martin, 15 June 1992.

46 Ottawa to NATO Paris, Tel. No. DL-2256, 10 November 1964, 27-4-NATO-12-1964-Fall, DFAIT.

47 Briefing Notes for NATO Ministerial Meeting [December 1964] *FOIA* Request 9202777.

48 McGeorge Bundy, Memorandum to A/Secretary of State George Ball, 16 December 1964, NSF, Country File: Canada, Box 165, Johnson Library.

49 Draft Memorandum for Cabinet, 29 March 1966 and Record of Cabinet Decision, 31 March 1966, DEA File 27-4-NATO-3-1-France, DFAIT.

50 Summary Record: Discussion between SSEA and British Minister for NATO Affairs, 18 May 1966, Martin Papers, Vol. 226, NA.

51 Ottawa to London, Washington, Brussels, and Bonn, Tel. No. DL-126, 20 May 1966, DEA File 27-4-NATO-12-1966-Spring, DFAIT.

52 External to NATO Paris, Tel. No. DL-1504, 1 June 1966, DEA File 27-4-NATO-12-1966-Spring, DFAIT.

53 Martin, *A Very Public Life*, vol. 2, 45–76.

54 Ottawa to NATO Paris, Tel. No. DL-1607, 15 June 1966, DEA File 27-4-NATO-12-1966-Spring, DFAIT.

55 Brussels to Department of State, Tel. No. Secto 46, 5 June 1966, *FOIA* Request 9202977.

56 Walt Rostow, Memorandum to the President, 9 June 1966, NSF, Memoranda to the President, Box 8, Volume 5, Johnson Library and Telegram from Secretary of State to the Department of State, 8 June 1966, in *FRUS*, 1964–68, Vol. 13: *Western Europe Region* (Washington: 1995), 410–11.

57 Pearson, "At the Atlantic Awards Dinner," 254–9.

58 H.B. Robinson, Memorandum for the Under-Secretary, 30 June 1966, DEA File 27-8-USA, DFAIT.

59 John Leddy (through s/s) to Ambassador L. Thompson, [September 1965], RG 59, Box 1979, File Pol. 1 Can, USNA.

60 American Embassy, Ottawa, to State Department, Airgram A-638, 6 January 1968, *FOIA* Request 9202777.

61 James Goodby, The Future of U.S.-Canadian Defense Relationships, April 1967, NSF, Country File: Canada, Box 165, Johnson Library.

62 R.B. Byers, "Canadian Foreign Policy and Selected Attentive Publics," 8 December 1967 (paper prepared for Defence Liaison (1) Division, mimeo), DFAIT Library, 68.

63 Lloyd Axworthy, "Canada and the World Revolution," 31–3; Warnock, "Canada and the Alliance System," 36–9.

64 John English, unpublished draft paper, "NORAD and Defence Cooperation with the United States," Historical Section, DFAIT, 5.

65 Cited in Saywell, *Canadian Annual Review for 1967*, 263.

66 Ibid., p. 266.

67 L.B. Pearson, Memorandum for the Hon. Paul Martin, Pearson Papers, Vol. 280, File 832 Secret, NA.

68 Paul Martin, Memorandum for the Prime Minister, 6 May 1967, ibid.

69 Walter Gordon, *A Political Memoir*, 285–6.

70 Ibid., 286.

71 English, *The Worldly Years*, 377.

72 John Leddy to the Acting Secretary of State, 22 September 1966, *FOIA* Request 9202777; Paul Martin, Memorandum for the Prime Minister, 30 September 1966, and Jacques Corbeil, Memorandum for Defence Liaison (1) Division, 3 October 1966, DEA File 27-14-NORAD-1, DFAIT.

73 Real Admiral R.W. Murdoch, Deputy Chief of Plans to Vice-CDS, 17 March 1967, Raymont Papers, File 343, DHist.

74 H.B. Robinson, Memorandum for Defence Liaison (1) Division, 10 February 1967, DEA File 27-14-NORAD-1, DFAIT.

75 Paul Martin, Memorandum for the Prime Minister, 19 May 1967, DEA File 27-14-NORAD-1.

76 Paul Martin, Memorandum to Cabinet, 31 May 1967, DEA File 27-14-NORAD-1, DFAIT.

77 Memorandum to the Cabinet, 31 May 1967, DEA File 27-4-NATO-12-1967-Spring, DFAIT.

78 H.B. Robinson, Memorandum for Defence Liaison (1) Division, 2 June 1967, DEA File 27-4-NATO-12-1967-Spring, DFAIT, and John English, "Problems in Middle Life," 47–66.

79 H.B. Robinson, Memorandum for Defence Liaison (1) Division, 1 June 1967, DEA File 27-14-1, DFAIT.

80 Paul Martin, *A Very Public Life*, vol. 2, 480; Gordon recalls this episode differently in his *Political Memoir*, 286.

81 Jim Nutt to H.B. Robinson, 28 July 1967, DEA File 27-14-NORAD-1; Gordon, *A Political Memoir*, 287. Martin claims that the views Gordon expressed at the time were more favourable to NATO; see Martin, *A Very Public Life*, vol. 2, 480.

82 Memorandum for the Cabinet, 5 September 1967, Pearson Papers, Vol. 280, File 830 Secret, NA.

83 Memorandum for the Cabinet: Canada and NATO, 5 September 1967, Pearson Papers, Vol. 280, File 830 Secret, NA.

84 Memorandum for the Cabinet: NORAD, 5 September 1967, Pearson Papers, Vol. 280, File 830 Secret, NA.

85 A.D.P. Heeney, Report on the PJBD Meeting, and H.B. Robinson to A.E. Ritchie, 6 October 1967, DEA File 27-4-PJBD-67-Fall, DFAIT; see also, Memorandum to Cabinet, 7 February 1968, Gordon Papers, Vol. 16, NA.

86 Walter Gordon to L.B. Pearson, 15 February 1968, Gordon Papers, Vol. 16, NA.

87 Walter Gordon's handwritten notes, 27 February 1968, Gordon Papers, Vol. 16, NA.

88 Cited in Axworthy, "Foreign Policy," 18.

89 American Embassy, Ottawa to State Department, Airgram A-772, 2 January 1968, FOIA request 9202777.

CHAPTER FIVE

1 There is an extensive historiography on Canada's role on the International Commission for Supervision and Control (ICSC) in Vietnam. Among the most important studies are the following: Taylor's polemical attack on Canadian policy, *Snow Job*; in the same vein, but grounded in a good deal more archival research, is Levant, *Quiet Complicity*; the tensions in early Canadian policy in Indochina are explored in a more balanced but still critical fashion in Eayrs, *In Defence of Canada*.

   The question is approached from a more analytical and comparative perspective in Thakur, *Peacekeeping in Vietnam*. The best work remains Ross's lengthy monograph, *In the Interests of Peace*. Canada's role in Vietnam is also examined in two important recent articles: Robert Bothwell dissects Canada's role in the ICSC up to the mid-1960s in his "The Further Shore: Canada and Vietnam"; John Hilliker and Donald Barry offer a comprehensive survey of Canada's role in Vietnam in their "Uncomfortably in the Middle: The Department of External Affairs and Canada's Involvement in the International Control Commissions in Vietnam, 1954–73," in Victor Howard, ed., *Creating the Peaceable Kingdom*, 167–95.

2 Robert McClintock to George Ball, 12 May 1966, RG 59, Box 1984, File POL 15-1 CAN, United States National Archives (USNA). See also Pearson, *Mike*, vol. 3, 137.

3 Washington to Ottawa, Tel. No. 1002, 16 March 1964, Department of External Affairs (DEA) File 20-22-Viets-2, Department of Foreign Affairs and International Trade (DFAIT).

4 Minutes of Rusk – Under-Secretary of State for External Affairs Meeting, 30 April 1964, DEA File 20-22-Viets-2-1, DFAIT. See also telegram from the Department of State to the Embassy in Vietnam, 1 May 1964, *Foreign Relations of the United States (FRUS)*, 1964–68, vol. 1: *Vietnam 1964*, (Washington, 1992), 281–2.

5 *FRUS*, 1964–68, Volume 1: *Vietnam*, 395.

6 Record of Conversation: Visit of Messrs Sullivan and Cooper to the Department, 3 June 1964, DEA File 20-22-Viets-2-1, DFAIT.

7 Ibid. In his memorandum of the conversation, Sullivan thought that Martin's nervousness about the domestic consequences of escalation was worth drawing to the attention of Ambassador Lodge. See *FRUS*, 1964–68, vol. 1: *Vietnam*, 395, n5.

8 Delworth, "A Study of Canadian Policy."

9 Herring, *America's Longest War*, 118–19.

10 Pearson, *Mike*, 137–8.

11 Washington to Ottawa, Tel. No. 2821, 5 August 1964, DEA File 20-22-Viets-2, DFAIT.

12 Ottawa to Saigon, Tel. No. Y-682, 28 September 1964, DEA File 20-22-Viets-2, DFAIT.

13 H.O. Moran, Memorandum for the Minister, 21 September 1963, Pearson Papers, Box 281, File 845/IV666 Crisis 1964, National Archives of Canada (NA). As a member of the Colombo Plan for Southeast Asian economic development, South Vietnam received $700,000 worth of Canadian assistance in the 1963–64 fiscal year. It would increase to $1.2 million in 1964–65.

14 Marcel Cadieux, Memorandum for the Minister, 6 October 1964, DEA File 20-22-Viets-1, DFAIT.

15 Washington to Ottawa, Tel. Nos. 4189 and 4190, 3 December 1964, DEA File 20-22-Viets-2-1, DFAIT.

16 Ottawa to Saigon, Tel. No. Y-885, 4 December 1964, DEA File 20-22-Viets-2-1, DFAIT.

17 Delworth, "Canadian Policy."

18 Pearson, *Mike*, 126–7.

19 Smart, *The Diary of André Laurendeau*, 127.

20 R.L. Rogers, Memorandum for the Under-Secretary of State for External Affairs, 9 February 1965, DEA File 21-13-Viets-ICSC.

21 Pearson, "Address to the Canadian Club of Ottawa," 10 February 1965. American observers missed this slight shift in Canadian policy and reported that Pearson, who "displayed a full understanding of the U.S. position and the western stake in the Vietnam situation," had "come

down strongly in support of U.S. objectives in Vietnam." See American Embassy, Ottawa to State Department, Airgram A-616, 15 February 1965, RG 59, Box 1989, POL 15-1 CAN, USNA.

22 New York to Ottawa, Tel. No. 349, 8 March 1965, DEA File 20-Viets-1-4, DFAIT.

23 Moscow to Ottawa, Tel. No. 324, 24 March 1965; Moscow to Ottawa, Tel. No. 334, 26 March 1965; Warsaw to Ottawa, Tel. No. 162, 23 March 1965, DEA File 20-22-Viets-2, DFAIT.

24 English, *The Worldly Years*, 367.

25 Reid, *Radical Mandarin*, 372.

26 Paul Martin, Memorandum for the Prime Minister, 29 March 1965, 20-Canada-9-Pearson, NA.

27 English, *The Worldly Years*, 362.

28 Hilliker and Barry, *Canada's Department of External Affairs*, 371–2.

29 Author interview with Michael Shenstone, 6 December 1996.

30 Pearson, *Mike*, 138.

31 Quoted in Hillmer and Granatstein, *For Better or For Worse*, 224.

32 Charles Ritchie, *Storm Signals*, 79–80. This kind of behaviour was not unusual. Rusk describes the "Johnson treatment" in the following terms: "Taller than most men, LBJ used his height to his advantage. He would draw close to his target, look down at him, stick a finger in the man's chest, and launch a barrage of extravagant language to make his point ... and he knew where his opponents vulnerable points were, when to appeal seductively, and when to apply pressure." *As I Saw It*, 333.
    American anger was compounded when they compared the circumstances surrounding Pearson's speech with those surrounding a speech that George Ball, the under secretary of state, was invited to give in Toronto in March. After consulting Canadian officials, Ball accepted Ottawa's advice and declined to make the speech lest it embarrass the government. See State Department to Ottawa, Tel. No. 1074, 6 April 1965, and Ottawa to State Department, Tel. No. 1258, National Security Files (NSF), Country Files: Canada, Box 166, Johnson Library.

33 State Department to Ottawa, Tel. No. 1074, 6 April 1965, NSF, Country Files: Canada, Box 166, Johnson Library.

34 Pearson, *Mike*, 156–7.

35 Marcel Cadieux, Memorandum for the Minister, 6 August 1965, DEA File 20-22-Viets-2-1, DFAIT.

36 American Embassy, London to State Department, Airgram A-3179, 22 June 1965, RG 59, Box 1989, POL 15-1-CAN, USNA.

37 Jack Valenti, Memorandum for the President, 2 August 1965, White House Confidential Files (WHCF), Johnson Library.

38 Ottawa to New Delhi, Tel. No. G-440, 20 December 1965, DEA File 20-22-Viets-2-1, DFAIT.

39 Washington to Ottawa, Tel. No. 4088, 30 December 1965, DEA File 20-22-Viets-2, DFAIT.

40 Author interview with Basil Robinson, 7 June 1994.

41 Heeney and Merchant, *Canada and the United States*, Annex A. For the reaction to the report see Heeney, *Memoirs*, 195–8; Hillmer and Granat-stein, *Empire to Umpire*, 275–6; Bothwell, *Pearson*, 176.

42 For a biographic sketch of Ronning, see Evans, "Ronning and Recognition," 148–67.

43 Paul Martin, Memorandum for the Prime Minister, 20 January 1966, DEA File 20-22-Viets-2-1-1.

44 Herring, *Secret Diplomacy*, 173; see also McNamara, *In Retrospect*, 247.

45 Author interview with Alexis Johnson, 8 June 1992.

46 Confidential interview.

47 Author Interview with H.B. Robinson, 7 June 1994.

48 Herring, *Secret Diplomacy*, 171.

49 Ibid., 176.

50 Saigon to Ottawa, Tel. No. 184, 11 April 1966, DEA File 20-22-Viets-2-1-1. For Ronning's account of the discussions in Hanoi see Ronning, *A Memoir of China*, 255–69.

51 Saigon to Ottawa, Tel. No. 184, 11 April 1966, DEA File 20-22-Viets-2-1-1, DFAIT.

52 Cited in Herring, *Secret Diplomacy*, 123.

53 Saigon to Ottawa, Tel. No. 184, 11 March 1966, DEA File 20-22-Viets-2-1-1.

54 Saigon to Ottawa, Tel. No. 188, 12 March 1966, DEA File 22-20-Viets-2-1-1, DFAIT. The verbatim text of the interview between Ronning and Pham was prepared and forwarded to Ottawa on 14 March 1966. In it, Pham's remarks are even more ambiguous. For instance, the translator had difficulty with what Pham meant when he talked of halting hostilities against the DRVN "for good and unconditionally." In the verbatim transcript the link between the 4th January statement and the offer to Ronning was far more explicit. Moreover, in an effort to be as precise as possible about the nature of his offer, Pham added that "when the USA have made a declaration corresponding to our requirements, we shall, for our part, contemplate it and decide what to do." Neither Ronning nor Moore reported this important qualification. By that time, of course, opinion in Ottawa had begun to coalesce on the basis of the first set of messages, and no one appears to have tried to factor in this new data that might have forced a new assessment of the evidence. See Saigon to Ottawa, Tel. No. 189, 12 March 1966, DEA File 22-20-Viets-2-1-1.

55 Paul Martin's marginalia on Marcel Cadieux, Memorandum for the Minister, 18 March 1966, DEA File 20-22-Viets-2-1-1, DFAIT.

56 Washington to Ottawa, Tel. No. 838, 21 March 1966, DEA File 20-22-Viets-2-1-1, DFAIT.

57 Ibid.

58 George Herring, *Secret Diplomacy*, 179. On Washington's reaction, see also FRUS, 1964–1968, vol. 4: *Vietnam* (Washington, 1998), 287–90. In his memoirs, *In Retrospect*, McNamara maintains that the North Viet-namese position was ambiguous but suggests nevertheless that the United States should have "probed the meaning of Pham's words more deeply" (248).

59 Washington to Ottawa, Tel. No. 1003, 2 April 1966; Washington to Ottawa, Tel. No. 1099, 14 April 1966, DEA File 20-22-Viets-2-1-1, DFAIT.

60 Saigon to Ottawa, Tel. No. 309, 16 April 1966, DEA File 20-22-Viets-2-1-1, DFAIT.

61 Marcel Cadieux, Memorandum for the Minister, 18 April 1966, DEA File 20-22-Viets-2-1-1, DFAIT.

62 Ottawa to Washington, Tel. No. Y-288, 22 April 1966, DEA File 20-22-Viets-2-1-1, DFAIT. The American record is reprinted in Herring, *Secret Diplomacy*, 187. Martin also raised the matter of a second Ronning mission with Averell Harriman on 20 April 1966. See A. Harriman, Memorandum of Conversation, 20 April 1966, RG 59, Box 1984, File POL 15-1, USNA.

63 Herring, *Secret Diplomacy*, 184–6.

64 Suggested Re-draft of U.S. Message (to be discussed in Washington), 30 April 1966 and Washington to Ottawa, Tel. No. 1361, 10 May 1966, DEA File 20-22-Viets-2-1-1, DFAIT.

65 Klaus Goldschlag, Vietnam: Operation Smallbridge, 2 May 1966, DEA File 20-22-Viet-2-1-1, DFAIT.

66 Ottawa to Saigon, Tel. No. Y-349, 14 May 1966 and Saigon to Ottawa, Tel. No. 409, 21 May 1966, DEA File 20-22-Viets-2-1-1, DFAIT; see also Herring, *Secret Diplomacy*, 193.

67 Klaus Goldschlag to Charles Ritchie, 24 May 1966, DEA File 20-22-Viets-2-1-1, DFAIT.

68 Ottawa to Brussels (for SSEA), Tel. No. Y-114, 4 June 1966, DEA File 20-22-Viets-2-1-1, DFAIT.

69 Nato Paris to Ottawa, Tel. No. 400, 5 June 1966, DEA File 20-22-Viets-2-1-1, DFAIT.

70 Saigon to Nato Paris (via Ottawa), Tel. No. 450, 6 June 1966, DEA File 20-22-Viets-2-1-1, DFAIT.

71 Ottawa to Nato Paris (for SSEA), Tel. No. M99, 6 June 1966, DEA File 20-22-Viets-2-1-1, DFAIT.

72 Ottawa to Brussels (for SSEA), Tel. No. Y-405, 6 June 1966, DEA File 20-22-Viets-2-1-1, DFAIT.

73 Nato Paris to Ottawa, Tel. No. 420, 7 June 1966, DEA File 20-22-Viets-2-1-1, DFAIT.

74 Ottawa to Saigon, Tel. No. Y425, 9 June 1966, DEA File 20-22-Viets-2-1-1, DFAIT.

75 Ibid., 192.

76 Washington to Ottawa, Tel. No. 1725, 10 June 1966, DEA File 20-22-Viets-2-1-1, DFAIT.

77 Ottawa to Saigon, Tel. No. Y-438, 16 June 1966, DEA File 20-22-Viets-2-1-1, DFAIT.

78 Saigon to Ottawa, Tel. No. 524, 18 June 1966, DEA File 20-22-Viets-2-1-1, DFAIT. Polish diplomats in contact with North Vietnam described Hanoi as "deeply disappointed by the proposals made by Ronning." See *FRUS*, 1964–68, vol. 4, 468.

79 Saigon to Ottawa, Tel. No. 525, 18 June 1966, DEA File 20-22-Viets-2-1-1, DFAIT.

80 Saigon to Ottawa, Tel. No. 529, 19 June 1966, DEA File 20-22-Viets-2-1-1, DFAIT.

81 Ottawa to Washington, Tel. No. Y-449, 21 June 1966, DEA File 20-22-Viets-2-1-1, DFAIT. See also Herring, *Secret Diplomacy*, 196–7.

82 Walt Rostow to the President, 8 June 1966, NSF, Memoranda to the President, Vol. 5, Box 8, Johnson Library.

83 Points to Be Put to State Department Representative, 20 June 1966, DEA File 20-22-Viets-2-1-1, DFAIT.

84 Herring, *Secret Diplomacy*, 197. See also *FRUS*, 1964–68, vol. 4, 448–9.

85 William Bundy, Memorandum for the Record, 22 June 1965, RG 59, Box 1984, POL 15-1 CAN, USNA. See also, P.H. Kreisberg, Memorandum of Conversation: Visit of Ambassador Ronning to Hanoi, 21 June 1966, *FOIA* Request 9202977.

86 A.E. Ritchie, Note for Mr Collins, 28 June 1968, DEA File 20-22-Viets-2-1-1, DFAIT.

87 Ottawa to Washington, Tel. No. 4476, 30 June 1966, DEA File 20-22-Viets-2-1, DFAIT.

88 English, *The Worldly Years*, 347, 357. See also Walter Gordon, Memorandum: Lunch with LBP, 30 March 1966, Gordon Papers, Vol. 16, NA.

89 Hellyer, *Damn the Torpedoes*, 209.

90 American Embassy, Ottawa to State Department, 6 January 1966, Airgram A-38, *FOIA* Request 9202977.

91 Robert E. Kantor, Memorandum for the President, 17 June 1966, WHCF, Country Files: Canada, Box 19, Johnson Library.

92 Benjamin H. Read, Memorandum to Ambassador J. Leddy, *FOIA* Request 9202977.

93 Dean Rusk, Memorandum for the President, 7 May 1966, NSF, Memoranda for the President, Vol. 2, Box 7, Johnson Library. For Butterworth's views, see also Telegram from the Embassy in Canada to Department of State, 27 April 1966, *FRUS*, 1964–68, vol. 12: *Western Europe* (Washington, 2001), 699–701.

94 Robert McClintock to George Ball, 12 May 1966, RG 59, Box 1984, File POL 15-1 CAN, USNA.

95 Francis M. Bator, Memorandum for the President, 10 August 1966, NSF, Memoranda for the President, Vol. 10, Box 9, Johnson Library.

96 Summary of Prime Minister's Meeting with President Johnson, August 21, for Consulates in the United States, 30 August 1966, DEA File 20-1-2-USA, DFAIT.

97 See American Embassy, Ottawa to State Department, Tel. No. 292 (in two parts), 23 August 1966, and American Embassy, Ottawa to State Department, Tel. No. 325, 26 August 1966, *FOIA* Request 9202977. Canadian officials were also pleased and thought that the meeting had "achieved very successfully the objectives which might have been hoped for on the Canadian side [and] ... further consolidated the personal relationship between the Prime Minister and the President." See H.B. Robinson, "Memorandum for File," 24 August 1966, DEA File 20-1-2-USA, DFAIT.

98 R. Smith, Memorandum of Conversation: Communist China and Admission to UN, 21 August 1966, NSF, Country File: Canada, Box 166, Johnson Library.

99 H.B. Robinson, Memorandum for File, 24 August 1966, DEA File 20-1-2-USA, DFAIT.

100 Mary Macdonald to J.E. Hadwen, 11 July 1966 and Marcel Cadieux, Memorandum for the Minister, 22 July 1966, DEA File 20-China-14, DFAIT.

101 Paul Martin, Memorandum for the Prime Minister and attachments, 22 July 1966, and Pearson's marginalia, Pearson Papers, Vol. 279, File 821/C539.11.Secret, NA. Emphasis in the original.

102 H.B. Robinson, Memorandum for File, 22 September 1966, DEA File 20-China-14, DFAIT. See also Telegram from Secretary of State Rusk to Department of State, 21 September 1966, in *FRUS*, 1964–68, vol. 12: *Western Europe*, 709–10.

103 Washington to Ottawa, Tel. No. 2791, 15 September 1966, and Washington to Ottawa, Tel. No. 2950, 29 September 1966, DEA File 20-China-14, DFAIT.

104 [P.A. McDougall], Chinese Representation: Notes on Three Possible Courses of Action, 21 October 1966, DEA File 20-China-14, DFAIT.

105 Cabinet Conclusions, 28 October 1966, RG 2, Vol. 6321, NA.

106 Ottawa to Washington, Tel. No. Y-745, 27 October 1966, and Washington to Ottawa, Tel. No. 3273, 28 October 1966, DEA File 20-China-14, DFAIT.

107 Dean Rusk, Memorandum for the President, 5 November 1966, *FOIA* Request 9202977.

108 Dean Rusk to L.B. Pearson, 9 November 1966, Pearson Papers, Vol. 7, File 821/C359.1.Conf., NA.

109 Canberra to Ottawa, Tel. No. 729, 11 November 1966, DEA File 20-China-14, DFAIT.

110 H.B. Robinson, Memorandum for the Prime Minister, 9 November 1966; Brussels to Ottawa, Tel. No. 785, 8 November 1966; and Rome to Ottawa, Tel Nos 1401 and 1409, 8 November 1966, DEA File 20-China-14, DFAIT.

111 H.B. Robinson, Memorandum for the Prime Minister, 11 November 1966, DEA File 20-China-14, DFAIT.

112 Ottawa to Rome, Tel. No. Y-125, 12 November 1966, DEA File 20-China-14, DFAIT.

113 H.B. Robinson, Memorandum for the Minister, 17 November 1966, DEA File 20-China-14, DFAIT.

114 Cabinet Conclusions, 18 November 1966, RG 2, Vol. 6321, NA.

115 H.B. Robinson, Memorandum for U.N. Division, 21 November 1966, DEA File 20-China-14, DFAIT.

116 Norman St Amour, "Sino-Canadian Relations," 120.

117 State to Taipei, Tel. No. 91450, and W.J. Stoessel, Memorandum of Conversation: Secretary's Conversation with Canadian Foreign Minister Martin: Chirep, 25 November 1966, *FOIA* Request 9202977.

118 J.G. Hadwen, Memorandum to Far Eastern Division, 30 November 1966, DEA File 20-China-14, DFAIT.

CHAPTER SIX

1 Litvak and Maule, *Cultural Sovereignty*, 30–31.

2 Royal Commission on Publications, *Report*, 74. See also O'Leary, *Recollections*, 138–40.

3 Litvak and Maule, *Cultural Sovereignty*, 65.

4 The pressure on the government was intense. See, for example, C.J. Laurin to Walter Gordon, 23 April 1963, Laurin to Gordon, 10 May 1963, and Laurin to Gordon, 28 May 1963, Gordon Papers, Vol. 10, National Archives of Canada (NA). The effort was ultimately counterproductive, as besieged officials tended to pass the epistles along, marginally dismissing them with notes that observed that the "situation is as usual extremely urgent." R.B. Bryce, Memorandum for Mr Gordon in Cabinet, 16 July 1963, RG 19, Vol. 5201, File 8891-07, NA.

5 A.F.W. Plumptre, Memorandum for the Minister, 25 April 1963, Gordon Papers, Vol. 10, NA.

6 See Bryce's marginalia on his Memorandum for Mr Gordon in Cabinet, 16 July 1963, RG 19, Vol. 5201, File 8891-07, NA.

7 R.B. Bryce, Memorandum for the Prime Minister, 12 August 1963, RG 19, Vol. 5201, File 8891-07, NA.

8 E.P. Zimmerman to R.B. Bryce, 4 September 1963, and Bryce to A.F.W. Plumptre, 4 September 1963, RG 19, Vol. 5201, File 8891-07, NA.

9 Tom Kent, Memorandum for R.B. Bryce, 9 September 1963, and attached Memorandum for the Prime Minister, 5 September 1963, RG 19, Vol. 5201, File 8891-07, NA.

10 Walter Gordon, Memorandum for the Cabinet, 30 September 1963, Privy Council Office (PCO) File T-1-20, PCO.

11 Tom Kent, Memorandum for the Prime Minister, 2 October 1963, Kent Papers, Box 3, Queen's University Archives (QUA).

12 L.B. Pearson, Memorandum for the Cabinet, 11 October 1963, PCO File T-1-20, PCO and Report of the Ad Hoc Interdepartmental Committee, 18 October 1963, RG 19, Vol. 5201, File 8891-07, NA.

13 Washington to Ottawa, Tel. No. 3796, 20 November 1963, DEA File 37-7-1-USA-1, DFAIT.

14 Memorandum of Conversation: Royal Commission on Periodicals, 22 January 1964, *Freedom of Information Act (FOIA)* Request 9202777.

15 Cited in Litvak and Maule, *Cultural Sovereignty*, 70. See also J.D. Daly to L.B. Pearson, 2 February 1964, PCO File C-2-3(g)-2, PCO.

16 *Toronto Star*, 24 February 1964.

17 Atkinson to L.B. Pearson, 20 March 1964, PCO File C-2-3(g)-2, PCO.

18 Floyd Chalmers to Mitchell Sharp, 26 March 1964, and Floyd Chambers to Mitchell Sharp, 4 May 1964, Sharp Papers, Vol. 19, File 6, NA.

19 R.G. Robertson, Memorandum for the Prime Minister, 14 April 1964, PCO File C-2-3(g)-2, PCO.

20 Kent, *A Public Purpose*, 319.

21 Azzi, "The Limits of Affluence," 227–8.

22 Cabinet Conclusions, April 16, 1964, RG 2, Vol. 6264, NA.

23 Marcel Cadieux, Memorandum for the Minister, 14 April 1964, DEA File 37-7-1-USA-1, DFAIT; See also R.G. Robertson, Memorandum for the Prime Minister, 14 April 1964, PCO File C-2-3(g)-2, PCO.

24 Marcel Cadieux, Memorandum for the Minister, 14 April 1964, DEA File 37-7-1-USA-1, DFAIT.

25 R.G. Robertson, Memorandum for the Prime Minister, 17 April 1964, PCO File C-2-3(g)-2, PCO.

26 Tom Kent, Memorandum for the Prime Minister, 11 May 1964, Kent Papers, Box 3, QUA. Kent owed some of the credit for the suggestions on

Canadian content to R.G. Robertson. See Robertson's Memorandum for the Prime Minister, 4 May 1964, PCO File C-2-3(g)-2, PCO.

27 Cabinet Conclusions, 21 May 1964, RG 2, Vol. 6264, NA. See also L.B. Pearson, Memorandum for the Cabinet, Cabinet Document 222/64, PCO File C-2-3(g)-2, PCO.

28 Cabinet Conclusions, 25 May 1964, Vol. 6264, NA. Cabinet members were also concerned that the proposal to give *Time* and *Reader's Digest* three years to meet their targets would expose the government to a three-year campaign against the legislation. See Tom Kent to Walter Gordon, 24 May 1964, Gordon Papers, Vol. 14, NA.

29 L.B. Pearson, Memorandum for the Cabinet Committee on Finance and Economic Policy, Cabinet Document 448/64, PCO File C-2-3(g)-2, PCO.

30 Marcel Cadieux, Memorandum for the Minister, 7 October 1964, DEA File 37-7-1-USA-1, DFAIT.

31 Cabinet Conclusions, 22 October 1964, RG 2, Vol. 6265, NA.

32 L.B. Pearson, Memorandum to Cabinet, 24 February 1965, PCO File C-2-3(g)-2, PCO.

33 See Tom Kent to the Prime Minister, 26 February 1965, Kent Papers, Box 4, QUA.

34 Cabinet Conclusions, 2 March 1965, RG 2, Vol. 6271, NA.

35 L.B. Pearson, Memorandum for the Cabinet, 8 March 1965, PCO File C-2-3(g)-2, PCO; Cabinet Conclusions, 9 March 1965, RG 2, Vol. 6271, NA.

36 Washington to Ottawa, Tel. No. 1134, 12 April 1965, DEA File 37-7-1-USA-1, DFAIT.

37 Ibid.

38 A.E Ritchie, Memorandum to Economic Division, 13 April 1965, DEA File 37-7-1-USA-1, DFAIT.

39 Ottawa to Washington, Tel. No. G-115, 26 April 1965, DEA File 37-7-1-USA-1, DFAIT.

40 Cited in Azzi, *Walter Gordon*, 123-4.

41 Washington to Ottawa, Tel. No. 1289, 26 April 1965, DEA File 37-7-1-USA-1, DFAIT.

42 Embassy Ottawa to State Department, Airgram A-638, 6 January 1966, *FOIA* Request 9202777.

43 The confusion surrounding this encounter is discussed in Fayerweather, *The Mercantile Bank Affair*, 50-77.

44 Draft Summary Record, Joint United States-Canada Committee on Trade and Economic Affairs, 4-5 March 1966, DEA File 35-4-5-1-1966, DFAIT.

45 T.C. Mann to Mitchell Sharp [March 1966], File LR 76-576-4-6, Rasminsky Papers, Bank of Canada Archives (BCA).

46 Walt Butterworth to Department of State, Letter No. A-941 and attached Memorandum of Conversation, RG 59, Box 838, FN 6, United States National Archives (USNA).

47 Embassy Ottawa to Department of State, Airgram No. A-1021, 15 April 1966, RG 59, Box 838, File FN 6 Can, USNA.

48 Walt Butterworth, Memorandum of Telephone Conversation, 2 May 1966, RG 59, Box 834, FN 6 Can, USNA.

49 Gordon, *A Choice for Canada*, 94–5. The response to this work is discussed extensively in Azzi, *Walter Gordon*, 143–4. For the Mercantile Bank's account of the July meetings, see Fayerweather, *The Mercantile Bank Affair*, 79–80.

50 Cabinet Conclusions, 17 May 1966, RG 2, Vol. 6321, NA.

51 The Minister of Finance to Cabinet, 2 May 1966, PCO File F-1-7, PCO.

52 Cabinet Conclusions, 9 May 1966, RG 2, Vol. 6321, NA.

53 Cabinet Conclusions, 17 May 1966, ibid.

54 Cabinet Conclusions, 9 May 1966, ibid.

55 Cabinet Conclusions, 24 June 1966, ibid.

56 Embassy Ottawa to Department of State, Airgram A-1342, 30 June 1966, RG 59, Box 838, FN 6 Can, USNA.

57 Saywell, *Canadian Annual Review for 1966*, 318–19. See also Ottawa to Washington, Tel. No. E-3167, 10 October 1966, DEA File 36-13-1, DFAIT.

58 Rufus Smith, Memorandum of Conversation: Discriminatory Canadian Banking Legislation, 2 November 1966 and Department of State to Embassy Ottawa, Tel. No. 719, 2 November 1966, RG 59, Box 838, FN 6 Can, USNA.

59 Embassy Ottawa to Department of State, Tel. No. 748, 3 November 1966, RG 59, Box 838, FN 6 Can, USNA.

60 Department of State to Embassy Ottawa, Tel. No. State 83614, 11 November 1966, RG 59, Box 838, FN 6 Can, USNA.

61 The text of the note and Ritchie's report on his discussion with Katzenbach are reprinted in Newman, *The Distemper of Our Times*, 515–18.

62 George Kidd, Memorandum for File, 18 November 1966, DEA File 36-13-1, DFAIT; See also, Department of State to Embassy Ottawa, Tel. 93230, 29 November 1966, RG 59, Box 838, FN 6 Can, USNA.

63 Department of State to Embassy Ottawa, Tel. No. 90666, RG 59, Box 838, FN 6 Can, USNA.

64 Embassy Ottawa to Department of State, Tels. Nos. 900 and 901, 30 November 1966, RG 59, Box 838, FN 6 Can, USNA.

65 *Toronto Star*, 1 December 1966.

66 Rufus Smith, Memorandum of Conversation: Controversy over Mercantile Bank, 2 December 1966, RG 59, Box 838, FN 6 Can, USNA and Washington to Ottawa, Tel. No. 3773, 3 December 1966, DEA File 36-13-1, NA.

67 Embassy Ottawa to Department of State, 5 December 1966, RG 59, Box 838, FN 6 Can, USNA. Sharp's efforts were not helped by all Canadian

officials. In the final paragraph of the above telegram, Butterworth reported that "under-secretary Cadieux had lunch with me. While avoiding being specific, he clearly conveyed predilection for the validity of our view. He asked about MacFadden and expressed hope that he would make a straightforward forceful defence of the right of First National City Bank to come in here and conduct legitimate commercial business under existing Canadian law."

68 Department of State to Embassy Ottawa, Tel. 103634, 15 December 1966, FN 6 Can, USNA.

69 Cited in Azzi, "The Limits of Affluence," 276.

70 Fayerweather, *The Mercantile Bank Affair*, 93.

71 Washington to Ottawa, Tel. No. 418, 30 January 1967, PCO File F-1-7(g), PCO.

72 A.E. Ritchie, Memorandum for File, 2 February 1967, DEA File 36-13-1, DFAIT.

73 John Fayerweather, *The Mercantile Bank Affair*, 113.

74 Cabinet Conclusions, 31 January 1967, RG 2, Vol. 6323, NA.

75 Ottawa to Washington, Tel. No. PCO 1, 1 February 1967, PCO File F-1-7(g), PCO. Pearson was obviously very worried about the Mercantile Bank affair. Visiting with the prime minister that evening, John Holmes found his friend "completely preoccupied by the problems of Canada–United States relations." See John Holmes to A.E. Ritchie, 3 February 1967, Holmes Papers, File A/1/26, Canadian Institute of International Affairs Archives (CIIAA).

76 Ibid.

77 Walter Gordon, Memorandum, 20 February 1967, Gordon Papers, Vol. 16, NA.

78 Walter Gordon, Memorandum, 24 February 1967, Gordon Papers, Vol. 16, NA.

79 Walter Gordon, Memorandum: Note of My Remarks to Cabinet, 24 February 1967, Gordon Papers, Vol. 16, NA.

80 Cited in Granatstein, *Yankee Go Home?* 179.

81 Cited in Azzi, *Walter Gordon*, 136.

82 Fetherling, *Travels by Night*, 113.

83 George Grant, *Lament for a Nation*.

84 Lee, "Third Elegy," 32–3.

85 Atwood, "Backdrop Addresses Cowboy," 10.

86 Cited in Granatstein, *Yankee Go Home?* 235.

87 Cited in Azzi, *Walter Gordon*, 133–4.

88 Owram, *Born at the Right Time*, 188, 194–5, 204–6, 262–4. See also Granatstein, *Yankee Go Home?* 179–80.

89 Hollander, *Anti-Americanism*, 416.

90 Ross, *In the Interests of Peace*, 259.

91 Marcel Cadieux, Memorandum for the Minister, 16 January 1967, DEA File 27-11-2-USA, DFAIT.

92 Pearson, "Canada," 121–5.

93 Paul Martin, Memorandum for the Prime Minister, 27 January 1967, DEA File 27-11-2-USA, DFAIT.

94 Canada, House of Commons, *Debates*, 13 February 1967, 12966.

95 Canada, House of Commons, *Debates*, 2 February 1967, 12361; 3 February 1967, 12617; 6 February 1967, 12679–80; and 7 February 1967, 12730.

96 Cited in Saywell, *Canadian Annual Review for 1967*, 208.

97 See, for example, Washington to Ottawa, Tel. No. 734, 21 February 1967, DEA File 20-22-Viets-2-1; and Washington to Ottawa, Tel. No. 1030, 16 March 1967, DEA File 20-22-Viets-2-1.

98 Canada, House of Commons, Standing Committee on External Affairs, *Minutes of Proceedings and Evidence*, No. 10, 11 April 1967, 312–14.

99 Ed Ritchie to Marcel Cadieux, and attachment, 20 April 1967, DEA File 20-22-Viets-2-1.

100 Permisny to Ottawa, Tel. No. 1087, 28 April 1967, DEA File 20-22-Viets-2-1.

101 London to Ottawa, Tel. No. 2385, 3 May 1967, DEA File 20-22-Viets-2-1.

102 Far Eastern Division to Under-Secretary of State for External Affairs, 16 May 1966, DEA File 20-22-Viets-2-1, DFAIT.

103 Walter Gordon, *A Political Memoir*, 281–2.

104 English, *The Worldly Years*, 377.

105 Walt Rostow, Memorandum for the President, 25 May 1967, National Security Files (NSF), Memoranda for the President, Box 16, Johnson Library.

106 Pearson, *Mike*, 144–7. See also, Walt Butterworth, Memorandum: Draft, 26 May 1967 and R.P. Davis, Memorandum of Conversation: President's Conversation with Prime Minister Pearson, 25 May 1967, in *FRUS, 1964–68*, Vol. 12: *Western Europe* (Washington, 2001), 715–19.

107 Talks between Prime Minister Wilson and Prime Minister Pearson, 1 June 1967, DEA File 20-22-Viets-2-1, DFAIT.

108 Smith, *Gentle Patriot*, 325.

109 Reid, *Radical Mandarin*, 372–5. On the origins of this appeal, see Escott Reid to John W. Holmes, 15 May 1967, John Holmes to Douglas LePan, and John Holmes to A.W.F. Plumptre, 16 May 1967, File c/IV/14, Holmes Papers, CIIAA.

110 English, *The Worldly Years*, 379.

111 Ottawa to New York, Tel. No. Y-537, 8 September 1967, DEA File 20-22-Viets-2-1, DFAIT.

112 New York to Ottawa, Tel. No. 2490, 22 September 1967, DEA File 20-22-Viets-2-1, DFAIT.

113 Martin, "Canada and the Universal Forum for Peace." In his memoirs, Martin calls his speech one of the earliest public calls for an unconditional bombing halt. See *A Very Public Life*, 454–5. However, in March 1968 he emphasized that his speech not only called for a bombing halt but "also comprised other essential elements." Paul Martin, Memorandum for the Prime Minister, 12 March 1968, DEA File 20-22-Viets-2-1, DFAIT.

114 H.B. Robinson, Memorandum for the Minister, 21 August 1967, DEA File 36-13-1, DFAIT.

115 Ottawa to Washington, Tel. No. E-3241, DEA File 37-7-1-USA-1, DFAIT.

116 Walt Rostow, Memorandum for the President, 10 October 1967, NSF, Country Files: Canada, Box 167, Johnson Library. For Butterworth's telegram, see Telegram from the Embassy in Canada to the Department of State, 23 October 1967, in *FRUS*, 1964–68, Vol. 12: *Western Europe*, 721–4.

117 Washington to Ottawa, Tel. No. 3993, 30 October 1967, DEA File 20-1-2-USA, DFAIT.

118 Washington to Ottawa, Tel. No. 4254, 17 November 1967, DEA File 20-1-2-USA, DFAIT.

119 R. Straus, Memorandum of Conversation: US-Canadian Relations, 16 November 1967, in *FRUS*, 1964–68, Vol. 12: *Western Europe*, 725–9. See also, Washington to Ottawa, Tel. No. 4254, 17 November 1967, DEA File 20-1-2-USA, DFAIT.

120 Briefing Paper for Mr Walt Rostow and Mr Ernest Goldstein, [19 October 1967], NSF, Country File: Canada, Box 167, Johnson Library; see also, Marcel Cadieux, Memorandum for the Minister, 11 October 1967, DEA File 20-1-2-USA, DFAIT.

121 Walt Rostow, Memorandum for the President, 26 October 1967, NSF, Memoranda for the President, Box 48, Johnson Library.

122 Paul Martin, Memorandum for the Prime Minister, 27 December 1967, DEA File 20-1-2-USA, DFAIT.

Bibliography

ARCHIVAL SOURCES

BANK OF CANADA ARCHIVES
Bank of Canada Records
Louis Rasminsky Papers

CANADIAN INSTITUTE OF INTERNATIONAL AFFAIRS ARCHIVES
J.W. Holmes Papers

DEPARTMENT OF NATIONAL DEFENCE, DIRECTORATE OF HISTORY
AND HERITAGE
Department of National Defence Records
Raymont Papers

GEORGETOWN UNIVERSITY LIBRARY
Foreign Affairs Oral History Collection
   Willis Armstrong
   Philip Trezise

JOHN F. KENNEDY LIBRARY
National Security Files
White House Confidential Files

LIBRARY OF CONGRESS
Averell Harriman Papers

LYNDON BAINES JOHNSON LIBRARY
Francis Bator Papers
National Security Files
  Administrative Histories
  Country Files
  Memoranda to the President
  President's Meetings
  Statements of LBJ
White House Confidential Files

NATIONAL ARCHIVES OF CANADA
Department of External Affairs Records
Department of Finance Records
Department of Industry Records
Department of Trade and Commerce Records
Privy Council Office Records
Walter Gordon Papers
A.D.P. Heeney Papers
Paul Martin Papers
L.B. Pearson Papers
H. Basil Robinson Papers

PRIVY COUNCIL OFFICE
Central Registry Files

QUEEN'S UNIVERSITY ARCHIVES
Tom Kent Papers

UNITED STATES NATIONAL ARCHIVES
Department of Commerce Records
Department of State Records

UNIVERSITY OF TORONTO ARCHIVES
Robert Bothwell Papers

INTERVIEWS

E.P. Black (9 November 1994): NATO Desk Officer, Department of External
  Affairs, 1962-65.

Tom Delworth (14 March 1997): Vietnam Desk Officer, Department of External Affairs, 1964–68.

John Fraser (9 June 1997): Canadian Trade Commissioner in Hong Kong, 1965–67.

U. Alexis Johnson (8 June 1992): Deputy Under Secretary for Political Affairs, United States Department of State, 1961–64 and 1965–66

George Kidd (29 June 1992): Minister, Canadian Embassy, Washington, 1964–67.

Paul Martin (15 June 1992): Secretary of State for External Affairs, Department of External Affairs, 1963–68.

Charles Ritchie (29 November 1992 and 12 May 1994): Canadian Ambassador to the United States, 1962–1966; Permanent Representative to the North Atlantic Council, 1966.

H. Basil Robinson (5 October 1993 and 7 June 1994): Minister, Canadian Embassy to the United States, 1962–64; Assistant Under-Secretary of State for External Affairs, Department of External Affairs, 1964–66; Deputy Under-Secretary of State for External Affairs, Department of External Affairs, 1966–70.

Walt Rostow (4 May 1992): Director, Policy Planning Staff, United States Department of State, 1961–66; National Security Advisor, National Security Council, White House, 1966–68.

Blair Seaborn (11 February 1992): Canadian Representative on the International Commission for Supervision and Control in Vietnam, 1964–66.

John Sharpe (24 September 1993): First Secretary, Canadian Embassy, Washington, 1961–64.

Michael Shenstone (6 December 1996): Counsellor, Canadian Embassy, Washington, 1964–67.

Philip Trezise (25 October 1995): Deputy Assistant Secretary of State for Economic Affairs, United States Department of State, 1964–65.

BOOKS, ARTICLES, AND THESES

Allard, Jean (with Serge Bernier). *The Memoirs of Jean Allard*. Vancouver: University of British Colombia Press, 1988.

Atwood, Margaret, "Backdrop Addresses Cowboy." In Al Purdy, ed., *The New Romans: Candid Canadian Opinions of the United States*. Edmonton, AB: Hertig Publishers, 1968.

Axworthy, Lloyd. "Canada and the World Revolution." *Canadian Dimension* 3 (March-April 1966): 31–3.

Axworthy, Thomas. "Soldiers without Enemies: A Political Analysis of Canadian Defence Policy, 1945–1975." Unpublished PHD Diss., Queen's University, 1978.

– "'To Stand Not So High Perhaps but Always Alone': The Foreign Policy of Pierre Trudeau." In Thomas Axworthy and Pierre Trudeau, eds., *Towards a Just Society: The Trudeau Years*. Markham, ON: Penguin Books, 1980.

Azzi, Stephen. "The Limits of Affluence: Walter Gordon, Foreign Ownership and the Politics of Independence Issue." Unpublished PHD diss., University of Waterloo, 1996.

– *Walter Gordon and the Rise of Canadian Nationalism*. Montreal and Kingston: McGill-Queen's University Press, 1999.

Ball, George. *The Discipline of Power: Essentials of a Modern World Structure*. Boston: Atlantic Monthly Press, 1968.

– *The Past Has Another Pattern: Memoirs*. New York: W.W. Norton and Company, 1982.

Beaton, Leonard. "The Canadian White Paper on Defence." *Internatinal Journal* 19 (Summer 1964): 364–70.

Beer, Francis A. *Integration and Disintegration in NATO*. Columbus, OH: Ohio State University Press, 1969.

Bercuson, David. "Canada, NATO, and Rearmament, 1950–1954: Why Canada Made a Difference (but Not for Very Long)." In John English and Norman Hillmer, eds., *Making a Difference? Canada's Foreign Policy in a Changing World Order*. Toronto: Lester Publishing, 1992.

Beschloss, Michael R., ed., *Taking Charge: The Johnson White House Tapes, 1963–1964*. New York: Simon and Schuster, 1997.

Blumenthal, Sidney. "The Ruins of Georgetown." *New Yorker*, 21 and 28 October 1996, 221–37.

Bothwell, Robert. *Canada and the United States: The Politics of Partnership*. Toronto: University of Toronto Press, 1992.

– *Pearson: His Life and World*. Toronto: McGraw-Hill Ryerson, 1976.

Brands, H.W. *The Wages of Globalism: Lyndon Johnson and the Limits of American Power*. New York: Oxford University Press, 1995.

Brecher, Irving, and Simon S. Reisman. *Canada–United States Economic Relations*. Ottawa: Queen's Printer, 1957.

Bryden, P.E. "The Liberal Party of Canada: Organizing for Social Reform, 1957–1966." In J.L. Granatstein and Gustav Schmidt, eds., *Canada at the Crossroads? The Critical 1960s*. Bochum, Germany: Univsitatsverlag Dr. N. Brockmeyer, 1994.

Bundy, McGeorge. "Canada, the Exceptionally Favored: An American Perspective." In Lansing Lamont and J. Duncan Edmonds, eds., *Friends So Different: Essays on Canada and the United States in the 1980s*. Ottawa: University of Ottawa Press for the America's Society, 1989.

Byers, R.B. "Canadian Foreign Policy and Selected Attentive Publics." Paper prepared for Defence (1) Liaison Division, 8 December 1967. Mimeograph, Department of Foreign Affairs and International Trade Library.

Canada. Department of National Defence. *White Paper on Defence*. Ottawa: Queen's Printer, 1964.

– House of Commons. *Debates*, 1963–68.

– *Sessional Papers*, 1967–68.

– Special Committee on Defence. *Minutes of Proceedings and Evidence*, 1963.

– Standing Committee on External Affairs and Defence. *Minutes of Proceedings and Evidence*, 1967.

Canada. Royal Commission on the Automotive Industry. *Report*. Ottawa: Queen's Printer, 1961.

– Royal Commission on the Economic Union and Development Prospects for Canada. *Report*. Ottawa: Supply and Services Canada, 1985.

– Royal Commission on Publications. *Report*. Ottawa: Queen's Printer, 1961.

Chalmers, Floyd S. *Both Sides of the Street: One Man's Life in Business and the Arts in Canada*. Toronto: Macmillan, 1983.

Clearwater, John. *Canadian Nuclear Weapons: The Untold Story of Canada's Cold War Arsenal*. Toronto: Dundurn Press, 1998.

Costigliola, Frank. "Lyndon B. Johnson, Germany and the 'End of the Cold War.'" In Warren I. Cohen and Nancy Bernkopf Tucker, eds., *Lyndon Johnson Confronts the World: American Foreign Policy, 1963–1968*. Cambridge: Cambridge University Press, 1994.

Dallek, Robert. *Flawed Giant: Lyndon Johnson and his Times, 1961–1973*. New York: Oxford University Press, 1998.

Delworth, Thomas. "A Study of Canadian Policy with Respect to the Vietnam Problem, 1962–1966." Mimeograph, Historical Section, Department of Foreign Affairs and International Trade.

Donaghy, Greg. "The Rise and Fall of Canadian Military Assistance in the Developing World, 1952–1971." *Canadian Military History* 4 (spring 1995): 75–84.

– "Domesticating NATO: Canada and the North Atlantic Alliance, 1963–68." *International Journal* 51 (summer 1997): 446–63.

– "Minding the Minister: Pearson, Martin and American Policy in Asia, 1963–1967." In Norman Hillmer, ed., *Pearson: The Unlikely Gladiator*. Montreal and Kingston: McGill-Queen's University Press, 1999.

– ed. *Canada and the Early Cold War, 1945–57*. Ottawa: Department of Foreign Affairs and International Trade, 1998.

Eayrs, James. *In Defence of Canada*. Vol. 5, *Indochina: Roots of Complicity*. Toronto: University of Toronto Press, 1983.

English, John. "Problems in Middle Life." In Margaret MacMillan and David Sorenson, eds., *Canada and NATO: Uneasy Past, Uncertain Future*. Waterloo, ON: University of Waterloo Press, 1990.

– *The Worldly Years: The Life of Lester B. Pearson*. Vol. 2, *1949–1972*. Toronto: Alfred A. Knopf Canada, 1992.

– "NORAD and Defence Cooperation with the United States." Draft paper, n.d.

Evans, Brian. "Ronning and Recognition: Years of Frustration." In Paul M. Evans and Michael B. Frolic, eds., *Reluctant Adversaries: Canada and the People's Republic of China*. Toronto: University of Toronto Press, 1991.

Evans, John W. *The Kennedy Round in American Trade Policy: The Twilight of the GATT?* Cambridge: Harvard University Press, 1971.

Fayerweather, John. *The Mercantile Bank Affair: A Case Study of Canadian Nationalism and a Multinational Firm*. New York: New York University Press, 1974.

Fetherling, Doug. *Travels by Night: A Memoir of the Sixties*. Toronto: Lester Publishing, 1994.

Galbraith, John Kenneth. *A Life in Our Times: Memoirs*. Boston: Houghton Mifflin, 1981.

Girard, Charlotte. *Canada in World Affairs*. Vol. 13, *1963–1965*. Toronto: Canadian Institute of International Affairs [1980].

Gordon, Walter L. *A Choice for Canada: Independence or Colonial Status*. Toronto: McClelland and Stewart, 1966.

– *A Political Memoir*. Toronto: McClelland and Stewart, 1977.

Granatstein, J.L. *A Man of Influence: Norman A. Robertson and Canadian Statecraft, 1929–68*. Toronto: Deneau Publishers, 1981.

– "Free trade between Canada and the United States: The Issue That Will Not Go Away." In Denis Stairs and Gilbert R. Winham, eds., *The Politics of Canada's Economic Relationship with the United States*. Ottawa: Supply and Services Canada, 1985.

– *Canada 1957–1967: The Years of Uncertainty and Innovation*. Toronto: McClelland and Stewart, 1986.

– "When Push Came to Shove: Canada and the United States." In Thomas Patterson, ed., *Kennedy's Quest for Victory: American Foreign Policy, 1961–1963*. Toronto: Oxford University Press, 1989.

– *Yankee Go Home? Canadians and Anti-Americanism*. Toronto: Harper-Collins, 1996.

Grant, George. *Lament for a Nation: The Defeat of Canadian Nationalism*. Toronto: McClelland and Stewart, 1965.

Hart, Michael. "Twenty Years of Canadian Tradecraft: Canada at the GATT, 1947–1967." *International Journal* 52 (autumn 1997): 581–604.

– "From Colonialism to Globalism." Unpublished manuscript.

Heeney, A.D.P. *The Things That Are Caesar's: Memoirs of a Canadian Public Servant*. Toronto: University of Toronto Press, 1972

Heeney, A.D.P., and Livingston Merchant. *Canada and the United States: Principles for Partnership*. Ottawa: Queen's Printer, 1965.

Hellyer, Paul. *Damn the Torpedoes: My Fight to Unify Canada's Armed Forces*. Toronto: McClelland and Stewart, 1990.

Herring, George C. *The Secret Diplomacy of the Vietnam War: The Negotiating Volumes of the Pentagon Papers.* Austin, TX: University of Texas Press, 1983.

– *America's Longest War: The United States and Vietnam, 1950–1972.* 2d Ed. New York: Alfred A. Knopf, 1986.

Hilliker, John F., and Donald Barry. *Canada's Department of External Affairs.* Vol. 2, *Coming of Age, 1946–1968.* Montreal and Kingston: McGill-Queen's University Press.

Hillmer, Norman, ed. *Partners Nevertheless: Canadian-American Relations in the Twentieth Century.* Mississauga, ON: Copp Clark, 1989.

Hillmer, Norman, and J.L. Granatstein. *For Better or For Worse: Canada and the United States to the 1990s.* Toronto: Copp Clark Pitman, 1991.

– *Empire to Umpire: Canada and the World to the 1990s.* Toronto: Copp Clark Longman, 1994.

– *For Better or For Worse: Canada and the United States to the Twenty-First Century.* Toronto: Copp Clark Pitman, forthcoming.

Historical Division, Joint Secretariat, United States Joint Chiefs of Staff. Chronology of JCS Involvement in North American Air Defence, 1946–1975. Mimeographed, Washington, 1976.

Hollander, Paul. *Anti-Americanism: Critiques at Home and Abroad, 1965–1990.* New York: Oxford University Press, 1992.

Ignatieff, George. *The Making of a Peacemonger: The Memoirs of George Ignatieff.* Toronto: University of Toronto Press, 1985.

Johnson, Lyndon B. *The Vantage Point: Perspectives of the Presidency, 1963–1969.* New York: Holt, Rinehart and Winston, 1971.

Kaplan, William. *Everything that Floats: Pat Sullivan, Hal Banks, and the Seamen's Unions of Canada.* Toronto: University of Toronto Press, 1987.

Keeley, James Francis. "Constraints on Canadian International Economic Policy." Unpublished PHD diss., Stanford University, 1980.

Kent, Tom. *A Public Purpose: An Experience of Liberal Opposition and Canadian Government.* Montreal and Kingston: McGill-Queen's University Press, 1988.

Kirton, John. "The Politics of Bilateral Management: The Case of the Automotive Trade." *International Journal* 36, no. 1 (winter 1980–81): 39–69.

Kirton, John, and Robert Bothwell. "A Proud and Powerful Country: American Attitudes toward Canada, 1963–1976." *Queen's Quarterly* 92, no. 1 (spring 1985): 108–26.

Kissinger, Henry. *The Troubled Partnership.* Toronto: McGraw-Hill, 1965.

Kunz, Diane. "Cold War Dollar Diplomacy: The Other Side of Containment." In Diane Kunz, ed., *The Diplomacy of the Crucial Decade: American Foreign Relations during the 1960s.* New York: Columbia University Press, 1995.

Lacey, F.H., ed., *Historical Statistics of Canada*. 2d ed. Ottawa: Statistics Canada, 1983.

LaMarsh, Judy. *Memoirs of a Bird in a Gilded Cage*. Toronto: McClelland and Stewart, 1968.

Lee, Dennis. "Third Elegy (Nathan Phillips Square Toronto)." *Canadian Dimension* 4 (September-October, 1967): 32–3.

Levant, Victor. *Quiet Complicity: Canadian Involvement in the Vietnam War*. Toronto: Between The Lines, 1986.

Levitt, Joseph. *A Vision beyond Reach*. Ottawa: Deneau [1982].

Litvak, Isaiah, and Christopher Maule. *Cultural Sovereignty: The* Time *and* Reader's Digest *Case in Canada*. New York: Praeger Publishers, 1974.

Mackenzie, Hector. "The ABC's of Canada's International Economic Relations, 1945–51." In Greg Donaghy, ed., *Canada and the Early Cold War, 1945–57*. Ottawa: Department of Foreign Affairs and International Trade, 1999.

McNamara, Robert S. (with Brian VanDeMark). *In Retrospect: The Tragedy and Lessons of Vietnam*. New York: Random House, 1995.

Mahant, Edelgard, and Graeme S. Mount. *An Introduction to Canadian-American Relations*. Toronto: Methuen Publications, 1984.

Martin, Lawrence. *The Presidents and the Prime Ministers: Washington and Ottawa Face to Face: The Myth of Bilateral Bliss, 1867–1982*. Toronto: Doubleday Canada, 1982.

Martin, Paul. "Canada and the Universal Forum for Peace: An Address to the United Nations General Assembly in New York on September 27, 1967." Department of External Affairs, *Statements and Speeches*, 67/30.

– *A Very Public Life*. Vol. 2, *So Many Worlds*. Toronto: Deneau, 1985.

Muirhead, Bruce. "The Development of Canada's Foreign Economic Policy in the Second Postwar Decade: Britain, Europe and the GATT." In J.L. Granatstein and Gustav Schmidt, eds., *Canada at the Crossroads? The Critical 1960s.* Bochum, Germany: Universitatsverlag Dr. N. Brockmeyer, 1994.

– *Against the Odds: The Public Life and Times of Louis Rasminsky*. Toronto: University of Toronto Press, 1999.

Newman, Peter C. *The Distemper of Our Times: Canadian Politics in Transition, 1963–68*. Toronto: McClelland and Stewart, 1968.

O'Leary, Grattan. *Recollections of People, Press and Politics*. Toronto: Macmillan, 1977.

Owram, Doug. *Born at the Right Time: A History of the Baby Boom Generation*. Toronto: University of Toronto Press, 1996.

Page, Don. "The Representation of China in the United Nations: Canadian Perspectives and Initiatives, 1949–1971."In Paul M. Evans and Michael B. Frolic, eds., *Reluctant Adversaries: Canada and the People's Republic of China*. Toronto: University of Toronto Press, 1991.

Patterson, Thomas. "Kennedy's Quest for Victory and Global Crisis," in Thomas Patterson, ed., *Kennedy's Quest for Victory: American Foreign Policy, 1961–1963*. Toronto: Oxford University Press, 1989.

Pearson, L.B., "Address to the Canadian Club of Ottawa, 10 February 1965." Department of External Affairs, *Statements and Speeches*, 65/6.

– "Canada, the United States and Vietnam," Department of External Affairs, *Statements and Speeches*, 67/8.

– "A New Kind of Peace Force." In J.L. Granatstein, ed., *Canadian Foreign Policy since 1945: Middle Power or Satellite?* Toronto: Copp Clark, 1969.

– "At the Atlantic Awards Dinner." In L.B. Pearson, ed., *Words and Occasions*. Toronto: University of Toronto Press, 1970.

– *Mike: The Memoirs of the Rt Hon. Lester B. Pearson.* Vol. 3, *1957–1968*. Toronto, University of Toronto Press, 1975.

Pickersgill, J.W. *The Road Back: By a Liberal in Opposition.* Toronto: University of Toronto Press, 1986.

– *Seeing Canada Whole: A Memoir.* Markham, ON: Fitzhenry and Whiteside, 1994.

Plumptre, A.F.W. *Three Decades of Decision: Canada and the World Monetary System.* Toronto: McClelland and Stewart, 1977.

Preeg, Ernest H., *Traders and Diplomats: An Analysis of the Kennedy Round of Negotiations under the General Agreement on Tariffs and Trade.* Washington, DC: Brookings Institution, 1970.

Public Papers of the Presidents of the United States: Lyndon B. Johnson, 1963–64. Book 1. Washington, DC: United States Government Printing Services, 1965.

Public Papers of the Presidents of the United States: Lyndon B. Johnson, 1965. Book 2. Washington, DC: United States Government Printing Services, 1966.

Public Papers of the Presidents of the United States: Lyndon B. Johnson, 1968–69. Book 1. Washington, DC: United States Government Printing Services, 1970.

Reid, Escott. *Radical Mandarin: The Memoirs of Escott Reid.* Toronto: University of Toronto Press, 1989.

Reisman, Simon. *The Canadian Automotive Industry: Performance and Proposals for Progress.* Ottawa: Supply and Services Canada, 1978.

Ritchie, Charles. *Storm Signals: More Undiplomatic Diaries, 1962–1971.* Toronto: McClelland and Stewart, 1983.

Robinson, H. Basil. *Diefenbaker's World: A Populist in World Affairs.* Toronto: University of Toronto Press, 1989.

Ronning, Chester. *A Memoir of China in Revolution: From the Boxer Rebellion to the People's Republic.* New York: Pantheon Books, 1974.

Ross, Douglas. *In the Interests of Peace: Canada and Vietnam, 1954–73.* Toronto: University of Toronto Press, 1984.

Rusk, Dean. *As I Saw It*. New York: W.W. Norton, 1990.

St Amour, Norman. "Sino-Canadian Relations, 1963-1968: The American Factor." In Paul M. Evans and Michael B. Frolic, eds., *Reluctant Adversaries: Canada and the People's Republic of China*. Toronto: University of Toronto Press, 1991.

Saywell, John, ed. *Canadian Annual Review for 1963*. Toronto: University of Toronto Press, 1964.

– *Canadian Annual Review for 1964*. Toronto: University of Toronto Press, 1965.

– *Canadian Annual Review for 1965*. Toronto: University of Toronto Press, 1966.

– *Canadian Annual Review for 1966*. Toronto: University of Toronto Press, 1967.

– *Canadian Annual Review for 1967*. Toronto: University of Toronto Press, 1968.

– *Canadian Annual Review for 1968*. Toronto: University of Toronto Press, 1969.

Schoenbaum, Thomas J. *Waging Peace and War: Dean Rusk in the Truman, Kennedy and Johnson Years*. New York: Simon and Schuster, 1988.

Smart, Patricia, ed. *The Diary of André Laurendeau*. Toronto: James Lorimer, 1991.

Smith, Denis. *Gentle Patriot: A Political Biography of Walter Gordon*. Edmonton: Hurtig Publishers, 1973.

– *Rogue Tory: The Life and Times of John G. Diefenbaker*. Toronto: Macfarlane, Walter and Ross, 1995.

Solomon, Robert. *The International Monetary System, 1945–1976: An Insider's View*. New York: Harper and Row, 1977.

Steinberg, Blema S. *Shame and Humiliation: Presidential Decision Making on Vietnam*. Montreal and Kingston: McGill-Queen's University Press, 1995.

Stewart, Gordon. *The American Response to Canada since 1776*. East Lansing, MI: Michigan State University Press, 1992.

Stone, Frank. *Canada, the GATT and the International Trade System*. 2d ed. Montreal: The Institute for Research on Public Policy, 1992.

Stursberg, Peter. *Lester Pearson and the American Dilemma*. Toronto: Doubleday, 1980.

Swift, Jamie. *Odd Man Out: The Life and Times of Eric Kierans*. Toronto: Douglas and McIntyre, 1982.

Taylor, Charles. *Snow Job: Canada, the United States and Vietnam (1954–1973)*. Toronto: House of Anansi Press, 1974.

Thompson, John Herd, and Stephen Randall. *Canada and the United States: Ambivalent Allies*. Montreal and Kingston: McGill-Queen's University Press, 1994.

Thakur, Ramesh. *Peacekeeping in Vietnam: Canada, India, Poland, and the International Commission.* Edmonton: University of Alberta Press, 1984.

United States Department of Commerce. Bureau of the Census. *Historical Statistics of the United States: Colonial Times to 1970.* Part 2. Washington, DC: United States Government Printing Office, 1976.

United States Department of State. *Foreign Relations of the United States, 1961–63.* Vol. 13, *West Europe and Canada.* United States Government Printing Office: Washington, DC: 1994.

– *Foreign Relations of the United States, 1964–68.* Vol. 1, *Vietnam 1964.* United States Government Printing Office: Washington, DC: 1992

– *Foreign Relations of the United States, 1964–68.* Vol. 2, *Vietnam – January to June 1965.* United States Government Printing Office: Washington, DC: 1995.

– *Foreign Relations of the United States, 1964–68.* Vol. 13, *West Europe Region.* United States Government Printing Office: Washington, 1995.

– *Foreign Relations of the United States, 1964–68.* Vol. 3, *Vietnam – June to December 1965.* United States Government Printing Office: Washington, DC: 1996.

– *Foreign Relations of the United States, 1964–68.* Vol. 4, *Vietnam 1966.* United States Government Printing Office: Washington, DC: 1998.

– *Foreign Relations of the United States, 1964–68.* Vol. 8, *International Monetary and Trade Policy.* United States Government Printing Office: Washington, DC: 1998.

– *Foreign Relations of the United States, 1964–68.* Vol. 7, *Western Europe.* United States Government Printing Office: Washington, DC: 2001.

Vipond, Mary. "Canadian Nationalism and the Plight of Canadian Magazines in the 1920s." *Canadian Historical Review* 58 (March 1977): 43–63.

Warnock, John W. "Canada and the Alliance System." *Canadian Dimension* 3 (March-April 1966): 36–9.

Willoughby, William R. *The Joint Organizations of Canada with the United States.* Toronto: University of Toronto Press, 1982.

Winham, Gilbert R. *The Evolution of International Trade Agreements.* Toronto: University of Toronto Press, 1992.

Wright, Gerald. "Cooperation and Independence: Canada's Management of Financial Relations with the United States, 1963–1968." Unpublished PHD diss., Johns Hopkins University, 1976.

Wright, Gerald, and Molot, M.A. "Capital Movements and Government Control." In A.B. Fox, Alfred O. Hero, and Joseph Nye, eds., *Canada and the United States: Transnational and Transgovernmental Relations.* New York: Columbia University Press, 1976.

Index